Incomes policy
and the
public sector

Incomes policy and the public sector

Campbell Balfour
Department of Industrial Relations
University College, Cardiff

Routledge & Kegan Paul
London and Boston

First published 1972
by Routledge & Kegan Paul Ltd
Broadway House, 68–74 Carter Lane,
London EC4V 5EL and
9 Park Street,
Boston, Mass. 02108, U.S.A.
Printed in Great Britain by
C. Tinling & Co. Ltd, Prescot and London
© Campbell Balfour 1972
No part of this book may be reproduced in
any form without permission from the
publisher, except for the quotation of brief
passages in criticism

ISBN 0 7100 7306 2

LIBRARY
FLORIDA STATE UNIVERSITY
TALLAHASSEE, FLORIDA

In memory of Jewel

Contents

Introduction

The attempt at incomes policy in Britain lasted some five years, from 1965 to 1970. The National Board for Prices and Incomes, commonly known as the PIB, was intended to be the instrument through which an incomes policy could be shaped and guided. The Board produced 170 reports, most of them concerning wages and salaries, and was the most wide-ranging attempt to influence incomes which has been seen in this country; and its influence on British incomes and inflation is now being studied in other countries which are seeking methods of combating inflation, which is now common to most industrialised countries.

This book does not set out to be either the history of the PIB, or an analysis of its effect over the whole of industry, though some overall comment and analysis of the effects of incomes policy on wages and salaries is introduced from time to time. The aim is more modest: to look at the reports of the Board, look at the criteria and judgments used, then to examine incomes policy by studying its impact in several areas in the public sector, of which the writer had detailed and lengthy experience.

The study arose from a growing sense of the unreality of teaching labour economics through the formal textbooks with their curves of demand, supply and marginal relationships. While few economists today hold the view that 'wage theory is only a special case of the general theory of value', much of the writing on wages tends to be abstract and analytic. While such books are excellent for training the mind to disciplined and logical thought, they tend to be far removed from the realities of contemporary collective bargaining in the period of incomes policy.

After the great contributions of economists to the work and wealth of our society in the last thirty years, it is unjust for some writers to be critical of their work in the last few years. Yet there is no doubt that there is less confidence in the economists' ability to solve the economic problems of our society than there was formerly, and these doubts are shared by some economists themselves. Professor Michael Poston wrote recently that 'the very quality of post-war economics, the greater sophistication of its theoretical constructions, its much refined statistical and econometric models, have put it out of touch with real economic situations'.

This statement is especially true of the period of incomes policy. While the economists and the statisticians were busy with slide-rule and computer, forecasting the possible growth of the national income and the amount that could be distributed in wages and salaries, related to the movement of other sectors of the national income, the trade unions or groups of their workers were frustrating or avoiding the aims of incomes policy by demanding increases far higher than the increase in productivity, thus leading to cost-push inflation. While the Cabinet and the Treasury were attempting to influence the economy through the budget, seen as the great economic regulator in the 1940s and 1950s, millions of workers were quietly, and not so quietly, negotiating to obtain greater increases in a month, through their wage packet, than the budget conceded them in a year, thus by-passing the intentions of Chancellor and Treasury. Traditional instruments for regulating the economy, taxes, bank rate, credit squeeze, higher unemployment, seemed to have lost their old effectiveness, and caused some economists to throw up their hands and say that the situation could only be improved by the psychologists.

This book tries to put the reader in touch with 'real economic situations' and looks at the progress of incomes policy. Some of the industries or services were seen from the inside, as a participant, others from surveys in industries. The bargaining situation in local government and municipal transport was seen as a city councillor and member of the finance, establishment, joint consultative and transport committees; in universities as a member of the Association of University Teachers salaries committee.

Experience in collective bargaining on both the employee and employer sides underlined for the writer the abstract nature of many formal textbooks. One recent, and rigorous, text says that collective bargaining is not the proper study of the economist, though it might be for the psychologist. Here again is the economist passing his unmeasurable, unquantifiable problems on to the shoulders of the absent, and unwilling, psychologist. Yet the study of incomes policy shows clearly that the results of collective bargaining were among the main factors which frustrated the predictions of the government and its economists. One is reminded of the sardonic remark of Bertolt Brecht: 'If the government is wrong, then change the people.' In this case, some economists say that people are not behaving in accordance with the laws of economics, that the degree of irrationality is such that an incomes policy has moved beyond the grasp of the economist and that solutions may only come from social psychologists and sociologists. Others argue that the answer is more law in industrial relations, and that while economics is still the queen of the social sciences, law is to be the prince consort.

What a number of writers and critics appear to have ignored is that if the well-established laws of economics do not explain the apparently irrational behaviour of workers as they quicken the wage-push inflation cycle by pressing for higher money wages which in turn raise prices, then we must look at the actual situations, drag out the available facts, cross-examine them and attempt to indicate new strategies or policies.

This procedure has already been followed by Dr Robin Marris, who says that many thousands of economics students are studying economics and are taught that the concentration of firms 'arises from circumstances which most economics textbooks ignore'. He adds that many texts have been published recently which 'frankly concede, in words, that the real world does exist, but their theories are nevertheless almost all founded on the assumption that individual firms cannot grow beyond a modest maximum size without becoming hopelessly inefficient' (*Guardian*, 13 April 1971).

This situation appears also in the fields of labour economics and industrial relations, where students are taught that there are limits to the level to which trade unions can raise wages. But in the inflationary world of the past twenty-five years, wages are less likely to adapt themselves to prices than are prices to adapt themselves upwards to meet wage increases. This has been particularly true in the last few years, where situations have developed with numerous mergers, larger firms and capital-intensive firms who find the cost of buying off a strike much cheaper than having expensive equipment standing unused, or hard-won markets or customers lost. Strong unions or groups in such industries negotiate wage demands which result in higher prices being passed on to a relatively passive consumer (cars, oil, newspapers, airlines, engineering) who in turn demands more as a wage-earner in order to keep abreast of rising prices which he feels passionately that other people's wage demands have generated. This is a paradox which the politicians have exploited rather than resolved.

It is the sense of resentment and deprivation felt among the groups who feel that others have been enriching themselves at the expense of their restraint, or lack of militancy, or effectiveness in bargaining, which makes a voluntary incomes policy virtually unworkable in an inflationary situation. The fact that many wage settlements are now political rather than economic, means that one union's pay increase is the signal for another union or group to demand comparable treatment. In this sense a study of incomes policy could be usefully done by using the sociological concept of reference groups, through which one group of people compare themselves with another group, and the concept of relative deprivation, by which people do not see themselves as better off economically each year, but compare themselves against the higher standards which other workers or groups have achieved. One of the consequences of the rising standards of living and greater social mobility and educational opportunity of the past twenty-five years has been to enlarge the number of reference groups with which people compare themselves. The universal television has expanded (backed by huge advertising expenditures) people's 'horizon of expectations'. The groups of workers who feel they are falling behind in the wages race feel a growing sense of deprivation; there is deepening anxiety about rising prices, and a feeling that others are profiting from any voluntary restraint which they may feel they have been exercising in their wage demands. The situation worsens as wage claims mount in size and are headlined weekly in the newspapers and mass media. The effects have been said well by Yeats—'Things fall apart; the centre cannot hold'—and an incomes policy begins to disintegrate rapidly.

If an incomes policy is considered to be desirable, then we need to know about the successes and failures of the 1965–70 attempt, and more about the actual workings of industrial relations in many industries. Allan Flanders, long an advocate of incomes policy and one-time adviser to the PIB, wrote recently in discussing factors in negotiation: 'The truth is that we have only recently begun to embark on the vast programme of empirical research that will be required to underpin any firm judgements on the determinants of the relative importance of these different factors in different situations' (*Collective Bargaining*, Penguin, Harmondsworth, 1969, p. 28). The lack of information about certain aspects of wages which are crucial to the operations of an incomes policy is put more bluntly by Derek Robinson: 'We probably know more about conditions on the surface of the moon than we do about the operations of local labour markets' ('Myths of the local labour market', *Personnel*, December 1967, p. 36).

This study points out that a voluntary incomes policy cannot work if a substantial number of firms and groups can slip through the restraining net of the government's '*x* per cent norm' and conclude their own agreements, publicly or privately, at a level which is both inflationary and causes other groups to claim comparable increases, while the 'norm' is imposed on weaker or public service unions. Nor can a government 'screw down' wage increases in the public services or public industries well below those in the private sector for any lengthy period without building up great resentment, militancy and eventual breaking of the wages dam. The results of this policy are also described in the following pages.

Last, the study of the years 1965–70 can also be seen as a shift from an incomes policy based on the co-operation of the unions to a legal policy for industrial relations against the wishes of the unions. The effects of legal restraints on collective bargaining, in relation to strikes, are as yet incalculable, but they serve to illustrate strikingly the transition in five years in government thinking from the advice of the economist to the advice of the lawyer.

Whatever the effects of the Industrial Relations Act 1971, the debate on incomes policy and methods of dealing with inflation is still an open one. Rival groups of experts advocate different methods, but none has been found to be politically palatable. It is hoped that this study will help towards an acceptable solution of what is likely to be a continuing problem.

My thanks are due to the employers, officials and trade unionists who answered my questions; my colleagues in the Department have helped me in many conversations, though they are not responsible for any faults or deficiencies in my analysis. I should also like to record my appreciation for the advice, over many years, of Professor George Thomason and Dr. Michael Fogarty.

1

Collective bargaining

The traditional picture of collective bargaining where unions and employers meet together and agree on the wage to be paid has now changed considerably. For the twenty-five or more years since World War II most industrialised countries have suffered from inflation in a variety of forms. Various causal factors have been put forward to explain this, centred around wages on the demand side as well as on the supply side. Whatever the dominant theory may be, the result has been that in most industrialised countries the government attempts to exercise some control or restraint on inflation.*

After 1945 the most popular explanation of inflation was that of 'demand-pull', a pent-up monetary demand suddenly being released and building up the price of scarce goods. Remedies for this were said to be higher direct and indirect taxes, raising bank rate, restrictions on credit, and possibly restrictions on the supply of money. 'Demand-pull' inflation could be endemic in a country where there were no trade unions.

'Cost-push' inflation occurs when the upward pressure on prices comes from the rise in costs. This can be either due to trade unions or groups of workers demanding and receiving large increases in money wages, or to the manufacturer raising prices to increase his profits, or to a combination of both, with the manufacturer acceding to a wage demand and passing the higher cost to the consumer in higher prices, to maintain his profit margins. This in turn faces the worker with higher prices as a consumer and he renews his wage demands in order to keep pace with rising prices. 'Cost-push' can also enter the economy through higher prices for imported raw materials, or through devaluation of the home currency.

There have been strong supporters of both theories since 1945,

* H. A. Turner and H. Zoeteweij, *Prices, Wages and Incomes Policies in Industrialised Market Economies*, ILO, Geneva, 1966; OEEC *Report on Rising Prices*, 1961; Fourth Report of the Council on Prices, Productivity and Incomes, 1961; Evidence to the Joint Economic Committee of the United States Congress, 1960–1.

although they are often difficult to separate in practice, and much inflation is a result of their interaction. However, by the late 1960s a number of influential reports were asserting that increases in costs through excessive wage increases had become a major factor in inflation. 'Excessive' in this sense means that increases in wages were not matched by increases in productivity.

Inflation has been endemic in many countries since World War II, though most western countries have kept price rises to manageable proportions. In some countries, notably Germany and Japan, rising wage rates have been covered by rising productivity and rapid economic growth. By contrast, the British economy has had a relatively low rate of economic growth in the past twenty-five years, which has made its inflationary problem more difficult than that of other western countries.

In Britain, the relationship between collective bargaining and inflation has been made more difficult by our position as a leading trading nation, heavily dependent on export earnings to finance the high imports bill. There is a continual balance of payments problem. Linked to this has been Britain's role as a world currency, which has subjected the pound to frequent international monetary speculation. This in turn has meant that sterling had to be underpinned by international funds and bankers who asked for strong measures to keep down inflation. This meant credit restrictions, raising taxes and bank rate and damping down wage increases in excess of productivity. The net effect was frequently to discourage economic growth.

Since 1945 successive British governments have followed a policy of full employment. Though there have been various definitions of this, the average figure of unemployed from 1946 to 1966 was well under 2 per cent. This can be contrasted with a figure for the years 1919–39 of some 14 per cent. The enormous difference between the two figures illustrates strikingly the change that has taken place in the labour market, from a surplus of labour to a shortage, and the consequent greater power of unions and workers in collective bargaining.

Collective bargaining and the public interest

The view that full employment would transform the system of industrial relations, collective bargaining and industrial discipline, was put bluntly in an article in *The Times*, 23 January 1943. This pointed out that unemployment was not an 'accidental blemish' but an important part of the economic system. It reinforced the authority of master over man and maintained industrial discipline. It also restrained wage demands and kept prices stable. The article said: 'If free wage bargaining as we have known it hitherto is continued in conditions of full employment there would be a continuous upward pressure upon money wage rates. This phenomenon also exists at the present time and is also kept within bounds by the appeal of patriotism. In peace-time the vicious spiral of wages and prices might become chronic.' Beveridge, in *Full Employment in a Free Society* (Allen & Unwin, London, 1944), agrees with this diagnosis and says there is no mechanism in the economic system for preventing this. He suggests either arbitration or some form of unified wage policy.

The first peace-time attempt by the government to represent the public interest came from Sir Stafford Cripps. As Chancellor of the Exchequer in 1948 he sent out a Treasury statement on incomes, costs, and prices which said: 'There is no justification for any general increase of individual money incomes.'* There were several exceptions to this general rule, such as skill differentials, underpaid workers and undermanned industries. The Statement had support from a TUC conference, and although the TUC has no legal powers of leadership, most of the unions exercised some restraint in wage claims in 1949 and part of 1950. This is evident from Table 1.

Table 1 *Changes in wage rates and earnings, 1949–52*

Year	% Changes in previous year	
	Wage rates	*Earnings per worker*
1949	3·4	4·0
1950	1·8	4·8
1951	9·4	9·3
1952	8·5	8·3

(Source: H. F. Lydall, 'Inflation and the earnings gap', Bulletin of Oxford Institute of Statistics in *The Labour Market*, ed. B. J. McCormick and E. O. Smith, Penguin, Harmondsworth, 1969, p. 336.)

Lydall says that 'both wage rates and earnings rose comparatively little in 1949 and 1950, when the trade unions were working with the government in the interests of price stability. In those years the average standard of living in this country was much lower than it is now, and the pent up demand from the war years was still pressing upon us' (op. cit., p. 343). He thinks that a wages policy

* For a good account of war-time and peace-time attempts at wage policy, see B. C. Roberts, *National Wages Policy in War and Peace*, Allen & Unwin, London, 1958.

would be much easier to implement under a government policy of expansion and rising living standards.

After the collapse of the government's wages policy, due to devaluation in September 1949, followed by the Korean War in mid-1950, the TUC withdrew its support and the new Conservative government appealed for restraint. This had no effect, as the above figures on wage rates and earnings show. Mr Butler, as Chancellor, then pursued a policy of expansion which included inflationary wage settlements and avoidance of strikes. Wages and prices rose side by side. The expansion was cut back after the general election of May 1955, and restrictions were put on hire purchase deposits and there was a general credit squeeze through the banks and on public spending. This was followed by an Autumn Budget which reclaimed most of the tax benefits of the April Budget.

From unemployment to full employment

The White Paper on employment policy of the war-time coalition government (Cmnd 6527, May 1944) was primarily concerned with the problem of avoiding large-scale unemployment in peace-time. The Government were so successful in this that by 1956 the White Paper, 'The Economic Implications of Full Employment', showed that inflation, not unemployment, was the central problem of the economy. Though there had been the difficulties of the transition from war to peace, devaluation, Korean War, the changing pattern of world trade, there had been 'a continuing tendency for prices to rise as incomes increase faster than output'. 'In these conditions it is open to employees to insist on large wage increases, and it is often possible for employers to grant them and pass on the cost to the consumer, so maintaining their profit margins.' It might be added that at a time of labour scarcity, employers compete for labour and offer higher wages. The building industry is a case in point.

The White Paper said that price stability is necessary to maintain full employment without inflation. It reiterated the theme of successive Chancellors and governments in the 1950s—'The solution lies in self-restraint in making wage claims and fixing profit margins and prices, so that total money income rises no faster than total output.' Many of the statements made in the White Paper of 1956 had been made for years previously and were to be said many times in later years.

Between the appeals for all citizens to exercise restraint in the interests of price stability there were moves towards deflation, notably by Mr Thorneycroft as Chancellor. He decided to pursue an effective credit squeeze by firmer control of the supply of money. This was after he had rejected unemployment as a solution. In his budget speech of April 1957, he said: 'There are some who say that the answer lies in savage deflationary policies, resulting in high levels of unemployment. They say that we should depress demand to a point at which employers cannot afford to pay and workers are in no position to ask for higher wages.' However, Mr Thorneycroft's deflationary measures did have the effect of raising the level of unemployment, which by January 1959 had risen to 620,000. April 1959 saw an expansionary budget with reductions in taxation in time for the general election which followed. As in 1955 this was followed in 1960 by credit restrictions and an attempt to halt expansion. The dilemma of the 1950s was that attempts to curb inflation by credit squeezes usually curbed production without raising unemployment, thus raising wage rates rapidly without a corresponding increase in productivity.

The movement away from exhortation towards the beginnings of an incomes policy came with Mr Selwyn Lloyd as Chancellor. Examples of economic planning from the continent, notably France, were being put forward along with 'league tables' showing comparative rates of economic growth with Britain lagging behind. The National Economic Development Council (NEDC) was set up, which developed some lines of long-term economic planning. In a framework of this kind, projections had to be made of the future rises in wages and earnings.

By the middle of 1961 the Government were thinking of influencing wages directly, and a 'pay pause' was imposed on the public sector. An incomes policy statement appeared in February 1962, and set out a 'guiding light'. This said that money incomes should rise at about $2\frac{1}{2}$ per cent per year. This policy did not work well in the private sector of industry, where employers were still free to negotiate with their employees. It was enforced in employment under government control and much resentment was felt by teachers and nurses at this apparent discrimination.

Mr Maudling, following Mr Lloyd, attempted to bring unions and employers together to support an incomes policy. He met with little success. Nurses and teachers demonstrated in the streets and post office workers had their first strike since 1926.

Conflicting views of incomes policy

The Council on Prices, Productivity and Incomes (Cohen Committee), which produced four reports, stressed throughout its concern with the relationship between 'expanding production and reasonable changes in prices', which meant surveying the whole field of incomes. By the third report they had agreed that the management of demand by fiscal and monetary measures might not be enough in itself and that the problem would be more manageable if there were some means of ensuring that money incomes rose in tune with rising output. As the inflationary pressure is caused by pay and prices reacting on each other, one solution is to reduce the pressure for pay increases. Demand can be cut back by monetary and other measures, but this has the adverse effect of slowing down economic growth and the rise of real income, and increases unemployment. An alternative to this is to attempt to act directly on money incomes, prices and profits. Price control is difficult, time-consuming and needs large-scale public support along with statutory enforcement (even in war-time there was some evasion). Profits can be tackled by company and personal taxation, but difficulties arise over the differences between firms: expanding, contracting and stationary. The cash flow position and the need to raise capital in these three categories (and many sub-varieties) could be very different.

Of the three factors, prices, profits, incomes, the third is the easiest, for the vast majority of earners, to influence at source. But the very fact that limitations on incomes can be shown to be more effective than on prices or profits, or at least affect the individual sharply and directly, makes many union leaders and wage-earners suspicious of a prices and incomes policy which appears to bear heaviest on wage-earners. Many workers find it hard to believe that wages and salaries are the major factor in national income, accounting for some 70 per cent of incomes, and that wage increases of 8 per cent, with productivity rising at 2 per cent per year, lead inevitably to price rises, inflation and balance of payments difficulties.

Nevertheless, it is acknowledged in all sectors of political and public opinion that inflation exists. The right wing, and moderate conservatives, point to the unregulated power of trade unions forcing wages higher than they might be. The left wing, and particularly moderate socialists, have shifted from the view that planning need only apply to profits, and that the country can opt out of defence expenditures, and now argue that 'The experience of sectional money wage bargaining in an unregulated, highly inflationary, and only intermittently expanding economy has had little to offer the trade unions' (*A Plan for Incomes*, Fabian Society, 1965, p. 12).

While common ground appeared between the political right and left, the differences arose over the reasons for an incomes policy. The centre-right wanted price stability, responsible collective bargaining, linked to output, and lower taxation to encourage business investment and expansion. The centre-left wanted to slow down price increases and raise output, but argued that an incomes policy allied to planning would raise real wages, provide balanced economic growth, reduce unemployment and lead to a juster and more equitable distribution of incomes. The latter themes were taken up by the Labour government of 1964.

Incomes policy

When the Labour government was elected in October 1964 some of the preliminary foundations for an incomes policy had been set up. There was the NEDC on long-range planning for growth and the short-lived National Incomes Commission. The trade unions had refused to serve on either of these bodies, arguing that wages were to be cut back while other groups in society, employers, landlords, shareholders, saw their incomes rise rapidly. The Labour government fought the 1964 election on a policy of growth, claiming that the British economy had been working on the 'stop-go' principle with uneven bursts of economic growth and stagnation for some fifteen years. One of the main planks in the Labour platform was to fashion an incomes policy into the pattern of growth.

A report by the TUC, *Productivity, Prices and Incomes*, April 1965, returns to the theme of the White Paper of 1956 on employment policy and points out that 'Since the end of the war wage and salary incomes have risen at an annual rate of $6\frac{1}{2}$ per cent but prices have risen by nearly $4\frac{1}{2}$ per cent per year. Real wages and salaries have therefore only been rising at a little more than 2 per cent a year.' The report concludes that 'a policy for planned incomes must be a part of overall planning; . . . and that it must include all incomes and allow room for the advancement of social equity. The General Council believe that the proposals now put forward meet these requirements and provide the basis for developing a more coherent policy on productivity, prices and incomes.'

There is an affinity here with the White Paper of 1956. But the difference is in the declaration of intent of 1965 as compared to the vague and unworkable moral exhortations of 1956.

The new Labour government of October 1964 had won the general election on a number of issues. One of these was the theme of expansion versus stagnation. This, together with the grave financial position, the large balance of payments deficit, and the announcement that the government would introduce long-term economic planning to raise the general standard of living, brought strong trade union support which had been lacking for the Conservative Chancellors, Mr Selwyn Lloyd and Mr Maudling.

Meetings were held with management and unions at a national level. A 'Joint Statement of Intent on Productivity, Prices and Incomes' was signed and issued on 16 December 1964. Some of the main points follow:

(a) The Government's economic objective is to achieve and maintain a rapid increase in output and real incomes combined with full employment. Their social objective is to ensure that the benefits of faster growth are distributed in a way that satisfies the claims of social need and justice. In this way general confidence will be created in the purpose of the national plan and individuals will be willing to make their utmost contribution towards its implementation . . .

Management and Unions
(i) We, the representatives of the Trades Union Congress, the Federation of British Industries, the British Employers' Confederation, the National Association of British Manufacturers, and the Association of British Chambers of Commerce accept that major objectives of national policy must be:
to ensure that British industry is dynamic and that its prices are competitive; to raise productivity and efficiency so that real national output can increase, and to keep increases in wages, salaries and other forms of incomes in line with this increase; to keep the general level of prices stable.*

This Statement was followed by an agreement setting up the machinery of Prices and Incomes Policy in February 1965. This was to be a National Board for Prices and Incomes (PIB), which would look at certain changes in incomes and prices and develop criteria for assessing them, in the light of Government policy. The

---

* The man most responsible for launching the Declaration of Intent is gloomy in his retrospective view of events. George Brown, Secretary of State for Economic Affairs, writes of George Woodcock (TUC General Secretary): 'He was continually warning me that while people might well sign the Declaration of Intent, I needn't have any illusions about their living up to it afterwards . . . it must be confessed that subsequent events have largely confirmed his judgement.' Lord George-Brown, *In My Way* (memoirs), Gollancz, London, 1971, p. 107

White Paper of February 1965 (Cmnd 2577) said that the PIB would be in two divisions, one dealing with prices, the other with incomes. The work of the Incomes Review Division was to be as follows:

Cases to be investigated

(p) As in the case of prices, the Government will retain direct responsibility for all references of claims, settlements and other questions to the Incomes Review Division. Some of these may be at the request of one or both parties, others may be directly selected by the Government as meriting investigation. It is hoped that in all cases the parties directly concerned will be willing to have claims brought before the Division where the Government consider this is desirable in the national interest.

Procedure and speed of investigation

(q) The Incomes Review Division, like the Prices Review Division, will decide its own procedure, including the extent to which it will sit in public. It will no doubt take evidence from the parties immediately concerned and from other interested parties. Reports should be available within two or three months of references being made, and if possible even more quickly in the case of claims.

Acceptance of Board's Findings and Recommendations

(r) The Government intend to give the voluntary method every chance of proving that it can be made to work. Accordingly, in the case of both prices and incomes, persuasion and the pressure of public opinion will be relied upon to ensure that the findings and recommendations of the Board are accepted by the parties concerned. The Government would resort to other methods only if they were convinced that the voluntary method had failed.

In November 1965 an early warning system for proposed price and pay increases was introduced. This was a voluntary notification system which gave the government an opportunity to look at such proposals. The government could then decide to refer the case to the PIB. In the case of proposed pay awards, information had to be given for all cases involving 100 or more employees, or cases which might have an effect on other groups or claims.

2

The work of the Prices
and Incomes Board

The PIB produced over one hundred reports in its first four years (1965–9). The General Report for 1965–6 (Cmnd 3087, August 1966) stated that they received twenty-three references from the government and produced eighteen reports. The references were fairly evenly divided between prices and wages and salaries, between the private and public sectors. The Board worked by deciding which organisations in a reference had to be approached, which statistics had to be collected, which parties or individuals had to be approached. Background papers were written and questionnaires were sometimes drafted to collect information. More typically the Board had a team working on a reference, who used outside help from universities and industrial consultants. Research was carried out 'in the field' using a common framework of inquiry and the various reports were then used to draft a final report which was approved by the members of the Board. This was usually done within three months so that the team worked under considerable pressure. The White Paper on Machinery (Cmnd 2577, February 1965) had hoped that industry and unions would co-operate on a voluntary basis. This seemed to happen in the majority of cases, but there were sometimes large gaps in some inquiries where co-operation was refused (e.g. by the unions, in the case of road haulage and buses, and by the road haulage industry, where 137 firms replied out of 330, of which only 38 replied in sufficient detail) or where the researchers had to spend much time digging for information which the organisations concerned could have supplied in a fraction of the time.

The strictures of the PIB in the August 1966 Report followed the general theme of the preceding twenty years. After pointing out that trade associations may raise prices unduly, it added that 'a trade union may use its power, possibly through the threat of a strike, to secure a particularly large wage increase which generates pressure for other wages to follow' (p. 4).

The Board saw itself as more than a judge in wage and salary arguments. It was also a jury, representing the public interest. It interpreted the government's policy in various White Papers, and expressed its aims under three headings: (a) to relate the claims to their implications for other claims; (b) to relate this to the community generally; (c) to change practices and habits in industry in the interests of higher output.

The third aim was the way in which the Board saw its productivity function, i.e. to increase output per head. In a sense this was also the reiteration of a theme which industry and unions had heard for twenty years and which had been thoroughly explored by the Anglo-American Productivity Teams of 1948–53, followed by the work of the British Productivity Council (BPC). The lack of success of productivity drives and propaganda can be seen from the pamphlet 'Aim for Prosperity—National Productivity Year 1962–63' (BPC, 1963) which reported: 'our rate of growth in productivity is smaller than that of many countries . . . the facts represent a threat to full employment, the value of earnings . . . and a great deal more besides' (p. 5).

The Board underlined this: 'We have found in many references that an increase in output per head could be achieved from existing capital equipment' (op. cit., p. 11). Unlike the BPC the Board achieved far more publicity and its recommendations had the effect of being related to wage and salary awards. While these were not always carried out, the ideas were planted. They summed up the aims of their policy: to relate earnings to output by adapting 'manning practices to current technology and to the fact of high employment rather than to continue to reflect on earlier technology and a lower level of employment. . . . The need to adapt the earnings structure so as to reflect the greater security that should go with high employment and thus help overcome resistance to change' (p. 13).

How far was the Board successful in its two aims, of keeping incomes related to productivity and of changing attitudes in industry?

Changing criteria in collective bargaining

The customary criteria of collective bargaining fall under at least six headings:

1 *The living wage argument:* This is used mainly by lower-paid groups. It was used in its classic form by Ernest Bevin in the

Dockers' Pay Claim of 1920, when he argued in court that dockers and their families could not live adequately on the wages paid.

2 *The cost of living:* This is related to (1) but can be used for any wage or salary group when prices are rising. The building industry was the largest industry to give official recognition to this argument. 'It has been the custom of the NJCBI in recent years to negotiate general increases to take effect in November of each year, followed 'by "sliding scale" increases with reference to the Retail Price Index to take effect in March. . . . The industry has now agreed to abandon the cost of living criterion for wage increases and the increase of March 1968 was the last to be made with reference to the Retail Price Index' (*PIB Report No. 92*, pp. 21–2). American agreements sometimes refer to this as an 'escalator clause' which means that money wages change by a specific amount if the Consumer Price Index shifts several points upwards in an agreed period. The intention is to protect the real buying power of wages.

3 *Relative earnings:* Wage- and salary-earners often measure, not their real earnings, but what some comparable occupation is getting, or what someone above, or below them in the industrial hierarchy is earning. Many wage claims contain this element of comparison.

4 *Profits:* of the firm or industry, or on the national level.

5 *Productivity:* of the firm or industry, though arguments arise over whether the productivity increase is due to worker effort or to capital investment.

6 *Shortage of labour—or the undermanning argument:* Used by various groups, mainly in public employment, e.g. armed forces, teachers, police, local government (notably bus crews and dust men).

The first three arguments are inflationary in their effects in a full employment situation. Increases based on high profits might also be inflationary, depending on the circumstances.* The shortage of labour argument depends on whether the existing labour force is being effectively deployed and used.

Though the Board did not analyse pay claims in this way, there was a firm rejection in their reports of (2), (3), (4) and (6) above. There was also a rejection of (1) in nearly all cases. Although provision had been made in the 'White Paper on Prices and Incomes Policy' (Cmnd 2639) for low-paid workers 'where there is a general recognition that existing wages and salary levels are too

---

* 'The extent to which profitability was determined by market power rather than by efficiency.' In this case the answer might be to reduce prices to the consumer.

low to maintain a reasonable standard of living' the Board seldom took action on this.

The climate of industrial relations

The PIB was set up at a time when the economy was facing difficulties after the inflationary push of 1964. The problems of industrial relations in 1964 were much as they are now, showing the deep-rooted nature of the difficulties and the impossibility of quick easy solutions. Proposals by the Minister of Labour for investigating unofficial strikes after the third day were turned down by the TUC and the BEC. They agreed to set up a fact-finding team. The TUC discussed amalgamations and closer working between unions, as it had done for sixty years, though some progress is now being made. The TUC also wanted an amendment of the 1906 Trade Disputes Act. The electricity supply industry made progress on salaries, staff status and productivity improvements.

The National Incomes Commission reported on the engineering and shipbuilding industries and commented strongly on the problem of 'wage drift', the gap between rates of pay and earnings. The Engineering Employers Federation (EEF) negotiated a three-year agreement with their trade unions on a $3\frac{1}{2}$–4 per cent increase in pay yearly. There were threats of an overtime ban by the Confederation of Shipbuilding and Engineering Unions (CSEU) annual conference. In mid-1964 there was a long dispute with the post office workers, unofficial strikes, bans on overtime and a national strike. The postmen received a $6\frac{1}{2}$ per cent award. Large scale redundancies were forecast in the steel industry. A strike in commercial television was narrowly avoided. The dockers rejected a 5·7 per cent offer and the teachers were given new negotiation machinery. The airlines made staff status, salary and hours improvements.

These events, which took place before the setting up of the PIB, were to be repeated; there was to be further tension in electricity supply, docks, postal services, buses, railways, engineering, airlines, and motor cars. These represent strategic pressure points on the economy and on the community. The PIB was faced with the task of improving not only wage structures, but the efficiency and attitudes of industry. The problems would have been enough in themselves. But the PIB set up its platform when some 6 million workers had been given pay increases under long-term agreements. *The Times* reported: 'There has never been a time when the nation was committed in advance to higher wages and shorter hours for such a large proportion of the labour force' (28 December 1964). It pointed out that those responsible for incomes policy 'will find their freedom of manoeuvre restricted by these prior commitments'.

Pay claims and the PIB

In its first year, April 1965–July 1966, the Board dealt with eleven references on pay claims. Seven of these were in the public sector: electricity supply, railways, armed forces, higher civil service, Scottish teachers, busmen, industrial civil servants. This left four references in the private sector: printing, bank staff, bakeries (2 reports). References on prices, however, sometimes included comment on the pay and productivity structure of the industry, e.g. road haulage and coal prices, with the latter report pointing to the manpower shortages and absenteeism in mining.

The Board's report on printing said that major changes in working practices were needed and that competition had failed to do this. They criticised the wage settlement of May 1965 and suggested that the Joint Manpower Committee of the industry should try to collect information, change working practices, relax apprenticeships quotas and restrictive practices. The two reports on the bakery industry asked for better use of manpower and re-fused an increase on the price of bread and flour. A strike followed and the second report looked at the wage structure. This was the first time that both sides of an industry had referred a dispute to the Board. The increase in earnings was refused subject to a major change in working practices, namely more flexibility on shift-working. The main achievement of the second report was to change the wages structure to a higher guaranteed minimum earnings rate, 'greater security and shorter hours'. Whether the other aim of better manpower use was achieved is doubtful.

The electricity supply report was interesting in that it arose from a productivity agreement for manual and technical workers. This led the administrative and clerical staff to press a pay claim and threaten a strike. The Board recognised 'a sense of grievance' and allowed some of the awards made although they were higher than the White Paper allowed for, 'on the grounds that they would assist in reducing the sense of disturbance amongst the staff concerned'. This was a strange finding for the Board in view of their strictures on 'The doctrine of comparisons . . . [which] . . . can frustrate the purpose of pay increases that are designed to improve productivity' (Report No. 19, p. 16).

The claim of the Midland Bank staff was based on two main grounds, productivity and the cost of living. The latter was dismissed as part of the inflationary pressure. The productivity claim was rejected as being based on general changes in the industry and not on direct changes by employees in their work. The finding was that the award made by the Banks was not justified, though some suggestions were made about changing the salary structure.

The report on railways staff dealt with a claim 'based wholly on specific comparisons with the pay of other workers'. This kind of claim had been used by the railway unions since the Guillebaud Report of 1960 had given some sanction to the comparative wage rates argument. The Board concluded that, while comparisons 'must play some part in wage determination' they should be less important in future. The recommendations dealt with pay and productivity, relaxation of restrictive practices, better use of manpower, reducing overtime. Pay and Productivity Councils should be set up. These suggestions resulted in a threatened national strike, averted at the last minute by the Prime Minister after some concessions as to the timing of the pay and hours (forty-hour week) award.

Reports 10 and 11 concerned the armed forces and the higher civil service. The criteria for the increases were based on comparative earnings by the Grigg Formula for the Forces, and by an independent review committee for the civil service. As the government were virtually bound in advance by the awards, the Board did not challenge them, although they observed that the government ought to apply the principles of the White Paper as an employer.

Scottish teachers' salaries brought in again the issue of 'comparability'. The Scots asked for a 'fair relationship' with teachers south of the border. The Board rejected this and the government carried out the original award.

The busmen's pay claim raised a number of traditional criteria. The claim of the London busmen based on a formula of comparative earnings; the comparison made with London busmen by the provincial busmen; the London Transport and union agreement based on labour shortage. The Board rejected the undermanning argument and said, as it had done before, that better use should be made of existing labour. Buses were a labour-intensive form of transport (staff costs 70 per cent of total cost) and a change should be made to one-man operated buses (omo). The London busmen got 6·6 per cent on undertakings of productivity changes, the provinces 3–3½ per cent unless productivity changes took place. In later months little progress towards omo was made and the buses remained a difficult problem for the PIB, erupting in go-slows, sanctions and strikes.

The report on industrial civil servants was another example of a wage structure based on comparisons with industry. There had been a failure to recruit and keep staff. The Board agreed there was a labour shortage and although it talked of better use of labour it agreed that 'pay . . . had fallen seriously out of line with that for similar workers' (p. 37). Suggestions were made about greater efficiency.

An analysis of the seven incomes references in the public sector shows that they were all concerned with comparability in one form or another. Although the Board had pronounced against the doctrine of comparisons it had to accept this as 'refined comparability'. Following the lead of the White Paper on Prices and Incomes, the Board objected to wage changes based on cost of living increases in two reports, those on printing and the Midland Bank. However, as the 'norm' of 3–3½ per cent had been calculated as a measure of the real income to be produced, this was clearly not achieved, as the cost of living rose by slightly more than the 'norm'. This caused pressure for wage increases throughout the economy, as we can see by looking at the negotiated changes in wages and salaries during this period.

The industrial background to the PIB's first year

Due to government action in cutting back demand through fiscal measures, output rose very little between April 1965 and July 1966. The Board itself called the rise 'insignificant'. Yet in spite of sluggish output the unemployment figures fell 'from 1·6 per cent in 1964 to 1·3 per cent in 1965, and to 1·2 per cent in the first half of 1966'. This was due mainly to the reduction in hours worked. Many industries moved on to the forty-hour week and standard hours were over 2 per cent less than the year before. This meant that more people were working to produce the same output. This was also the year of the 'double deal', when a number of industries negotiated both a rise in wages and a fall in hours worked. This helped to increase hourly earnings, which rose by 10·8 per cent (Ministry of Labour Index).

An analysis of collective bargaining in the Board's first year was carried by Incomes Data Services (*IDS Panorama April 1965–July 1966*). Out of 189 settlements examined, the report concluded 'less than a third of the 189 settlements had percentage increases in rates below 3–3½ per cent. Only 52 (28 per cent) provided pay increases below the norm, 33 (17 per cent) were between 3 and 3·9 per cent, and the remaining 104 (55 per cent) were all, to varying extents, above the norm.' Of those above, 24 per cent were double the norm.

In view of the allegations made during the Selwyn Lloyd 'pay pause' of the early 1960s, where many complained that the 'pause' operated only in the public sector on nurses, teachers, local government and nationalised industries, it is ironic to read in the above survey: 'As one would expect, it was in areas where the Government could exert a more direct influence—in the nationalised industries and public services—that the crude "norm" was most likely to be observed.'

The TUC set up a committee to vet wage claims and examined 174. The Transport and General Workers Union (TGWU) said they would inform the TUC of some wage claims, but would not let that body interfere with their collective bargaining negotiations.

The government moved on with its reforms in industrial relations. The Redundancy Payments Act, which related redundancy pay to length of service with the same employer, had been passed in December 1965. This was followed by the wage-related sickness and unemployment benefit scheme which gave additional payments over the flat rate benefit up to £7 per week for those earning between £9 and £30 per week (National Insurance Act 1966). The Industrial Training Act of 1964 also provided means for training and retraining workers and encouraging mobility. By August 1967 twenty training boards had been set up in various industries.

Standstill and severe restraint

In the first year of the PIB there was a 'voluntary' incomes policy. The Board's recommendations were advisory and the parties could accept or reject them. But the economic climate changed and there was from July 1966 to August 1967, for the first six months a standstill on wage, price and dividend increases, followed by a period of 'severe restraint' for the second half of the period. The Board's powers to delay a wage increase extended to seven months. If the Board were against a pay increase after its investigation, the government could prevent the increase for a further three months. But the increase could be paid retrospectively after that time.

The standstill affected agreements which had not been implemented, professional fees, rents, rates, fares and prices, 'except where necessary because of marked increases which cannot be absorbed' due to rising import costs, or increased taxation. About 6 million workers who had been expecting either a rise in pay or fall in hours from recent agreements were affected. There were exceptions such as incremental payments, piecework increases, promotions. Productivity deals were ambiguously treated.

The government took powers to enforce the standstill from one to four months by fines. Mr Cousins resigned from the Cabinet over this issue. The government argued that 'the new powers will be used very selectively, but they need to be potentially wide-ranging if they are effectively to deter the selfish minority who are not prepared to co-operate, and no less important, to reassure those who are observing the policy that they will not be penalised for doing so' (*Ministry of Labour Gazette*). This last phrase was significant in that, whatever the partial success of the 'freeze', the later weakness of incomes policy was due to groups and unions feeling that they were being by-passed by the strong and ruthless.*

The TUC supported the standstill by a small majority. The government brought in Part Four of the Prices and Incomes Act, the 'penal clauses' which gave them power to fine up to £500 on indictment on 6 October 1966. This was due to the challenge of the Association of Supervisory Staffs, Executives and Technicians (ASSET), who successfully appealed through an employee who claimed his £1 a week increase since the standstill, which his employer had refused to pay (Allen *v.* Thorn Electrical Industries Ltd, *The Times*, 30 September 1966). The order was also used against the Newspaper Proprietors Association. A number of other cases arose in November.

The government's deflationary measures increased the total of unemployed to its highest level for thirty-two months, to 437,229 or 1·9 per cent. *The Times* of 21 October even had an article 'Can a Serious Recession be Avoided?' The PIB in its Second General Report, Cmnd 3394, August 1967, showed that the unemployment level rose substantially over the year from under 300,000 in June 1966 to around 500,000 in June 1967. Total industrial production fell, but output per person rose by $2\frac{1}{2}$ per cent. Unit labour costs were stable compared with an increase of '6 per cent between 1964 and 1965 . . . and with an average annual rise of $2\frac{1}{2}$ per cent in such costs in the past 10 years' (op. cit., p. 5).

The Board concluded that the standstill in wages and prices had been effective. Prices rose by only 1·4 per cent in the Retail Price

---

* Mr Aubrey Jones was well aware of this. In mid-1965 he said: 'The problem of inflation is not just a problem of money; it is also a problem of social customs' (*The Times*, 12 July 1965).

Index in each of the two six-month periods. Wages rose scarcely at all. The government's statutory powers were hardly used. The Board rightly said: 'though compulsory powers existed in the background, it was not they which made the policy effective; it was the willingness of people to co-operate.' It was against the background of this year and in this economic climate, that the Board's second year of reports must be seen.

The PIB Reports, July 1966–August 1967

The Board now began to see its role as the supreme watchdog. In examining the role of wages councils, the Board was disturbed at the divergence of attitudes between the councils and the Board. Minimum wage awards set a new floor in some industries and became pace-setters for new claims from others, 'setting at nought . . . Governmental policy with regard to prices and incomes'.

The Board was concerned about the possible 'maverick' role of Wages Councils and also about other bodies, presumably independent review committees such as Kindersley and Plowden. This implied that other bodies connected with incomes and prices policy should defer to the Board which 'is in a sense a final court, needing screening procedures in advance of it' (op. cit., p. 20).

We could say that this was the year in which the PIB developed a two-prong thrust, on productivity and low wages, as a number of references referred to these.

In 'Wages and Conditions in the Electrical Contracting Industry' (Cmnd 3172, December 1966) the agreement referred to the PIB covered 56,000 operatives. This was to be a three-year agreement starting with a 13 per cent increase which had been deferred. Electricians' mates were to be eliminated and workers regraded. Pay rises over the three-year period could be up to $33\frac{1}{3}$ per cent. The industry argued that the agreement was valid as the industry 'was underpaid and undermanned and that the proposed regrading of operatives constituted a major change in working practices' (op. cit., p. 26). The Board disagreed with the argument on the grounds that the increases were exceptional and the public would find the costs passed to them in higher prices. But the 13 per cent first stage was allowed. The second and third stages had to be re-negotiated later. A new Joint Industry Board was to grade workers, and the second stage was not to be paid until each worker had been graded by the JIB. This report was strongly criticised by the ETU and the job-grading made little progress.

The next reference dealt specifically with the problem of low

C

pay in agriculture (Cmnd 3199). The Agricultural Wages Board had decided to increase the minimum wage at the end of the 'standstill period'. The Board considered the possibility of establishing a 'standard of need' for low-paid workers, but decided instead to compare average earnings in agriculture with those in other industries. Not surprisingly, the Board found that agricultural workers were poorly paid and that their fringe benefits of vegetables, food, housing were also low. The Board agreed with the Agricultural Wages Board award of 6s weekly. (It is interesting to compare the difficulty the farm worker had in getting a rise of 6s weekly compared with the dockers ability to negotiate much higher increases through unofficial strikes, without reference to the PIB; yet would anyone argue that a docker works harder or is more skilled than the average farm worker?) It can be added that earnings in the low-wage industries rose less than the national average from 1960 to 1966. (See P. Townsend, *Poverty, Socialism and Labour in Power*, Fabian Society, 1966; also *A Plan for Incomes*, Fabian Society, April 1965, which states (p. 8): 'For both manual workers and "administrative, technical and clerical" employees there has been a tendency in the 1960s for the gap between the lowest earnings industries and the highest to widen.')

A new wage structure for different grades of worker was proposed. From agriculture, the Board moved to look at low pay in the retail trades (Cmnd 3224). The Wages Council had recommended an increase of 15s for men and 12s 6d for women. It was found that the workers were not so badly paid as was claimed, but there was a minority who were amongst the lowest-paid. The Board agreed with awards of 12s and 10s respectively to men and women and introduced 'tapering' increases which disappeared 'when earnings were more than £3 (for men) or £1 (for women) above the minimum'. The Wages Councils were criticised for sticking to their last, which was to consider the level of minimum wages in the industry, without considering 'national policies on prices and incomes'. But the Wages Council did not agree with the PIB and went ahead with its recommendations. This caused the Minister of Labour to send out a notice to employers agreeing with the PIB's suggestions. How far the employers complied with this is not known, but this made the Government more anxious to deal with the autonomy of Wages Councils after the Donovan Commission had reported.

After two references on low pay, the Board moved to its third one. 'The Pay and Conditions of Manual Workers in Local Authorities, the National Health Service, Gas and Water Supply'

(Cmnd 3230, March 1967). This report dealt with over a million workers, the largest group of low-paid workers in the country. There was much evidence of under-utilisation of labour, the 'Council Stroke'* of workmen, and much scope for work measurement and incentive schemes. Advisory services and consultancy services for smaller authorities could be set up. The main objective of the report was to see that future pay increases were linked to productivity.

Refusals by the Board to grant pay increases always led to union protest and sometimes to industrial action. An example of this was the ten weeks 'go-slow' by artificial limb fitters from May to July 1967 when a £2 per week increase agreed on by the employers was vetoed.

Although the PIB did not favour the labour shortage argument for pay increases, it had to bend its principles from time to time. One example was the report on Fire Service pay (Cmnd 3287) where the finding was that pay had fallen behind earnings in industry and men had left the fire service because of this. The Board not only agreed with the employers' side offer from the National Joint Council of 7½ per cent, they improved it at certain points. This was to encourage firemen to be available for duty over a longer period, making possible 'a smaller more highly paid service'. In this sense the fire-fighting service differed from general industry and represented a special case. This was one of the cases where the Board had to recognise the pressure of labour market forces.

Although the PIB had set itself against the relative pay argument, this was allowed in a modified form in the 'Pay and Conditions of Merchant Navy Officers' (Cmnd 3302, June 1967). The National Maritime Board had awarded an increase to officers of 10 per cent. The officers based their claim on the 9½ per cent increase for seamen after the 1966 strike, and argued that there should be a 'proper relationship' between the pay of officers and men. The PIB agreed with the award and said 'the officers' agreement could not reasonably have been for much less than 10 per cent on National Maritime Board rates'. But they also argued that better use could be made of manpower, especially the skilled. Suggestions were made about changing the salary structure.

This year, July 1966–August 1967, began with the 'standstill' for six months and was followed by six months of 'severe restraint'. The Board laid down guidelines for pay increases justified by

* A colloquialism for the unhurried and intermittent digging of roadworkers in local authorities.

productivity agreements. It was felt that such agreements were possible, not only in the capital-intensive industries which were the most spectacular examples, such as Fawley, but also in labour-intensive ones. Labour/management discussions on such agreements were encouraged, as was the training of union representatives and the circulation of more information about productivity bargaining.

The Report (No. 36, 'Productivity Agreements', June 1967) is best known for its seven guidelines, which tried to link pay and productivity under the following headings.

(i) It should be shown that the workers are making a direct contribution towards increasing productivity by accepting more exacting work or a major change in working practices.

(ii) Forecasts of increased productivity should be derived by the application of proper work-standards.

(iii) An accurate calculation of the gains and the costs should normally show that the total cost per unit of output, taking into account the effect on capital, will be reduced.

(iv) The scheme should contain effective controls to ensure that the projected increase in productivity is achieved, and that payment is made only as productivity increases or as changes in working practice take place.

(v) The undertaking should be ready to show clear benefits to the consumer through a contribution to stable prices.

(vi) An agreement covering part of an undertaking should bear the cost of consequential increases elsewhere in the same undertaking, if any have to be granted.

(vii) In all cases negotiators should beware of setting extravagant levels of pay which would provoke resentment outside.

These guidelines were meant to close as many loopholes as possible against the inflationary pay award. Yet in practice there must have been a number of pay increases smuggled through them or around them. The first rule runs up against the difficulty of precise measurement, and can depend on a number of subjective estimates, as the minutes of any establishment committee in a local authority would show. So with (ii), in the absence of work-study officers or departments, or in their inability to enforce their standards (see Report No. 65, 'Payment by Results'). The third rule assumes that costing in British industry is far more advanced than it is. Report No. 65, commenting on payment by result systems, talked of 'the widespread ignorance we found among managements about the implications of their pay systems for costs' (p. 14). The fourth rule is the one most likely to be winked at. A number of productivity agreements have paid on promises rather than productivity, but the nature and extent of the 'phoney' productivity agreement is not known. So far, the books and articles have been about the successful ones.* Rule five appears to have been dropped quietly overboard, as has rule six, as increases for manual workers have invariably led to claims by white-collar workers, and vice versa.

Rule seven brings us back to comparative wages, on which the Board took so firm a stand. The extravagance of the level may depend on the importance of the productivity deal to management, or on market or strike threat factors which have become increasingly important recently. The TUC reaction to the seven rules offered them was chilly, and the implication was that they would not be taken seriously. However, the argument about criteria for pay increases has been influenced by these rules, whatever Mr George Woodcock has said about them.

The third year of the PIB

After the year of 'standstill and severe restraint' there was bound to be a spate of pay claims. This natural tendency was reinforced by the devaluation of the pound in November 1967, although both the government and the Board warned against the erosion through pay increases of the benefits to exports which this would generate. A nil norm for pay increases from July 1967–March 1968 was replaced by a ceiling on pay increases set out in 'Productivity, Prices and Incomes Policy—1968 and 1969' (Cmnd 3590). This emphasises pay increases linked to productivity, either through increased output per man, or through 'a major revision of the pay structure'.

In spite of these warnings, and despite a rise in unemployment from the post-war average of $1\frac{3}{4}$ per cent to 2·4 per cent, earnings went up by 8 per cent, against the average post-war increase of 6 per cent.

One explanation of the sharp rise was that there was a back-log of pent-up pay claims released after the standstill and severe restraint period was over.

The Board looked at salary structures in the General Accident

* Though a strongly critical note appears in H. A. Clegg, *How to Run an Incomes Policy*, Heinemann, London, 1971, p. 38.

Group (Cmnd 3398). This was an agreement between the Group and employees for an increase of about 8 per cent, on the grounds that there was high staff turnover and a failure to get high-grade staff. This was adversely affecting business. It was found that salaries had fallen behind, as they had risen in similar companies, but the Board felt that the lower scales should be increased and the higher ones reviewed annually. Suggestions were made about efficiency and use of manpower. This showed the possibilities of job evaluation for clerical workers and extending work measurement techniques.

Signs that both sides of industry were now beginning to bargain about productivity is found in 'Pay of Electricity Supply Workers' (Cmnd 3405) where the employers had offered 3 per cent for more flexible working arrangements. The unions claimed 5 per cent for their co-operation in work-study. Talks had broken down when the PIB was given the reference. The Board recommended a 9·5 per cent increase in manual workers' schedule salaries (3·7 per cent in earnings). This was based on the industry's estimated increase in productivity of 4·8 per cent. It was suggested that the Electricity Council should draw up a register of best working practices and devices for measuring labour productivity. Agreements were reached on these suggestions: there is now a register of best labour practices and the National Joint Industrial Council (NJIC) has advised on incentive schemes. But there has been more bargaining than productivity, and the schemes are still in an amorphous state.

The Board frequently advised industry on better use of manpower. But industry sometimes does not, or cannot, follow the advice fully. This is evident in the newspaper industry, where the *Daily Mirror* admitted that it could reduce manning costs by 25–30 per cent (Cmnd 3435). Although the report said some progress was being made, this is bound to be a slow process in an industry controlled by tightly-knit trade unions (note the successful opposition of the National Union of Journalists (NUJ) to Clive Jenkins's debut as a journalist).

Salary structure was dealt with in Report No. 45 on chief and senior officers in local government. Suggestions were also made about job evaluation.

Strains and issues in incomes policy

The Donovan Report commented that there were two systems of collective bargaining, national and local. The PIB agreed with this view and analysed it in two reports, those concerning engineering workers (Report No. 49) and payments by results (No. 65). Engineering is an industry with a comparatively low basic wage (the Donovan Report gives examples of this), so that the local or factory agreement becomes more important than the national one. Whilst this system means that the negotiated pay bears a closer relation to reality, it also leads to inter-factory comparisons and claims based on relative pay.

The payment by results reference showed how local fragmented bargaining could yield earnings that were 'high and loose' and not related effectively to output. The Board put this forward as one of the reasons for the fact that 'earnings have been increasing faster with a higher level of unemployment than they did at a lower level' (Report No. 77, p. 142).

Besides the 'whip-saw effect' of national and local bargaining interacting on each other, the PIB had to face growing union and market pressures. The huge engineering industry and the powerful Amalgamated Engineers and Foundryworkers (AEF) were a case in point; municipal transport and the Transport and General Workers' Union (TGWU) were another.

This introduces the political aspect of incomes policy, not its background. The AEF has been strongly opposed to incomes policy and Mr Scanlon has made a number of speeches denouncing it as 'anti-worker' in its content and emphasis. The reports on the pay and conditions of engineering workers (Cmnd 3495) and staff workers (Cmnd 3495-1) formed a large-scale survey which looked, in the first report, at the effect of the three-year agreement, between EEF and CSEU, on earnings, costs, productivity, prices and differentials, in the industry, and in the second report, at the pay and conditions of staff workers. The intention of the two reports was to provide a long-term framework for the wage and salary structure of the industry.

As might be expected from a study of the diverse firms and groupings in the industry, there were many anomalies in the pay structures, even in a single establishment. The Board recommended that there should be a one-year agreement for manual workers 'which would deal with minimum earnings levels and certain guidelines for domestic increases' (Report No. 77, p. 33) (based on productivity agreements). For staff workers, there should be a development of better salary structures and grading schemes. Suggestions were also made about the role of national agreements in developing minimum conditions and pay levels and establishing relationships between different grades. The report attempted to bring some rationality and order into a chaotic pay structure, but it cut across well-entrenched attitudes in a powerful trade union grouping. Subsequently, in Autumn 1968, strike threats brought another breach in the incomes policy.

The important role of the Board in promoting efficient working and better use of labour and capital equipment, and the strong resistance offered to this ideal which all support in the abstract, can be seen in Cmnd 3498, 'Productivity Agreements in the Bus Industry'. Municipal transport has deep-set problems with a declining demand, low basic wage, excessive overtime, falling morale and high labour turnover. For years management and other experts have pointed to the great savings to be made from one man operation (OMO) of buses. On touring buses, in the private company sector, there had been a marked shift to OMO, but little progress had been made in the municipalities. The industrial relations in the industry were not good and there were fears about widespread redundancies.

The Board made suggestions about the scale of payment for the change to OMO (20 per cent above basic rates for driver-operators in urban areas; a 10s bonus payment to all platform staff in areas where agreement was reached about OMO). Suggestions were also made about changes in working practice. The TGWU, who represent most of the platform staff, had made large pay demands based on the 'Busmen's Charter'.* The Board rejected this: 'these claims (with the exception of OMO) were unrelated to productivity, and their acceptance would have raised labour costs substantially' (Report No. 77, p. 35).

The TGWU at the time of the report (December 1967) were pressing for local bargaining (they had left the NJIC some months before) and an all-round national increase. There were widespread strikes and sanctions. An increase of £1 on basic rates was agreed with the employers' side of the industry. This was referred to the PIB in January 1968, and a later report examined this claim. There were to be a number of strikes, and high turnover and absenteeism, in municipal transport throughout 1968.

The Board made some advances in productivity agreements in the Atomic Energy Authority (see Cmnd 3499). The unions were concerned at the proposals for flexibility in working practices. There were fears of redundancies. A central committee was set up to check the savings made in the new agreement.

The Board were less successful with their foray into the legal profession. 'Remuneration of Solicitors' (Cmnd 3529) looked at

* The TGWU Journal *Record*, June 1967. The bus industry is analysed later in this book.

professional fees for the first time. After a survey of earnings they decided that there was no case for an increase in solicitors' total income, but that its distribution could be changed, with conveyancing fees over most property sales reduced and County Court fees increased. The aftermath of the report shows how little effect it had on the legal profession.

Market factors, shortage of labour and public sympathy were evident in the recommendations on the pay of nurses (Cmnd 3585) where suggestions about increasing efficiency and changing the pay structure went along with a 9–14 per cent pay increase which followed an 11 per cent increase in mid-1965, an increase of over 20 per cent in three and a half years. Further pressure by the nurses since then has led to more changes in pay and conditions.

The main resistance by the Board and the government to pay increases in 1967–8 was focused on municipal transport. The Board took up this reference after the strikes and sanctions of Autumn 1967 had produced the £1 basic increase. This agreement came under a standstill order from the government originally for three months and later extended to delay the £1 increase for a year. This pay freeze meant that, sensible though the PIB's suggestions for greater efficiency and a better pay structure were, they were almost completely rejected by the union side of the industry.

The Board found that the £1 increase did not meet the criteria for exceptional pay increases in the White Paper. There were labour shortages, but they could be overcome by the more efficient manning of buses, and looking at other sources of labour supply (lorry drivers to bus drivers, women drivers, etc.). Suggestions were made about higher pay for better use of manpower and speeding up the change to OMO.

'We also made proposals for a number of changes in working practice, including greater flexibility between grades; more use of part-time labour; and of women drivers and conductors; and the removal of local restrictions on standing passengers. . . .' (Report No. 77, p. 50). The report found no argument for raising the general pay level.

The report led to a good deal of trouble in municipal transport and other reports followed on individual cities and towns. One report covered Belfast, Glasgow and Liverpool. The three cities had reached agreement with their transport staff in November 1967, when industrial relations in the industry had broken down and local pressures were being applied by the busmen. The agreements would have raised the basic pay, and overtime in two cases, in the way the national agreement would have done. As the PIB had already rejected the national increase, they had to find special arguments for an increase in Liverpool and Glasgow. This was found in the 'effort and strain' of work in a large city, which justified the Board passing the two agreements. It was claimed that this would have happened anyway if the bus industry had agreed to a tiered system of basic rates. It is difficult to believe that the 'effort and strain' of work in Liverpool and Glasgow is markedly different from that in Belfast. What is different is the labour market situation in Belfast compared with Liverpool, which had a strike of busmen for eleven weeks, and Glasgow. The Board found no serious manpower problems in Belfast, and did not accept the agreement made there.

The Board faced the difficulty of measuring the work of draughtsmen in Cmnd 3632, May 1968. The Engineering Employers' Federation had offered DATA (Draughtsmen's and Allied Technicians' Association) a 10 per cent increase on minimum salary at age twenty-one, and 5 per cent at age thirty and over. DATA wanted plant bargaining for increases of $33\frac{1}{2}$ per cent at twenty-one, and 9 per cent at age thirty and over. The Board approved some agreements as satisfying their criteria, but turned down others for their lack of national salary structure. They insisted that greater efforts should be made to measure the work of draughtsmen. New agreements were drafted which met the Board's requirements of increasing productivity and efficiency. Certain criteria for greater efficiency were laid down, as most drawing offices could increase efficiency greatly. The agreement with the Beckman Company was based on a big improvement in productivity and the fact that rates were low.

Other white-collar staff agreements that were examined were those of the Prudential and the Pearl Assurance Companies. The agreements were designed to keep salaries comparable to work in other fields. The Board, in Report No. 77 (Third General Report, Cmnd 3715, July 1968), showed that work measurement of staff work was still in an elementary stage: 'We felt that increases based on comparisons with pay elsewhere would only be justified if clerical output could not be measured to serve as a guide to pay improvements.' The Board felt that some measurement was possible and that something had been done in this direction, but added reluctantly 'although it was difficult for us to identify precisely the contribution by the staff to increased efficiency'. They passed the agreements with the promise that there would be measured increases related to effort, responsibility or skill in the future.

One of the most far-reaching and valuable surveys done by the Board was their inquiry into payment by results systems (Cmnd 3627). This arose from the widespread view held by economists and some managers that PBR was responsible for a certain amount of wage drift due to the number of badly measured or badly administered pay systems. The inquiry followed three lines:

(a) to survey the many different payment systems, examining the operation of each in different, and changing work situations.

(b) to examine the relationship between PBR systems and earnings, with special reference to the problem of wage 'drift'.

(c) to deduce from the above the implications of PBR systems for the policy of productivity, prices and incomes.
(Report No. 77, p. 51.)

After examining a wide variety of wage systems allegedly based on some form of PBR, the Board found there was a need of more statistics on the coverage and forms of PBR. One of their conclusions was that wage drift accounted for about half of the annual increase in average hourly earnings (manual workers). Wage drift of this kind did not yield genuine productivity increases. A number of guidelines were given which would show when a PBR system was not functioning properly. These included comments on the 'learning curve' or 'improvement effect', the wider use of work-study or measured standards, pay anomalies between groups or departments in the same factory, greater separation of negotiations over standards and over pay; but more important, perhaps, were the two yardsticks which could be used to measure 'loose' systems. The first of these warning signals would be when the rate of increase of average hourly earnings exceeded $2\frac{1}{2}$ per cent per year (leaving out overtime, official negotiated increases, and genuine productivity increases). The second when 'the proportion of average earnings (excluding overtime) which takes the form of variable output bonus is over one-third;' (op. cit., p. 53).

Another important reform suggested was that the Department of Employment and Productivity (DEP) should set up a small advisory unit in each region of officers who would collect information and advise firms on PBR systems.

The Board attempted, in an appendix at the end of its Third General Report, to meet the growing chorus of criticism over the alleged failure of incomes policy. There is a lengthy and complex discussion as to what the increases in incomes and prices would have been in the absence of an incomes policy. Their conclusion, which was seized on by the newspapers and by critics of the policy, was: 'it appears that incomes policy has on the average reduced the rate of rise by rather less than one per cent in those years when it has been in operation.' But they went on to say: 'This is probably an underestimate of the true effect', which they qualified by saying, 'All of these results are provisional, and they record what is our first excursion into a difficult and controversial field' (op. cit., p. 67).

Whatever the effects of incomes policy were on the level of prices and incomes, there is some evidence that it was having a pervasive effect on productivity and that management was becoming more cost-conscious. The labour correspondent of *The Times Review of Industry*, looking back over eight years of reporting on industrial relations, wrote: 'It can be said, on the whole, that productivity bargaining is now fashionable and that it is an enormous step forward' (op. cit., October 1967, p. 60). While this view was too optimistic, the language of productivity, though not always the results, was in common use in collective bargaining.

Industrial relations in the Board's third year

The third year of incomes policy showed a rapid increase in the volume of wage demands—a thaw after the 'freeze and squeeze' as the Press had explained it to the rank and file trade unionists, or the 'standstill and severe restraint' as it had been termed by the government. The Board pointed out that earnings rose by over 8 per cent between April 1967 and April 1968, while rising unemployment, from 1·9 per cent to 2·3 per cent, had not acted as the restraint advocated by some economists.

The third year also saw a growing disenchantment with the incomes policy on the part of some of the large or powerful unions, and a growing number of small and unofficial strikes as local leaders sought to make gains based on good bargaining positions. The Board itself complained of being misunderstood even by bodies who were well equipped to understand incomes policy. This appears in their summing up of their third year's work (Report No. 77) where they find 'widespread misunderstanding . . . exemplified by the Donovan Commission's Report on Trade Unions and Employers' Associations', which stated that incomes policy is more concerned with the short run than with the long. The Board retorts that its objectives are long-term as well as short-term. An observer might feel that if the incomes policy was misunderstood by the Donovan Commission it was even less likely to be understood by the ordinary worker. The left wing of the Labour movement had been critical of incomes policy for some time, as can be seen from the pages of *Tribune* in the summer of 1966, following the resignation of Mr Frank Cousins who returned to lead his union, the TGWU, in opposition to wage restraint.

By the autumn of 1967, and before devaluation came in November, labour stoppages were beginning to cause anxiety in government circles. This followed a year when disputes had been diminishing and an improvement had been hoped for. But this was not to happen. If we look at the figures over a few years (Table 2), the trend can be seen. The number of stoppages increased as well from 1,951 in 1966 to 2,133 in 1967.

Table 2 *Number of days lost through industrial disputes (per 1,000 persons employed)*

1958	1959	1960	1961	1962	1963	1964	1965	1966	1967
260	420	240	220	440	140	170	220	170	250

Source: *Ministry of Labour Gazette*, January 1968, p. 13.)

The docks accounted for the largest number of work days lost in 1967, with a total of 500,000 work days, of which 200,000 were lost in the lengthy disputes in October–November in London. Under the colourful and newsworthy Mr Jack Dash, the London dockers used their bargaining power to great effect at a time when rising exports were said to be our main chance of bridging the trade gap. Liverpool dockers were influenced by this display of successful militant action. In September, the *Observer* was writing of 'The Great Docks Robbery' and quoting docks employers as saying that wage costs in the docks had gone up by thirty per cent since the previous year yet there had been next to no gain in productivity.

There was also trouble on the railways for a short time, and in the Liverpool docks. While the Press talked of restrictive practices, the core of the problem could be found in the fears of redundancy in the docks and the railways, out-of-date and inefficient pay structures and excessive overtime. Allied to this might have been the increased interest in productivity measurement and the shift in control from national trade union officers to local shop stewards and unofficial leaders as management pushed for cost reductions and greater efficiency.

Mr Gunter's 'bed of nails' was refurbished in Christmas Week 1967, when the million strong AEF and the Confederation of Engineering and Shipbuilding Unions, said they would reject the PIB refusal to endorse their demand for a long-term wage agreement with a big increase for two and a half million workers. Mr Scanlon, the new and militant president of the AEF said that he would fight for the freedom to negotiate without outside interference. There were a number of stoppages in municipal transport in the autumn, and a number of important strikes in the car and car supply industries through the year.

A government White Paper of 3 April 1968, 'Productivity, Prices and Incomes Policy in 1968 and 1969' (Cmnd 3590), said that devaluation had underlined the necessity of an incomes policy. There would be a ceiling of $3\frac{1}{2}$ per cent for all wage and salary increases on or after 20 March. There was to be no general blessing for increases. All increases below $3\frac{1}{2}$ per cent would have to be based on productivity or low pay. Labour shortage and comparability arguments could only be used in certain instances. Productivity agreements were to be encouraged. The government could delay price and pay increases up to twelve months with a reference to the PIB.

The TUC produced its own economic review, which was markedly different to the view of the government. They suggested an increase in gross domestic product of 6 per cent, a rise of 5 per cent in productivity yielding the same rise in incomes. This would be a general $3\frac{1}{2}$ per cent, 14s weekly on average. The extra $1\frac{1}{2}$ per cent was to allow for local bargaining and wage drift. The TUC argued that an incomes policy was still necessary. This report was accepted with a small majority, against the large votes of the AEF and the TGWU, who opposed the incomes policy.

By April the TUC economic committee were opposing the government White Paper of 3 April. A number of unions objected to the White Paper at their Easter conferences and at later ones. The TUC wage vetting committee continued to meet and consider wage claims in the context of the TUC's new economic policy.

On 2 May the Ministry of Labour changed its name and focus into the Department of Employment and Productivity. One new aspect was the Manpower and Productivity Service, set up in the autumn of 1968, under an experienced industrialist, Mr George Cattell. He controlled a central consultancy service with ninety or so Manpower Advisers on a regional basis. The aim was to give advice to industries and firms on industrial relations and manpower and improve management techniques. Its services were for the use of both industry and the unions. The White Paper 'The Reform of Industrial Relations' suggested an expansion of this role.

The fourth year of the PIB

For the first three years of its existence the Board had worked with the sponsorship of the DEA (Department of Economic Affairs). In its fourth year it came under the sponsorship of the Department of Employment and Productivity. This represented a change in emphasis from the Board's role in a strategy of overall economic planning, with wage levels as a primary interest, to a closer working with industry, with productivity bargaining and wage structure. It also brought the Board under the eye of Mrs Barbara Castle, Secretary of State for Employment and Productivity, who had more force and determination than the Board had met for some time.

1968–9 was the 'fifth phase' of the productivity, prices and incomes policy. It was an extension of the 'fourth phase' which followed the devaluation of November 1967, with the difference that there were greater statutory powers over incomes, prices, rents and dividends, given by the Prices and Incomes Act, 1968, passed in July. This Act had given the government powers to hold up price or wage increases for up to twelve months, in consultation with the Board (as they had done in the case of the municipal busmen). These powers had come in for criticism by the trade unions and the government moved to a more flexible policy when it said in April 1969 that the deferment of pay increases would be three months (with reference to the PIB).

The Board, in its Fourth General Report (No. 122, Cmnd 4130, July 1969), said that its calculation that the Board's activities had resulted in incomes rising at 1 per cent less than they otherwise would have done, had important consequences for labour costs per unit of output. Following Professor Solow of MIT (Massachusetts Institute of Technology) the Board assumed that 'a reduction of 1 per cent in the rate of growth of money incomes translated into a reduction of 1 per cent in the rate of growth of labour costs per unit of output' (op. cit., p. 2) would have altered the balance of payments position considerably. There are a number of qualifications which might be made about this equation, but the Board insisted that a reduction in labour costs could help to decrease the unemployment figures.

The Board noted a number of qualitative changes: 'expectations with respect to the growth of incomes had increased and were increasing independently of any policies' (op. cit., p. 4). Some of these expectations were due to greater hire purchase, the drive towards equal pay, a long period of full employment. (The Board might also have considered the influence of newspaper comment on the cost of living, whether factual or speculative, rather than the standard of living. The cumulative effect is to discourage savings and increase spending, which in turn raises prices and generates wage demands.)

The Board criticised indirectly one school of thought, when they said: 'a rise in the level of unemployment did not moderate the rate of growth in money earnings as much as it had on previous occasions' (op. cit., p. 4). Professor Paish, who had written for a number of years on the relationship between the rate of growth of money incomes and the level of unemployment, and had argued that a higher rate of unemployment, e.g. around $2\frac{1}{2}$ per cent, would slow down the rise in money incomes, offered an explanation of the apparent failure of the 'Paish Effect'.* He said that this was due to (a) the monopoly effect of trade unions; (b) redundancy payments and 'more generous unemployment benefits'; and (c) increase in structural unemployment.

Between April 1968 and April 1969, unemployment was between 2·2 and 2·6 per cent compared with an average of 1·7 per cent in the previous decade 1958–67. The Board said: 'The index of weekly wage rates rose by 5·0 per cent and of average weekly earnings by 8·8 per cent as compared with averages of 3·7 and 5·5 per cent respectively in the previous decade' (op. cit., p. 4). By this form of measurement, the incomes policy had not succeeded in controlling wage levels. However, one hopeful development was that productivity had risen by 3·7 per cent, 'whereas the average annual increase in productivity in manufacturing over the previous ten years was 2·7 per cent' (op. cit., p. 4). This was too short a period to declare that a rising trend of productivity existed, although the Board claimed that the productivity criteria on which they had been insisting were beginning to have some effect. They did admit, however: 'What may have happened is that the "squeeze" of 1966 brought about a "shake-out" of labour and the emphasis on productivity later contributed to stricter manning standards' (op. cit., p. 8). The conclusion was that output per head had gone up from an average annual percentage increase of 2·2 per cent, 1957–66, to 4·0 per cent in 1968, and wages and salary costs per unit of output had gone down from 3·1 (average annual percentage

* F. W. Paish, 'The Rise and Fall of Incomes Policy', *Hobart Paper 47*, London 1969, pp. 49–56.

increase) in 1957–66 to 2·4 increase in 1968 (op. cit., p. 8). This
was a hopeful trend for the economy, but other West European
countries had better records here and some had achieved actual
reductions.

It was pointed out that the prices and incomes policy did not
function in isolation to other factors in the economy, and that the
effect of fiscal or monetary changes, e.g. a rise in indirect taxation,
might be to induce a greater pressure for wage increases.* The
Board was also concerned with the fact that the number of
references on incomes had declined, and more significantly, that
the number of references on prices had gone down more sharply.
It was thought that this trend would be changed as rising prices in
the shops caused people to believe that prices were rising more
sharply than wages 'though in fact the opposite is the case' (op.
cit., p. 14). The Board thought that it ought to have more price
references sent to it. In the year under discussion, 1968–9, they
published twelve reports on prices and thirty-two on incomes.
More 'efficiency audits' were suggested, both in private as well as
public industry. References to the Board, they said, would be
better sent in the intervals between pay claims and not after a
settlement had been reached and the parties' claims had hardened.

Reports and criteria in the fourth year

The output of reports from the Board was now substantially
increased over previous years, as can be seen from Figure 3† of
Report No. 122, p. 15, although, as previously noted, the rate of
references, especially in prices, had slowed down. The heavier
work-load now handled by their staff had also meant the use of
more sophisticated techniques, from management consultants to
computer analysis. In addition, there was the need to carry out
surveys to establish the necessary statistical data, on which there
is often far less information than is available, for example, in the
United States. Much of the work was carried out in the field,
frequently by part-time staff; but the numbers involved, with, at
times, up to forty or more working on a reference, meant that
many of the reports were far superior to most of the work previously done on particular industries.

* The government had raised both direct and indirect taxation, as well as prices. In
October 1964, an import surcharge had been applied; in April 1965 some £200m had
been raised in extra taxes; in May 1966, Selective Employment Tax (SET) had been
introduced. In July 1966, a summer budget had aimed at a £500m deflation.
† The number of references received during each quarterly period 1965–9 were at their
peak in the first quarter of 1968. They fell to about half this number a year later, although
references in incomes remained high.

D

The 'ceiling' on pay increases remained at $3\frac{1}{2}$ per cent. Some of the references which the Board examined during the year had calculated their expectations of back pay in terms of the 'ceiling', but the Board said this had to be measured against 'four criteria relating to the following circumstances: where employees make a direct contribution towards increasing productivity; where the distribution of manpower needs in the national interest to be changed; where pay is too low to maintain a reasonable standard of living; and where pay is widely recognised to have fallen seriously out of line with pay for similar work and needs in the national interest to be improved. Exceptional above-ceiling increases may be allowed in two cases: first, in the case of an agreement which raises productivity and efficiency sufficiently to justify more than the "ceiling" when measured against the guidelines set out in Report No. 36; and secondly, in the case of a major reorganisation of a pay structure justified on productivity and efficiency grounds' (op. cit., p. 19).

The productivity criteria remained, although, as we shall see later, the question of measurement was often very difficult, and there were a large number of 'phoney' productivity bargains. The distribution of manpower argument rested on the interpretation of the 'national interest', a concept on which Dr Johnson has been frequently quoted. The low pay argument remained, although relatively few groups used it (what is a 'reasonable' standard of living?) as the official view was 'somewhere less than unemployment benefit'. The fourth criteria, like the second, brought back a docile form of comparability, 'widely recognised' as well as 'needs in the national interest'. Exceptional increases were allowed on the well-known criteria of productivity and efficiency and where a pay structure had been improved in the same interests.

Some of the above criteria left the Board with a great deal of scope for their judgments, a number of which were severely criticised, e.g. the University pay award, top salaries in the private sector and nationalised industries, among others.

The thirty-two reports on incomes fell into certain groupings. Those on the busmen continued the inquiries of the past year, which had reflected much of the unrest and trouble in municipal transport.

Busmen and other transport groups

Report No. 78 (Cmnd 3723) looked at a local agreement in Rochdale. The Council had agreed to pay 15s as a 'productivity' payment to its busmen. This had been subjected to a standstill order after the DEP had passed it to the Board. It is interesting, in view of the criteria on low pay, that the report noted that 'Among the Rochdale non-craft depot staff, 26 per cent earn less than £14 per week' (op. cit., p. 3). The report found that the award should not be made as it stood, as it would increase unit costs. Recommendations were made about efficiency and productivity. Report No. 85 (Cmnd 3791) dealt with the pay and conditions of Dundee busmen, who had also concluded a local agreement. It was found that productivity could be much improved, and ways and means were recommended. The men were not to be paid any acceptance bonus for OMO over the national agreement of £1 weekly when it was reached by the NJIC.

Reports Nos. 95 and 96 dealt with the busmen of Wigan and Great Yarmouth, respectively. Each local agreement had been under a standstill order. The Board was critical of both agreements. The recommendations followed the lines of the previous ones for other local bus agreements. In the case of Great Yarmouth, the 'settlement was regarded by both the Union and the management as a once-for-all payment to end a strike which had arisen largely as a result of misunderstandings' etc. (op. cit., p. 2). The Board said the settlement went against incomes policy. The Wigan agreement had been agreed to by both parties as being in line with 'White Paper criteria relating to comparability, low pay and man-power shortage' (op. cit., p. 7). The report on Wigan concluded that earnings were not out of line, that the pay was not low, and that there was no serious staff shortage. The maintenance workers in the bus industry were more fortunate, as Report No. 99 (Cmnd 3868) suggested an increase in pay of 2 per cent over the ceiling of $3\frac{1}{2}$ per cent. The reason for the reference was the agreement by the NCOI (National Council for the Omnibus Industry) which had increased the basic rate of skilled workers by $8\frac{1}{2}$ per cent and of the less-skilled by 6 per cent (both groups were in the company sector). Both employers and unions had accepted the criteria of labour shortage and comparability. The report found no 'serious general labour shortage' and rejected comparability, but said that an agreement on productivity improvements would justify $5\frac{1}{2}$ per cent. A list of recommendations on those lines followed.

A contrast can be made between local employees on bus undertakings and those working on docks. Report No. 81 (Cmnd 3752) on staff employed in the Bristol docks, showed that while comparability was not an argument for the busmen, it was allowable for staff on docks. After concluding that the pay of staff must be influenced by the pay of dockers, the report said: 'it is clear that the nature of the reference gives rise to large questions—notably the question whether pay in the dock industry should be determined primarily by events within it or events outside it' (op. cit., p. 2). The Board decided, after listing the large increases gained by dockers, that the £1 a week award to the Bristol docks staff should stand, although suggestions about productivity were made. It is significant that the £1 award by the City of Bristol had been preceded by a ban on overtime and a threatened strike, as in the case of busmen in some authorities. However the market position and the effect on exports is different between dockers and busmen and this may have been one of the reasons why comparability was allowed.

Another aspect of transport was examined in Report No. 94 (Cmnd 3847) on productivity agreements in the road haulage industry. A number of agreements were examined and an attempt was made to lay down guidelines for productivity agreements. Most of the agreements which had been referred had been developed by the unions and arose from the refusal by the Wages Council for the industry to grant a £1 weekly increase in the minimum rate and the government's proposals 'for reducing the legal limits on drivers' hours in road haulage' (op. cit., p. 9), which would have lowered earnings in view of the long hours worked by drivers. A number of suggestions were made to improve productivity, with staggered hours, shift working and standards for work, including the use of the tachograph to measure speed, distance and time.* The industry were urged to stop the system of 'pay hours' or payment for hours not worked. Work study and incentives were suggested instead of this practice.

Report No. 103 (Cmnd 3929) on pay and productivity in the car delivery industry, which was treated as a specialised branch of the road haulage industry, illustrates the difficulties of implementing incomes policy in an industry with a large number of small firms, a comparatively small labour force (about 3,000 operating staff) and a strong union. The market position of the workers is a powerful one and 'go-slow' or other sanctions can affect the car industry. This was not a specific pay reference but an examination of pay and productivity generally. Among the findings were that 'Very few of the pay agreements made recently in the industry have been notified to the Department of Employment and Productivity' (op. cit., p. 8) and that men were being paid for more hours than they had worked. A number of pay agreements examined showed that 'the current incomes policy sits lightly on the industry'

* The TGWU opposed this device strongly as 'the spy in the cab'.

(op. cit., p. 10). The survey found a great many loopholes in the relationship between pay and productivity, e.g. 'not one firm costed with any accuracy the increases in wage rates which resulted from the negotiations in Birmingham last year. Nor do prices charged bear a true relation to costs' (op. cit., p. 12). A number of suggestions for improving this system were made.

Engineering and chemicals

The engineering industry showed another gap in incomes policy. Report No. 104 (Cmnd 3931) looked at the effect of the three-year agreement in engineering on earnings levels and differentials, productivity, costs and prices. The survey found a lack of data: 'We were disappointed in the earnings information that was available to us in the plants investigated' (op. cit., p. 7), and that 'few firms would have been able accurately to assess the impact of the Package Deal (the long-term agreement) on costs' (op. cit., p. 14). The effect of the agreement had 'added roughly $9\frac{1}{2}$ per cent to the wage bill of firms belonging to the EEF, but because of wage drift average earnings rose between January 1965 and January 1968 by 20·9 per cent for skilled and 19·3 per cent for unskilled workers. The rise in earnings outstripped improvements in productivity with the result that, contrary to the intention of the package deal, costs rose. Little or no success was achieved in realising another aim of the package deal—to improve the relative position of women and low-paid workers in the industry' (Report No. 122, Fourth General Report, Cmnd 4130, p. 57). The report on engineering workers said that the failure of the long-term agreement to create a link between earnings and productivity was due mainly to the two systems of collective bargaining, commented on for some years by labour economists and given the *imprimatur* by the Donovan Commission. In engineering this had meant that small groups of workers or plant committees had negotiated substantial pay increases which had contributed to the wage drift in the industry. It was found that, because of the lack of basic wage data and information in the industry, 'managements were often determining wages in the dark . . . rational wage structures and control of the wage bill were impossible' (op. cit., p. 26). After this indictment, it is hardly surprising to read that 'Apart from two firms, few seemed to be greatly concerned at these increasing labour costs' (op. cit., p. 13). Advice was given on the improvement of negotiating machinery.

Imperial Chemical Industries were more successful with the

results of their pay and productivity agreements, although the survey was faced with the refusal of all the craft unions involved in the agreements (with one exception) to give evidence. ICI's settlements with its unions had been referred to the Board as the firm had agreed a rate of pay increase above the $3\frac{1}{2}$ per cent ceiling allowed. This was a case where the justification was that productivity was increased by 'accepting more exacting work, or a major change in working practices'. As the settlements reached meant pay increases of 6·8 per cent on the average, the productivity increases were assessed. It was found that the agreement, with a new pay structure, Manpower Utilisation and Payment Structure (MUPS) 'is potentially of great benefit both to the company and to the employees covered by it because of the increased efficiency coupled with higher earnings and improved status which it makes possible' (op. cit., p. 11). The agreements were approved.

Low pay

The criteria of low pay arose in the case of the agricultural workers (Report No. 101, Cmnd 3911), but the Board were faced with the difficulties of interpretation. As 'the needs of individual workers are largely determined by the extent of their family commitments . . . the Government have raised the level of family allowances'. The report goes on to say: 'This means that it is not possible to lay down a particular earnings figure which divides workers who qualify for an increase in pay under the existing low pay criterion from the rest' (op. cit., p. 8). However, their pay could be compared with average earnings elsewhere, as well as the distribution of earnings within the low-paid group. Agriculture had the biggest group of low-paid workers, with 3s 3d an hour less than the average for all the industries surveyed. Not only were they the lowest-paid, but they also worked the longest hours. It was pointed out that the wage gap would continue to grow. This was the second time the Board had looked at the agricultural workers' pay. In January 1967 they approved a 3 per cent increase; in February 1968, there was a 7 per cent increase which was not referred to the Board; the survey arose from the decision of the Agricultural Wages Board to award another increase of 7 per cent in the minimum weekly rate. The PIB could not find that the award was justified under the criteria for exceptional increases, although they accepted that both sides thought that productivity might be improved. The award was approved on the grounds that 'it will make it possible to fulfil one of the underlying aims of the incomes policy which would otherwise be frustrated, namely to safeguard and improve the relative position of workers with very low pay' (op. cit., p. 10). For this reason a 'special exception' to the White Paper had to be made.

Report No. 110 (Cmnd 4002) and Supplement (Cmnd 4002–1), on the clothing manufacturing industries, also dealt with the criteria of low pay, as well as with the role of Wages Councils in this respect. The reference was concerned with a number of voluntary agreements and complementary Wages Council's awards. The reference was not under the early warning system but was an opportunity for the Board to look at the question of pay and productivity in the industry. There were ten Wages Councils in the industry with a coverage of 440,000 workers. The reference also dealt with low pay in an industry with a high proportion of women workers. The market situation was one of a large number of firms and a relatively weak union organisation. There was little pressure from shop stewards and very little negotiation, either formal or informal, on the shop floor. In the majority of firms the union was non-existent, and there was little evidence of productivity bargaining. The survey was critical of the Wages Council system in clothing. It had failed to encourage the development of voluntary bargaining. The Fourth General Report commented: 'We discovered that the Wages Councils were being used to secure the application over most of the industry of across-the-board wage increases . . . in other words, a system designed to give special protection to the low-paid was being used to transmit general pay increases to large bodies of workers who did not have low pay' (Report No. 122, p. 65). It was proposed that the Wages Councils be gradually phased out of the industry and that better voluntary machinery should be developed. In the near future the Wages Councils should try to raise the minimum rates for the lowest-paid by awarding over the 'ceiling' and giving less to the higher-paid.

A group of reports dealt with pay and conditions in the building and construction industry. Reports 82 and 84 (Cmnds 3768 and 3784) dealt with related groups, the former with sawyers and woodcutting machinists, the latter with workers in the thermal insulation contracting industry. The conclusion in the former report was that there should be greater flexibility and more productivity agreements; that wage increases in the building industry should not lead immediately to a rise in this sector. The latter report, like the former, approved the agreement examined. There were suggestions for more job evaluation and productivity encouragement through payment by result schemes.

The construction and electrical industries

The other, and more substantial, reports dealt with the civil engineering, building, and construction other than building industries (Reports 91, 92, 93 and Supplement, Cmnd 3836, 3837, 3838 and 3982 respectively). The three industries were closely related in their pay and conditions and the Board was asked to look at the industries before the settlement was reached. In the case of the first two references above, the terms of inquiry asked the Board to examine 'wage drift' and 'scope for improving productivity'. This meant that the pay settlements for the industries were postponed and an interim settlement arranged. The conclusion was that there was no case for an improvement on the interim settlement for another six months and then only if performance were improved, as there were many opportunities for raising productivity. Pay and occupational structures needed reform, as the incentive systems were not suitable. There was too much overtime, often used simply to raise earnings, and workers were productively employed for only two-thirds of their time. The smaller firms often gave 'unofficial additions' to pay. Guidelines were needed to improve negotiations. Training of management and job evaluation techniques were also suggested. In Report No. 93 on construction it was found that measures were also needed to raise productivity. Another group of reports dealt with electricity supply and the electrical contracting industry. The first (Report No. 79, Cmnd 3726) dealt with national guidelines covering productivity payments and specifically with the criteria used in recent incentive bonus payments (of March 1968) on the distribution side of the industry. The Board suggested that the schemes be called 'incentive' rather than 'productivity' as the latter term means a fundamental change in working patterns, whereas the former means more pay for better performance. Different electricity boards had interpreted performance in different ways, and there was a lack of performance in work measurement. Labour performance could be much improved but the hasty introduction of unsuitable schemes should be avoided. A better use of manpower could mean that the labour force could be reduced by 25 per cent. Although the report does not say so, this was an industry where a strike or sanctions could cause a good deal of disruption, which may be one reason why haste was being made so slowly.

Pay and conditions in the electrical contracting industry in Scotland were dealt with in Report No. 108 (Cmnd 3966). The conclusions were not as far-reaching as they might have been, as the agreement being examined was, in essence, comparability in pay with electrical contracting elsewhere in the United Kingdom, and the Board had just begun its survey of the industry as a whole. The Scottish agreement had been reached after a number of official strikes over the September 1968 $3\frac{1}{2}$ per cent award. These had led to a December agreement based not on 'wage-for-age' principles, but on comparability with other parts of the UK. The report said that the separate negotiating machinery in Scotland ought to reach its own pay and conditions agreements rather than rely on comparability. The productivity agreement could be much improved.

This was followed three months later by Report No. 120 on the electrical contracting industry (Cmnd 4097). The industry had just concluded its second three-year agreement. In reviewing the 1963–6 one, the report said that the aims had not been achieved, either in raising productivity or relative wages. The 1966–9 agreement saw the average hourly earnings of electricians rising by 22 per cent in the first $2\frac{1}{2}$ years after excluding overtime payment. There was virtually no wage drift, although the survey found a number of firms paying more than the allowed rates. The agreement did not specify greater productivity but set out to improve the atmosphere of industrial relations so that greater efficiency might be reached through, e.g. the new proposals for grading, the elimination of the grade of mate, the reduction of time lost through disputes. In these aims, and in setting up the Joint Industry Board (JIB) the agreement had been successful. However, the use of labour could be improved greatly, although much of the misuse arose from poor work organisation at the work-place or site.

Another of the difficulties of incomes policy was shown by the government's annual appeal to strong groups not to exploit their bargaining position. There is little evidence that this appeal had much effect, either on the side of the worker or the employer. Report No. 117 (Cmnd 4088) on the exhibition contracting industry shows the power of groups in a strong bargaining position. The exhibitor has to have his stands and equipment set up and taken down in a short time, due to shortage of suitable halls. Labour costs are a fraction of total costs and it is no surprise to find that the survey concluded that exhibitors are not cost-conscious. The situation is one of strong unofficial groups facing many small firms in a weak management situation, so that unofficial strikes and bans on overtime have cancelled and postponed exhibitions. There is strict demarcation, high mid-week absenteeism and excessive overtime working for this reason. To some extent this reflects the insecurity of a labour force which is partly seasonal and casual. The Board concluded that the agreement of February 1969 in the industry, which gave increases well above the 3½ per cent, was not justified. The industry was advised to cut down the use of casual labour and inefficient working practices. It did not seem likely that these injunctions would have much effect, in view of the strong bargaining position of the unofficial groups and the refusal of the unions to take part in the survey. Nonetheless, contractors were advised to improve management and supervision, and the unions to bring about closer liaison with shop stewards.

Pay of staff workers

The next references dealt with staff (numbers of whom are salaried) whose working conditions and benefits are often different from those of other groups of weekly-paid workers. These raised the problem that, while productivity agreements were spreading among manual workers, it was more difficult to devise techniques for work measurement in white-collar jobs (though these are now being developed) 'Pay of Staff Workers in the Gas Industry' (Report No. 86, Cmnd 3795), examined a claim for a 5 per cent increase related to productivity. The staff side claimed an increase on three grounds: (1) the length of time from the last general increase measured at 3½ per cent per year—this was at least 5 per cent; (2) comparability—equivalent grades in local government, nationalised industries and the civil service had moved higher in the salary scale with increases based on comparability, and manual workers in Gas had also moved ahead 10 per cent in the same period; (3) productivity—all staff had given full aid to productivity measures, without restrictive measures.

The employers had accepted these points. The report, however, simply noted (2) and (3) as claims based on the White Paper criteria. Comparability was ruled out, and although it was agreed that manual workers in the industry had moved ahead, this, said the report, was due to their greater participation in incentive schemes. The pay of staff workers had not fallen seriously out of line. This left the claim on productivity grounds. The report agreed that the staff had co-operated in changes, and after proposing that the agreement should contain a clause on the development and application of work-study, work measurement and job evaluation, recommended that the employers' offer of 4·2 per cent should be accepted.

In the opinion of the writer, who observed some of the changes recently taking place in the industry, the impetus for the staff claim arose chiefly from the increases awarded to the manual workers, a number of whom had engaged in some form of incentive or productivity bargaining.

Report No. 109 (Cmnd 3981) on the pay of salaried staff in Imperial Chemical Industries (ICI), had some similarities with the situation in the gas industry. The manual workers in ICI had an increase of 6·8 per cent approved by the Board (see Report No. 105) on the grounds of their increased productivity. The staff naturally claimed on the same grounds and the company proposed to pay them an increase of 6 per cent. This was the subject of the survey, which agreed with a $3\frac{1}{2}$ per cent increase on the grounds that the staff had assisted in increasing productivity. The report found that there were no grounds for an exceptional increase based on White Paper criteria. The salary structure was designed to reward individuals fairly. The salary bill had already risen over the $3\frac{1}{2}$ per cent allowed, as individual increments had added 4·2 per cent. There also appeared to be 'salary drift' of 1–2 per cent. The next argument advanced was that it would be unfair to allow the manual workers such a rise and deny it to staff. The Board disagreed, and pointed out that one of the aims of MUPS was to bring manual workers closer to the status and attitudes which the staff had. Referring to the ICI argument that the staff had few restrictive practices to surrender, the Board replied that they had their present salaries precisely because of this co-operative attitude, and they hoped that the rise given to the manual workers would also change their attitudes.

The Board agreed with $3\frac{1}{2}$ per cent but refused the addition up to 6 per cent. The company said it would withhold the balance for the maximum period of a statutory standstill, i.e. until the end of November. It also announced that it would then pay the full amount retrospectively from 1 January. The net effect of the Board's intervention was only to delay what the company wanted to pay, and did pay. This appeared to lay down the precept for a number of industries that if a productivity bargain was concluded for manual workers, the net differentials within the company remained roughly the same since the staff workers moved in their wake, albeit with some concessions to efficient working.

The staff in the London clearing banks, dealt with in Report No. 106 (Cmnd 3943) were unfortunate in not having a large group of manual workers to precede them in a productivity bargain. The report, in fact, pointed out that the staff were co-operating fully in all changes and that it was 'neither necessary nor desirable' to pay them more for agreeing to 'specific changes in working methods' (op. cit., p. 14). The claim, agreed to by the Joint National Council for Banking (JNC), gave an average overall increase for male bank clerks (16–31) of 7 per cent, and, as a move towards equal pay, a 10·9 per cent increase in basic pay for female bank clerks in the same age range as the male clerks. Minimum retirement salaries would have increased by 7 per cent for men and 17·4 per cent for women. Bank managers' minimum salaries would have increased by 6·8 per cent. The JNC argued that the agreement was based on all four of the criteria in the White Paper (Cmnd 3590), justifying $3\frac{1}{2}$ per cent, and that there were also grounds for an exceptional increase on grounds of higher productivity. The Board went through the claim point by point and rejected the plea of labour shortage on the grounds that were was no excessive overtime, that Saturday closing would help the staff position, and that a rise in staff pay in banking would set in motion claims from other industries who compete with banks for staff. The claim that pay was 'seriously out of line' was rejected, the Board showing no sympathy for the plea that bank salaries had fallen badly out of line in the past twenty years. Nor did they accept the 'low pay' plea for younger bank employees. On productivity, as indicated above, the Board pointed out that the staff were already co-operating, and that much of the increase was due to heavy capital expenditure on computerisation. However, an award of $3\frac{1}{2}$ per cent was held to be justified on the grounds of productivity. The argument that computerisation had led to 'a major reconstruction of the routine procedures of banking' was rejected. There were no grounds, the Board said, for an exceptional increase. It was agreed that $3\frac{1}{2}$ per cent could be paid.

The Federation of Bank Employers decided to observe a pause in their agreed increase (they were already paying with permission the $3\frac{1}{2}$ per cent on a provisional basis) and then to proceed with the full increases originally agreed and paid retrospectively to 1 July 1968, 'thus implementing in full an agreement which does not meet the requirements of the Government's incomes policy' as the Board ruefully commented in Report No. 122. In this decision, the Federation of Bank Employers were marching in step with the ICI decision, which also ignored the recommendations of the Board.

Professional groups

The analysis of the reports so far has shown that the Board had more influence on the public sector than on the private sector, except where the public sector employees could exercise effective pressure through strikes or other sanctions on exports or foreign earnings, or could cause serious inconvenience to the public or industry, e.g. gas, electricity, rail—but not bus transport.

The following reports on professional groups illustrate varying positions of market power. These are university teachers, the armed forces (in so far as they are a profession), journalists and airline pilots.

'Pay of University Teachers in Great Britain' (Report No. 98, Cmnd 3866) was a standing reference, i.e. it was continuously before the Board. The Association of University Teachers (AUT) had agreed to this reluctantly, as they would have preferred to have proper negotiating machinery. The claim was for 15 per cent back-dated to 31 December 1967, with 21 per cent at the bottom of the lecturer scale. The claim rested chiefly on the criteria of comparability: to 'restore that competitive equivalence between salaries and prospects in the universities and in other occupations drawing on the same pool of recruits which your predecessors the National Incomes Commission . . . judged to be in the public interest' (AUT submission in evidence). The PIB, however, clearly felt no filial loyalty to the National Incomes Commission (NIC) and replied that the argument from comparability was a contributory cause of inflation. A stand had to be taken 'to break the endless chain of increases'. The university teachers became one of the links which had to be broken. The report said there was no recruitment or retention problem in universities. The claim met none of the criteria of the White Paper, except possibly in the case of the quality of new entrants to university teaching. The recommendations were that assistant lecturers should receive 10–17 per cent, lecturers between 4 and 10 per cent (4 per cent at the top of the scale), readers and senior lecturers 3 per cent, and professors 2 per cent. A number of suggestions were made, the most controversial being that the universities should encourage a shift from research to teaching. This suggestion, linked as it was to the view that the primary function of a university is to teach students, therefore good teaching should be encouraged and rewarded, was much more complex than it appeared and the Board offered few details on how this was to be done. The AUT, and the Committee of Vice-Chancellors and Principals, were hostile to the suggestion. There was a good deal of campaigning and pressure on parliament to improve the award and reject some of the recommendations. The award was accepted by the government without any comment on the improvement of teaching, which was not insisted upon. After several months of negotiations, the award was improved to the bare minimum, e.g. a lecturer at the top of the scale (the normal career grade) had received a 13 per cent increase over five years. Frustration in the universities mounted sharply on the awards of the Kindersley Review Body for doctors which ignored incomes policy and found no difficulty in giving substantial increases based on comparability.

Armed forces' pay (Report No. 116, Cmnd 4079) was also a standing reference to the Board. The report makes interesting reading for a number of reasons. In comparison to the report on universities, the one on the armed forces was a far-reaching and comprehensive survey, including attitude surveys. It also brushed aside the White Paper criteria with a perfunctory wish that the government should apply it to the Forces in the future. Comparability was acknowledged, not as a defect as in the case above, but as a right of the Forces to have their pay measured by the Grigg formula—'a commitment to be honoured'. While the Board was not enthusiastic about the Grigg formula, it felt justified by the next reason, the need to increase Service pay which was necessary to end the manpower shortage. This was examined in some detail, as were the working conditions and promotion prospects in the Forces. The conclusion was that 'The extensive rank hierarchy is partly needed to provide a means of rewarding individual ability' but that it also offered better prospects for advancement than existed in industrial life.

Comparability also appeared in the case of doctors and dentists, who were linked to the pay of doctors in civilian life. In 1966 the government had reduced the pay lead which the Service doctors had had since 1962 over GPs in the National Health Service. The BMA promptly 'blacklisted the Service career' (ibid., p. 35). This was a striking illustration of the market power of doctors against, for example, university teachers, although both are paid mainly out of public funds. Service pay was to be changed and single men to be on a par with married men. Job evaluation was to be used, although the Board conceded that it would be difficult to assess the danger, effort and fatigue involved in battle or active service. Active service was to be subsumed under the 'X' factor, and regarded as a major change in pay structure. The award was for 7 per cent, two years at the full $3\frac{1}{2}$ per cent.

'Journalists' Pay' (Report No. 115, Cmnd 4077) examined the pay settlement of December 1968 between the Newspaper Publishers' Association (NPA) and the National Union of Journalists (NUJ), the effects of this on the national and London evening newspapers under the agreement and the relations between this settlement and the pay of other groups of journalists. At one time, Fleet Street had been the peak of the journalistic profession, but by now the whole range of opportunities had been widened to include more highly paid work for journalists in television, public relations, advertising and the whole range of the communications industry. High rates elsewhere in the mass media had affected rates in journalism. There was also discontent at the 'merit' pay for certain journalists, at the expense of a stable salary and a career structure for the older journalist. The pressure from without on wage rates was added to by pressures from within the newspaper industry as productivity agreements spread through the groups of manual workers employed by newspapers. This was a situation analogous to that described in gas and ICI, as well as in other industries where increases based on productivity for manual workers had bred discontent and demands for rises from the white-collar workers or the salaried staff. Difficulties arose in attempting to measure journalists' work by 'the column inches of editorial matter printed per unit of staff' (ibid., p. 11), although this method had been used by the Economist Intelligence Unit in 1966. There was also the issue that increases in the minimum rate spread upwards throughout the profession; 'actual increases and actual earnings differ considerably from those laid down in the national agreement' (ibid., p. 6). The total cost of the first stage of the agreement was to be 9·1 per cent, the second stage 5 per cent. The Board allowed the first stage of the settlement, with minimum increases. They said that the pay of journalists should also be restructured through method study and job analysis, with salary grading schemes. Fragmentation of negotiating structure had to be overcome.

While the Board noted that the salary levels of journalists had been rising by 5 per cent per annum, we were not given an estimate of the rate at which the pay of airline pilots had been rising. Report No. 88 (Cmnd 3789) on the pay of pilots employed by the British Overseas Airways Corporation (BOAC) looked at the pay and productivity of this group. The British Airlines Pilots Association (BALPA) had shown increasing militancy since December 1967 when they had had a two-day strike (their first). In June 1967, BALPA had withdrawn from the National Joint Council for Civil Air Transport (NJCCAT), and rejoined it again in March 1968 after two Courts of Inquiry (Cmnds 3428 and 3551). An agreement was reached on increases in pay of 10 per cent, 7½ per cent and 7½ per cent on January 1968, 1969, and 1970, respectively.

Argument arose over the cost savings in the agreement and BALPA withdrew from it. There was a two-week strike before the matter was referred to the Board, and in the course of the inquiry joint negotiations were begun under the chairmanship of Professor John Wood. This resulted in the Wood Agreement which set out a new system of payment for airline pilots in BOAC. The main feature of this was a shift from an annual salary to an hourly rate of pay and BOAC constructed a bid-line system (blocks of work which pilots could bid for in order of seniority). BALPA agreed to reductions in pilot staff up to 20 per cent. Further savings in manning could be made by reducing the number of pilots on planes from 3 to 2. The PIB agreed to a 10 per cent increase in the current salary bill, with possible rises in the pay of other BOAC employees. Another strike took place after the report was published, then the minimum pay guarantee and the hourly rate was agreed upon. Further disputes have occurred over the bid-line system, and the pilots' claim for international comparability of pay.

These negotiations are an illustration of the quasi-monopoly power of airline pilots. Like busmen, they also transport passengers, but whereas striking busmen have only a marginal effect on domestic travel due to substitutability, air travellers suffer greater inconvenience and have little choice of alternatives unless they can switch to other airlines, in which case the strike-bound airline suffers large losses in foreign as well as domestic currency. The Board's inability to keep the pay of airline pilots within the White Paper's criteria illustrates the reality of market power against moral exhortations to strong groups to refrain from using their power.

An unusual survey by the Board examined the pay and duties of light-keepers (Report No. 114, Cmnd 4067) and the comparability claimed by them with seamen's pay, which had been improved along with a reduction in the basic working week. It was found difficult to apply ordinary working hours, plus overtime, for light-keepers and it was suggested that the level of pay should recognise this. The settlement noted that the pay structure would be revised to take account of this and an award above the $3\frac{1}{2}$ per cent was given. Job evaluation was suggested, as well as the possibility of comparing pay with that of coastguards.

Top salaries

The next report to be examined is of unusual importance for its possible political repercussions rather than the number of people concerned. 'Top Salaries in the Private Sector and Nationalised

Industries', (Report No. 107, Cmnd 3970) brought the Board in its fourth year from one end of the spectrum with its examinations of low pay in agriculture and clothing, with pay in the area of £10 weekly (full-time), to the salaries of £100 weekly for part-time work, and up to £1,000 weekly, sometimes more, for full-time work. The sample was perhaps not so large as it might have been and the firms were perhaps not quite so representative as was assumed, although the nationalised industries were fully covered. Fringe benefits appeared to be low compared with what information there was about them, e.g. company cars are estimated against their cost to the company and not on the pre-taxed income the individual has to earn to buy and maintain one. The report said that 41 per cent of top executives receive bonuses between £3,000 and £1,095, but this is not considered to be a significant part of their pay. Private sector pensions are now drawing ahead of the public sector, though this is mainly due to the lower salaries in the latter. Another reason for this is that 'less use is made in the public sector of discretionary arrangements permitted by the Inland Revenue rules' (op. cit., p. 10). The survey asked for quantitative measures of each job: annual expenditures controlled, value of goods produced or sold, the number of employees under the executive's direction.

One consultant who tried to assess differences in comparative responsibility between top jobs in the private and public sectors commented that although top executives in the public sector have heavier responsibilities 'the pay is often less than half' (ibid., p. 14). Some private companies had made international comparisons, according to their connections, with US-based firms. The report recognised this and regretted it, but found it acceptable if the comparisons were 'contained'.

One of the statistical tables shows the increases in gross pay over the years 1965-8: members of main Boards 8 per cent, executives 15 per cent, employees in these undertakings 19 per cent. The corresponding figures for nationalised Boards were: 2 per cent, 10 per cent, 16 per cent. The report found that 'some restraint has been shown', (ibid., p. 18), although when we consider that the greater part of the companies surveyed were well through the White Paper's ceiling of 3½ per cent, this is hardly believable. Even if only the top salaries had been referred to in this context, the executives in the private sector, which covers the greater part of the economy, had averaged 5 per cent per annum.

The Board appeared to accept this by drawing up their criteria for executive pay as compared to operatives' pay; the salary structure must adequately reward promotion and induce people to take jobs which have more responsibility than before—for such moves people should have greater pay; high performance should be rewarded. The Board had been dealing with largish companies but the White Paper did not ask for increases to less than a hundred workers to be referred to the Board. Those that were referred in small numbers could go through the 'ceiling' if the increases were due to 'added experience, increased responsibility or special effort, or to increases resulting from promotion to work at a higher level' (ibid., p. 21). These criteria gave a great deal of scope for many executives.

The conclusions of the report, which aroused much comment in newspapers as well as in parliamentary and trade union circles, were that differentials have to be widened in the nationalised industries at the higher levels, due to the need to encourage promotion, to relate reward to performance, and to stimulate recruitment from outside the industry. Salaries were to be substantially raised at the top levels, so that they could be raised in the supporting levels of management. Chairmen of Group A Boards were to rise from £12,500 to £20,000 yearly and of Group B Boards from £11,000 to £17,000, with suitable adjustments in the executive range. These increases were to be realised in three stages. The government accepted the report and announced that the first increase was within the 3½ per cent level.

Last, we consider the report on job evaluation (Report No. 83, Cmnd 3772), where the Board attempted to quantify the problems of measuring work and rewarding performance. One aspect of this had been dealt with in the report on payment by results systems. Job evaluation attempts to rationalise the wage structure and set jobs in a relationship to each other, in contrast to piecemeal bargaining by groups of workers pressing wage claims based on pay relativities between groups in the same factory or industry. Job evaluation compares jobs, ranks them according to duties, difficulties, performance, or responsibilities, and relates this to the pay structure. There are four main methods used: ranking, and grading or classification, which are usually described as non-analytical and can be used for simple job ranking; factor comparison and the points rating method, which give numerical values to the rankings.

The Board carried out a survey to discover the extent of job evaluation. This showed that 'some 25 per cent of the nearly 6,500,000 employees in the sample were covered by job evaluation' (op. cit., p. 10). It was expected that this method would be extended in the future. Surprisingly, more than 70 per cent of the employees in coal mining were covered, as was tobacco manufacture. Oil and chemicals had 50 per cent, and air transport 40 per cent of its employees. Job evaluation was least used in 'timber and furniture, construction, printing and publishing, leather and fur, shipbuilding and marine engineering—all industries where job relationships seem deeply rooted in tradition and craftsmen are numerous' (op. cit., p. 11).

The survey found that the method was used mainly by large organisations for evaluating 'managerial' groups (30 per cent) and 'staff' (27 per cent). Non-craft manual employees, with 26 per cent coverage, came next, and craftsmen came last, being more hostile to job evaluation, with 11 per cent.

The Board, as we have seen, recommended the introduction or extension of job evaluation in a number of industries as a means of increasing pay and productivity. This would have the effect of hastening the shift from national or industry-wide collective agreements to local and work-place negotiations. This could lead to a breach between firms and the national federations and the report suggests that job evaluation schemes might be developed on industry-wide lines, available to firms and unions. Federations should develop a new role and relationship with firms and unions. One of the defects of job evaluation is that it leads to a short-term increase in costs, although, as we have already noted from a number of reports, few firms were able to give the actual costs or percentage additions to wages from any new system or method. The survey showed that only seven companies out of ninety-one were able to give percentage cost additions to the wage-bill from a job-evaluated pay structure. These additions ranged from 2 per cent to 12 per cent.

The PIB clearly hoped that the wider use of job evaluation would bring a greater sense of rationality and fair play or justice to pay differentials. They recommended that trade unions should be involved in the negotiations and implementation of the method.

Industrial relations in the Board's fourth year

The beginning of the fourth year was overshadowed by the appearance of the report of the Royal Commission on trade unions and employers' associations (Cmnd 3623). The Donovan Report, as it is now known, after Lord Donovan, the Chairman, is too lengthy to summarise here. The main findings are well-known: the analysis of the 'two systems' of industrial relations, one at the national or industry-wide level, the other on the local or shop-floor level, and the consequent shift in power with its effects on trade unions and particularly on unofficial strikes. The Commission called for an Industrial Relations Act and a 'complete overhaul of industrial relations'. Many suggestions were made for the reform of collective bargaining, mainly through the improvement of contracts and procedures, the process of reform to be assisted by the setting up of an Industrial Relations Commission with powers of investigation into various union/management problems. Companies above a certain size would have to register their collective agreements with the Department of Employment and Productivity. The main interest of the industrial and political world centred on the report's views on the legal aspects of strikes and disputes. In brief, their view was that the law should be kept out of the field of industrial relations as much as possible, though there was a suggestion that more effective legal action might be taken against unofficial strikers by making them legally responsible for damages incurred through such strikes. A minority group on the Commission argued that the imprisonment of unofficial strikers would merely make matters worse; in any event, trade unions might decide to change their rules to make all strikes official until the union executive decided otherwise. Discussions on this point continued through the year and influenced the White Paper 'In Place of Strife' (Cmnd 3888), which discussed the enforceability of agreements. Contracts could be legally enforced if this were written into the contract and agreed to by both parties to the arrangement. The White Paper proposed that there be: a Commission on Industrial Relations, a register of industrial agreements for the larger companies, the right to belong to a trade union, the right of a trade union to be recognised by an employer, safeguards for employees against unfair dismissal. The controversial aspects of the White Paper were the suggested remedies for unofficial strikes: an Industrial Board which could impose sanctions for breach of an order by the Secretary of State, a twenty-eight-day 'conciliation pause' in some cases, refusal to obey which would lead to sanctions, possibly fines. 'The Board (the "Industrial Board") will have power to impose financial penalties on an employer, union or individual striker as it found appropriate . . . in the appropriate County Court by attachment of earnings and other civil remedies for the collection of debts . . .' (op. cit., p. 21).

In the early months of 1969 the lengthy and damaging strike in the Ford Company, coupled with several others, sharpened the national argument over unofficial strikes (although the Ford strike had been, for the most part, an official one). The Prime

Minister criticised the 'irresponsibility' of the Ford strikers, and said that it justified the government in its attempts to reform trade union law. He mentioned the strikes at Girlings and Vauxhall's, Ellesmere Port, and said that they might lead to future developments going abroad (*Guardian*, 15 March 1969). The White Paper had started an extensive debate in parliament as well as in the country. The Conservative Party had gone further than the government in its proposed legal curbs. *Fair Deal at Work*, published by the Conservative Central Office in April 1968, suggested a cooling-off period of sixty days; in the case of a strike threatening the national interest, a secret strike ballot would be taken in this period; collective agreements would be binding in law, and certain types of strikes would not have protection in law against civil action for damages. By contrast, the government White Paper was less far-reaching, but much argument took place over the possibility of strikers being fined, or sent to prison for non-payment of fines. Months of wrangling inside the Cabinet, the Parliamentary Labour Party, and the Labour movement, including the trade unions, led to the proposed legal sanctions being dropped. The TUC gave what the Prime Minister described as a 'solemn, binding promise', 'copper-bottomed' and with the weight of the TUC General Council behind it. This was the TUC's 'Programme for Action' with which they would intervene in unofficial strikes which were important and damaging to the economy. Much was expected from this programme (though not apparently by Mr Feather, Acting General Secretary of the TUC, who explained modestly that he was not a miracle-worker but would do what he could) although in its first serious test, the blast-furnacemen's strike at Port Talbot in July–August 1969, the TUC intervention had little effect.

The TUC published its 1969 Economic Review, which suggested a higher rate of growth in the economy than the government had forecast. The unions proposed that the growth rate should be 6 per cent in the next year, and that the awards for wages and salaries could rise by about 12*s* to 18*s* per head per week. Collective bargaining machinery could be improved and taxation changed to benefit the lower-paid workers at the expense of the better-off. A better strategy for keeping down prices should be developed. The TUC were also critical of the White Paper on strikes; of the secret ballot, and of the possible attachment of earnings to pay fines incurred.

Evaluation of the PIB's fourth year

The Board had reached the point where it saw itself as the supreme arbitral body on wages and salaries. This implies that they examined a pay claim in the context of the industry's structure and industrial relations, and gave their verdict, interpreting the criteria of the government's White Paper and the ceiling of $3\frac{1}{2}$ per cent. In general, the reports of the Board were of a high standard, considering the shortage of time in which the survey teams had to work, i.e. around four months, and the great shortage of statistics and information about wages, salaries, collective agreements and conditions of work. Some of the reports were poor, although technically competent, due to lack of knowledge or understanding of the work situation or context. They also failed, at least in print, to recognise the forces of market power and industrial action; there is almost no mention in the many reports of the Board, or in their annual surveys, of the industrial troubles which could take place before, during, or after a reference had been submitted to them. Neither did the Board say whether they ever discussed the possible consequences of a reference in terms of the effect on industry or exports if a substantial increase in pay were not given. There is also the curious matter of the various groups who drove breaches through the incomes policy, ranging from the dockers to the pilots, some of whom escaped official notice or reference.

When we look at the three outstanding increases of the year in the public sector, the BOAC pilots, the top salaries of top executives, and the higher civil servants, we find that the pilots' increase was due mainly to their ability to inflict great losses on the airline and cause inconvenience to important travellers. The high capital costs of the airlines and the relatively low labour costs made some newspapers argue that the increases demanded by the pilots were relatively small seen against the total cost of running the airline. The Board were prepared to concede increases of three times the ceiling in the first year and double the ceiling for the next two years, in return for the doubtful promise that there would be demanning. This indicates that the more over-manned an industry is, the greater the concessions that can be got. The pilots, through further strike action, improved their pay considerably above what the Board and the employers had originally agreed to.

The other two large increases in pay were achieved without any industrial action, and apparently on criteria which the Board had rejected for lower-paid people. These increases were outlined in the report on top salaries, which gave increases up to 60 per cent over three years, and the report on higher civil servants, which listed increases up to 63 per cent over three years. The higher civil servants had their pay increased by the recommendations of the Standing Advisory Committee, one of the committees which the government and the Board wished could come under more centralised control. Yet the Board itself recommended that top salaries for chairmen and others on nationalised industries should also rise up to 60 per cent over three years.

The electrical contracting industry had little difficulty in negotiating 9 per cent per annum, and the same industry in Scotland, after having its claim on comparability grounds with England rejected, went on strike and was given the comparability it had demanded. Doctors and dentists achieved increases of 8 per cent or so from the Kindersley Committee which, like a number of other committees, ignored the criteria of the Board and made an award which they thought suitable. There were the awards in private industry of ICI and the London Clearing Banks, which, although refused by the Board, simply went ahead with the full award, paid retrospectively, after a pause. There were the industries which, although examined by the Board, did not allow its recommendations to influence their pay increases to any great extent. These were the engineering industry and the car delivery group, with the engineers reaching an average of 7 per cent increase per annum. Agriculture reached 7 per cent per year on the criteria of low pay.

All the industries examined by the Board in its fourth year received increases of $3\frac{1}{2}$ per cent per year or more, with two exceptions. These were the municipal busmen and the university teachers. Significantly, both are in the public sector, and although the busmen's strikes and sanctions inconvenienced numbers of the public, the government and the Board resisted the pressures. The university teachers have never followed a policy of sanctions or strikes, as their ability to influence the economy or the government in this way is relatively small.

The verdict on the Board's fourth year can be put briefly: if the industry or group was paid from public moneys or was under public regulation, and had no effective market or political power (through strikes, sanctions, or effect on parliament or the public) then the Board or the government could give them less than the $3\frac{1}{2}$ per cent per year. An exception to this statement was where pay in the public sector was determined by a committee or agreed formula, e.g. Kindersley Committee, the Standing Advisory Committee for Higher Civil Service Pay, Civil Service Tribunal,

Burnham Committee, the Grigg Formula; these bodies often awarded more than the Board would have done; they seldom awarded less. For this reason, the Board and the government wanted to abolish the various committees mentioned above and set up one body for pay in the public sector.

In the private sector, the Board had influence on wages and rates, but little influence on earnings, as was evident from the reports on car delivery, electrical contracting, the exhibition industry, building and construction, BOAC pilots, ICI, London Clearing Banks, journalists. This does not mean that the public sector was entirely dominated by the Board or by the government. Strikes or sanctions in the public sector, where effective, had results. The fuel industries had above 'ceiling' increases, although coal was a special case for a number of reasons; gas and electricity supply did well, as they possessed considerable market power and disruptive potential, along with some, though not as much as claimed, increases in productivity. The railways had steady increases for the same reasons, especially that of effective industrial action. Doctors and dentists had substantial increases due to considerable market power, assisted by a controlled scarcity of recruits and an international market for our medical graduates. The top salaries group in the public and private sectors owed their good fortune partly to the discovery by the Board's top executives that they were earning more than the top echelons in public industry, and to a rather different set of criteria from that used on lower ranges of salaries (Report on top salaries, Cmnd 3970, p. 33).

Municipal busmen were probably the least fortunate of the local government employees. Municipal transport has to be self-financing. A rise in wages today leads to a rise in fares soon afterwards, a fall in passengers, an increase in the deficit on the undertaking, and indignant public and political reactions. Other local government employees did better as the Board had little knowledge of the workings of the establishment committees in local authorities—as little, in fact, as the local authorities themselves.

University teachers had less success in percentage terms than the busmen had: if a 'league table' of the Board's awards for the year had been drawn up, they would have been the wooden spoonists.

The verdict of the newspapers and the commentators on the Board came before the end of the fourth year. April was the cruellest month, with a number of articles noting the demise of the Board with muted regret. Peter Jenkins of the *Guardian* who had noted the weakening pulse of the patient for some time, wrote:

'The incomes policy is dead, long live the PIB' (*Guardian*, 11 April 1969). Mr Jenkins's view was that the government had fought the wrong war at the wrong time, and had been forced to retreat after their bluff had been called. The 1 per cent restraining effect on incomes (possibly only 0·7 per cent) might even have had a disproportionate effect on costs by worsening industrial relations, and causing strikes and unrest, besides stimulating wage claims. The incomes policy 'became a collection of loopholes tied together with string. There grew up incomes policy avoidance, which like tax avoidance was legal though often unfair, and incomes policy evasion, which was illegal but often went unpunished.' The industrial editor of *The Times* wrote that the top salaries reference had buckled the 'structure of consent' on which incomes policy had been based. 'Whatever the logic, nothing could be more offensive to a man denied his few pennies an hour than an award of perhaps several times his total earnings as an increase to, say, nationalised industry chairman' (*The Times*, 8 April 1969, p. 22). The *Guardian* agreed with this viewpoint, saying in an editorial that 'Ministers are allowing their incomes policy to be whittled away piecemeal, like slices of salami' (*Guardian*, 7 April 1969).

In writing 'the present as history' journalists of quality newspapers are often the best observers. They are on the scene, they talk to the protagonists, and with their wide-ranging contacts and information as to what is happening elsewhere in the industrial scene, they can make a synthesis which, though often overstated, conveys much of the union feeling about the issues. (These observations by the newspapers were found to be largely correct by the writer, who went to a number of trade union and political meetings before and during this period.) There is little doubt that once the Board examined, and published, their recommendations on the salaries of top executives, the 'structure of consent' and voluntary restraint on which incomes policy must rest, moved from an already weak position to one of disintegration. The few remaining defenders of the incomes policy were Labour MPs, and while they naturally spoke about the achievements of their government, they found it difficult to justify a 60 per cent award at the top of the salary scale, even when spread over three years and declared to be 'within the $3\frac{1}{2}$ per cent ceiling'.

The other weakness of incomes policy was that it was conceived in the expectation that it would function in an expansive economic climate. The constant restrictions which economic events forced on the strategy of growth led an increasing number of trade unions to look upon incomes policy as a brake on their legitimate demands.

At the end of the fourth year the TUC had moved from a position of restrained agreement with a voluntary incomes policy, while objecting strongly to legal sanctions, to one of opposition to the whole policy. At the TUC Conference in September 1969, against the advice of the General Council, the following motion was passed by 4,652,000 votes to 4,207,000: 'Congress reaffirms its opposition to anti-trade union legislation and other forms of interference in trade union affairs. We therefore demand the repeal of the Prices and Incomes Act of 1966' (*Guardian*, 4 September 1969). Although the decision rested on a narrow majority, it was nonetheless decisive, as it was supported by a group of the larger and more powerful unions, notably the TGWU and the AEF. This placed the government in a difficult position as the Chancellor of the Exchequer, in his budget speech in 1969, had said that they would not retain the power to delay wage and price increases for twelve months, but would use instead Part II of the 1966 Prices and Incomes Act, which gave the government powers of delay, on reference to the PIB, of three months. The Chancellor followed this statement by a Letter of Intent to the International Monetary Fund on 24 June, indicating that pay or price increases could be deferred up to three or four months (PIB Fourth General Report, pp. 1–2).

The fifth year of the PIB

The Fifth and Final Report of the PIB (Cmnd 4649, April 1971) was in the nature of a requiem for the Board, as the Conservative government of 1970 had decided to dissolve it by March 1971. The obituary, being written by the victim, showed insight into the reasons for the demise. The Board said that as early as the beginning of 1969 the government were accepting 'wage increases of up to $3\frac{1}{2}$ per cent almost automatically'. As they put it (and others had done so long before them), the ceiling of $3\frac{1}{2}$ per cent had become a floor. They might have added that it was a spring-board for others.

The 'softening' of the policy had occurred at the end of the long, contentious struggle in the bus industry, with the bus maintenance workers having a large increase, followed by the clearing bank employees, then the exhibition contracting industries. Strikes or difficulties with the first two groups had made difficulties for the public face of the government. The latter group had been able to put strong pressure on business, and also the government, before large and important exhibitions.

The Board traced further 'softening' after the end of 1969. This was evident from the large increases given earlier to the manual workers in local authorities and to government industrial workers, who both received $8\frac{1}{2}$ per cent. Much of this had been compensation for the effects of devaluation working through the economy, raising prices and costs. Prices had been pushed up further by the government raising taxation as a deflationary measure and also, although from the best of motives, increasing the social security contribution in order to raise the standards of the social services. The net effect of these measures had been to cause the price level to rise, with rents, rates and bus fares in the local authority sector also rising, so that the average worker felt that his real standards were falling at a time when some groups of workers appeared to be getting higher wage increases. Hence the growing pressure of wage demands which faced the Board in their final year.

The government White Paper of December 1969, 'Productivity, Prices and Incomes Policy after 1969' (Cmnd 4237), raised the norm to the range of $2\frac{1}{2}$ to $4\frac{1}{2}$ per cent, though it could be said that in this case the higher level became the floor. Questions in parliament in the early months of 1970 showed that many wage increases were now running at 9·7 per cent (Parliamentary Answer, 4 March, cf. Cmnd 4649).

Reports and criteria in the PIB's fifth year

In its final year the Board was less involved in controversial decisions, as the rigours of incomes policy had faded. It was now more able to engage in studies of special areas, where its expertise and wide coverage could bring together a wide range of field studies throwing light on deep-rooted problems and practices of industry; productivity agreements, salary structures; hours of work, overtime and shift-working; low pay. There were, in addition, studies of professions and industries.

Productivity

Productivity or efficiency agreements remained the corner-stone of the Board's policy. In their third report in this field (No. 123, 'Productivity Agreements', August 1969, Cmnd 4136) they suggested new guidelines, which included the development of existing agreements, and tackled the problems of sectional agreements in firms, along with the old problem of measuring clerical and non-manual work so that such groups can take part in the benefits of productivity. Finally, there was the question of devising agreements reaching across companies and industries.

The Board's emphasis on productivity or pay structure changes can be traced through a number of reports. The efficiency of staff based on job evaluation, common grading for male and female clerks, and salary restructuring, are dealt with in Report No. 125, 'Salaries of certain staff employed by British Insulated Callenders' Cables Ltd' (Cmnd 4168). The salary award was 6 per cent, which was also a move towards equal pay for male and female.

As the 6 per cent was nearly twice the 'norm' of $3\frac{1}{2}$ per cent the Board had to search for 'exceptional treatment' or productivity criteria. They were critical of the information offered on these grounds, but felt that the changes would lead to more efficiency. This conclusion was typical of many of their reports.*

Work-study, as an aid to efficient working, was suggested in Report No. 140, 'Pay and Conditions of Workers in the Milk Industry' (Cmnd 4267). Significantly, this reference arose from unrest in the industry, whose problems were low basic pay, high turnover and long hours. These varied between regions, but the industry was a labour-intensive one based on a seven-day week. Labour costs would continue to rise and efficiency had to be improved and overtime reduced. Minimum earnings for a standard week were suggested.

The Board was correct in its advice on efficiency and some industries and firms accepted this. Others were more obdurate, either from fear of a strike or slow-down or because of a tight labour monopoly which refused to give up a favourable position; the two reasons were functionally related, each reinforcing the other.

This is evident in Report No. 141, 'Costs and Revenue of National Newspapers' (Cmnd 4277), which returned to the earlier themes pursued in Report No. 43, which discovered over-manning of some 25–30 per cent in at least one national newspaper. Sectional bargaining in the industry led to a 'see-sawing' of rates between newspapers, and plant-wide bargaining with guidelines

---

* The DEP seem to have allowed large numbers of 'productivity' bargains to pass, partly because of insufficient information, and partly for expedient or tactical reasons. Professor Clegg is critical of the numbers of productivity agreements of the 'spurious' variety and quotes a pilot survey in *The Times*, 28 September 1970 (H. A. Clegg *How to Run an Incomes Policy*, Heinemann, London, 1971, p. 38). An example of this was a major survey done by the PIB, 'Costs and Efficiency in the Gas Industry' (Report No. 155, Cmnd 4458). Though this was one of the best reports of its kind, it is evident that the Area Boards did not have the data on which effective incentive payment and productivity schemes could be based. Although improvements have since taken place, many of the schemes studied by the PIB had to be taken on trust or on informed guesses.

set out by the industry was suggested. Wage structures were to be based on job evaluation and work-study. These recommendations have had relatively little effect on the industry, where the major changes have come about through the disappearance of newspapers and subsequent mergers.

Another example of the failure to penetrate a tight labour monopoly appears in Report No. 126, dealing with Smithfield Market (Cmnd 4171). The self-employed porters or 'bummarees' had long been a classic case of a tightly organised group of workers over which the union had little influence (as was also the case in the London and Liverpool docks). There were wide and unjust differences in earnings between groups and labour entry was highly restrictive with a closed shop. Labour costs were nearly 68 per cent. A Market Joint Board was suggested which would produce a comprehensive agreement, with arrangements for redundancy and run-down of the labour force. The Board's recommendations faced the same difficulties as they had done in the newspaper industry. The 'bummarees' had defied government committees and even a High Court judgment in the past, and the remarks of the union official on the ruling of the judge who ordered them to allow meat traders to carry their own meat to their vans deserve wider publicity: 'He said they could; we said they couldn't; and they didn't.'

The labour monopoly was not confined to manual worker groups, as many professional groups bristle with monopolistic characteristics disguised as professional standards. Such groups included the airline pilots. Report No. 129 on BOAC pilots recommended that 'the practice of relating pilots' pay to the type of aircraft should be discontinued and common scales of pay for all pilots should be introduced regardless of the type of aircraft flown'. This had little effect on the bargaining over jumbo jets. Nor had the Board's suggestions much effect on the legal profession, as has already been noted, although they devoted three reports to this.

There were also three reports on the armed forces, which resulted in large-scale job evaluation being carried out as a basis for pay structure. They ended with the confident assertion that 'job evaluation is now firmly established as a technique for continuing use in connection with the Armed Forces' (Fifth General Report, p. 14).

An important by-product of the Board's interest in efficiency and in structural changes was the major survey on hours of work, overtime and shift-working (Report No. 161, Cmnd 4554). It had been evident for over twenty years that there was too much overtime in British industry and that this had resulted in inefficient working in normal hours so that overtime would be available. Many productivity agreements had, as their major aim, the reduction of overtime, while the introduction of shift-working has been the main proposal of many management consultants for numbers of companies in recent years. It was found that high levels of overtime were a reminder that there could be much wastage of resources. One variation on overtime working is the practice of 'moonlighting', where workers may have two jobs. There are a number of varieties of this. (See Campbell Balfour, 'The Missing Millions', *Management Today*, March 1971.)

The Board noted that numbers of companies who wished to cut down overtime and ineffective payment by result systems and move to shift-work and effective pay systems were handicapped by the lack of effective costing systems relating pay to productivity. This statement is found in a number of their reports over the years.

Low pay

Earlier, we suggested that the traditional criteria for wage increases used by unions and employers had been criticised by the PIB, who stated that their twin objectives were productivity improvements leading to pay increases and social justice for the lower-paid. As indicated, the Board did much work on the productivity factor, with uneven results, but were less successful in their research and recommendations on low pay.

The last group of reports issued by the Board may represent a belated attempt to grapple with the problem, and we may wonder why this issue was left to the penultimate report, 'General Problems of Low Pay' (Report No. 169, Cmnd 4648). Like the survey on hours of work, the report drew together a range of interesting statistics and made a number of observations. Whilst some of these border on the banal, such as the statement that low pay is an important factor in causing low family income among men in the sample, there does emerge a multiplicity of reasons for low pay, among which are: the inefficiency of the industry or firm; declining public demand; large numbers of unskilled workers in the industry unable to find more pay elsewhere; lack of effective trade unions or of arrangements for determining wages.

Apart from indicating that the social income of the lower-paid was assisted by redistributive taxation and social security measures, the report recommended that Wages Councils (which had been dealing with the lower paid since 1909 and in their modern form from 1945) should have more information about earnings than they then had. That there might be a national minimum wage, although too much should not be hoped for here, as experience from other countries showed. Manpower services and job training could help, although trade union help would be needed in this, as well as in the general problem of differentials between jobs and industries. (In our opinion, however, trade unions would be unlikely to accept the proposition that raising the wages of the lowly-paid must mean 'a relative worsening of the position of others'.)

Evaluation of the fifth year

The final year's work of the Board was influenced by the 'succession of political and economic developments outside its control, concluding with a decision by the new Government that the Board should be dissolved' (Fifth General Report, p. 1). The dissolution of the Board had become an article of faith with the Conservative Party in the run-up to the general election of 1970, as part of the institutional superstructure of the Labour Government which they intended to sweep away. The authority of the Board had also been seriously undermined by the obvious collapse of incomes policy from mid-1969 onwards; the effects of devaluation and rising costs and prices working through the economy; the Labour government's desire to create a minor boom before the election, along with the rejection of incomes policy by the TUC.

In spite of these factors, some good surveys were carried out in the last year and have provided useful material for industry, unions and arbitrators. Like much good work this was largely unacknowledged by the politicians, by the public or by the press. The latter, having exhausted their obituary notices on the impending death in the Board's fourth year, simply noted the passing, although both *The Times* and the *Guardian* said that there was still a role for the PIB and that it could well be revived. Even lengthy articles of an analytical nature had morbid photographs: 'RIP for the PIB'. (Cover photo, *Personnel Management*, February 1971.)

Unfortunately for the Board, which had done good work in providing the ground rules for genuine productivity agreements, the industrial unrest and accompanying 'wage explosion' of the period made groups of shop stewards in strong bargaining positions reluctant to undertake negotiations which traded higher wages in return for less overtime and a possible reduction in the labour force. During 1970 wage earnings rose by some 15 per cent and the number of strikes to over 2,000. This was in spite of the higher unemployment figures of the same year.

In this situation, the Board adopted a less militant posture towards references than it had done in past years and saw itself in a more consultative role with its reports on special issues such as hours of work, low pay, equal pay and salary structures. It had also played a role in improving negotiating machinery in a number of industries.

Incomes policy and collective bargaining

So far we have traced the origins of the Board and its work in its five years of existence. All the reports dealing with the incomes aspect of the policy have been looked at, briefly in the first three years of reports, in more detail in the fourth year when the method of the Board's surveys had become more sophisticated and some continuity had been achieved in the attempts to interpret the criteria of the White Papers, in less detail in the fifth year, when the functions and public standing of the Board were altered by the 'wage explosion', the pre-election and post-election situation, and its last nine months under the shadow of its dissolution. But the reports, because of the short time available for research, and the restrictions and inhibitions of official comment, were incomplete. There was a lack of official information about the events which led to the pay claim, the methods or strategy which may have been employed in pursuing it, and the action, if any, after the publication of the report. This gives an incomplete picture of the effects of incomes policy on the workings of collective bargaining in a particular industry. Professor Dunlop has written: 'A wage-price policy . . . comes down to detailed micro-problems' (PIB Fourth General Report, p. 16). We now propose to look at the effects of incomes policy on several industries (bus transport, universities, local government, air transport) and examine them in much greater detail. These industries or services are all in the public sector, under direct government pressure or control, and should serve as a test of the government's success or failure in following its own pronouncements on incomes policy, and that of the PIB in interpreting them.

3

The bus industry

The strains and stresses, and partial successes of incomes policy appear clearly in the bus industry. The difficulties in the industry were there, of course, before the National Board for Prices and Incomes was created in 1965. The last few years also show another interesting trend, the move away from national agreements to more localised ones.

In 1963 there had been a Committee of Inquiry into pay and conditions of employment for bus crews in London Transport, headed by Professor E. H. Phelps Brown.* Another Committee of Inquiry, chaired by Sir Roy Wilson, QC,† looked into the dispute between the two sides of the National Council for the Omnibus Industry. There had also been an arbitration on disagreements on the NJIC, heard by a board led by Professor D. J. Robertson.

The bus industry itself covers four main groupings. PIB Report No. 50 (Cmnd 3498) defines them as follows:

(i) London Transport Board, operating about 7,700 vehicles in the Central and County Area fleets, and employing some 33,000 drivers and conductors.

(ii) Municipally-owned undertakings with some 16,800 buses and 52,000 platform staff. All except five of these undertakings are members of the Federation of Municipal Transport Employers.

(iii) Company undertakings, which are members of the Conference of Omnibus Companies and are mostly owned either by the Transport Holding Company (THC) or the British Electric Traction Group (BET). The THC is publicly owned and is at present in process of

---

* Committee of Inquiry to Review the Pay and Conditions of Employment of the Drivers and Conductors of the London Transport Board's Road Services; appointed jointly by the Ministers of Labour and Transport on 20 November 1963.
† Committee of Inquiry into the Causes and Circumstances of the Difference Existing between the Two Sides of the National Council for the Omnibus Industry; appointed by the Minister of Labour on 10 March 1965.

F

purchasing BET. The two groups together operate about 26,500 buses and coaches and employ some 73,000 platform staff.

(iv) 'Independent' companies outside the Conference with about 23,700 vehicles, and 21,000 'off-season' staff. Some of the coach operators are members of the Passenger Vehicle Operators' Association, but negotiations on pay and conditions are all conducted locally, though agreements tend to follow those of the Conference Companies (op. cit., p. 3).

This was the situation in December 1966. This analysis will concern itself mainly with (ii) above, muncipal transport, and (i) London Transport, with some reference to (iii) company undertakings. The TGWU is the sole union representing busmen in London Transport, and the union has all the seats save one (occupied by the National Union of General and Municipal Workers) on the union side of the NJIC.

Economic and social factors in the bus industry

The framework in which the bus industry functions shows in detail the inter-relationships between market forces, the methods of transport operation, and the power structure of local authorities responsible to the electors. Municipal transport is a declining industry as measured by consumer demand. There are a number of factors at work here (see Table 3). The industry can do little

Table 3 *Percentage change in number of passengers carried 1955–65*

Period	Change (%)
Monday to Friday	−35
Saturday	−47
Sunday	−53
Total	−39

(Source: PIB Report No. 16, p. 6.)

about these changes which lead to a falling output per unit of cost. Nor can it do much about its own cost structure. Revenue is derived from bus fares and bus companies are not free to vary these. Applications for fares increases have to be made to the Road Transport Commissioners, who hold a public hearing, and the application may be refused or deferred. A fares increase can also lead to a fall in total revenue, as consumers make marginal decisions to buy cars, e.g. council estates are increasingly built on the outskirts of cities, and higher bus fares become a daily prod to workers, the main bus-users, to buy cars. There is also a growth in 'car pools' or groups using one car or several cars on a rota.

Because of the growth of cars, the decline of the railways and the development of heavy road transport, congestion has increased greatly. This prevents the buses from running to schedule, which leads to public frustration and less confidence in the bus service, and increases the drift to car ownership or usage through 'car pools' or daily 'lifts'. This, in turn, leads to a fall in bus revenue, a need to raise fares, and a further fall in bus usage, leading to increased congestion. The bus industry is caught in a narrowing circle of falling revenue and rising labour costs, given the present method of manning buses with a two-man crew, as a quarter-full bus needs as much labour as a full one.

The PIB estimated in 1965 that 'the pay of drivers and conductors represents $5\frac{1}{2}d$ out of a 1s fare' (see Table 4). In spite of a great fall in public demand for bus transport in the 1950s and 1960s 'the size of the labour force in the industry . . . remained practically unchanged' (Report No. 16, p. 7).

Table 4 *Costs represented as elements of a shilling bus fare in 1965*

	Provincial buses (12 undertakings)	
	Per cent of revenue	Cost in pence
Drivers	26	3
Conductors	21	$2\frac{1}{2}$
Traffic and administrative staff	7	1
Cleaning, maintenance and repairs (including labour)	14	$1\frac{3}{4}$
Tyres	2	$\frac{1}{4}$
Fuel	10	$1\frac{1}{4}$
Insurance, licences, operating and administration overheads	9	1
Depreciation of vehicles	6	$\frac{3}{4}$
Total cost	95	$11\frac{1}{2}$
Surplus	+5	$+\frac{1}{2}$
	100	1s

Source: PIB Report No. 16, p. 7.)

The bus industry dilemma is due partly to social costs, and if the move away from car usage to bus usage could be halted, this would have a great effect on the shape of our cities and on heavy public expenditure on roads. There has been a good deal of interest in the problem, stimulated mainly by the Buchanan Report. More immediately, the question of costs lies either with the government, or with local authorities in the form of subsidies from the government or the rates or through deficit financing.

The PIB and the bus industry

The PIB took more time over, and produced more reports about, the bus industry than it did for any other industry in the country. The reasons for this attention arose from the deep-seated nature of the problem as well as the recurring disputes in the industry and the subsequent fragmentation of collective bargaining.

There are three main reports on the bus industry. The first (Report No. 16, 'Pay and Conditions of Busmen', Cmnd 3012) appeared in May 1966, and dealt with all three sectors of the industry, the basic pay rates and the relationships between the sectors. The first report arose from a claim by the TGWU to the London Transport Board (LTB) for a review of wages under their agreement which made annual reviews possible. The negotiations resulted in a pay claim which the LTB said would come to an increase of 6·6 per cent on the basic rate of pay for Central London drivers.

Shortly before the London negotiations in February 1966, a claim for a substantial increase in pay had been made to the National Joint Industrial Council for the Road Passenger Transport Industry (NJIC) on behalf of the employees in municipal transport. Negotiations in February were influenced by the progress of the London Transport negotiations. In the third sector, a claim was made to the National Council for the Omnibus Industry (NCOI) on behalf of the employees of the larger bus companies.

The claims were referred by the government to the PIB on 4 March 1966 for a report on the criteria in the pay claim, and the pay relationship between the three sectors. The inquiry showed the difficulties which the Board sometimes encountered. The employers and the unions co-operated with the exception of the TGWU, which as the main representative of the busmen, and the sole representative in London, faced the Board with a problem in collecting the necessary evidence. They said: 'We have as a result been hindered in forming a judgement about the attitudes of busmen themselves to the conditions of their work' (op. cit., p. 2).

Before examining the pay claim, the Board began by looking at the structure of the busmen's pay. This is made up differently from that of the factory worker, as busmen have two main peaks of demand, morning and evening. There are early turns and late turns, and a number of 'spread-over duties' where a man works in the two peak periods, and has an interval in between. There are also 'rostered earnings', where a roster is made up and men are given schedules of duties. These may be varied from week to week, as earnings vary on different schedules. As the buses provide a seven-day service, special arrangements have to be made for week-end work. Apart from the basic rate for a standard week, there are a number of premium rates which make up an average earnings figure for January 1966 in London in the manner shown in Table 5.

Table 5 *Central bus driver's average earnings, January 1966*

	s	d
Basic wage	305	6
Sunday pay	11	2
Saturday afternoon pay	6	9
Early and late pay	6	1
Scheduled overtime	2	4
Spread-over allowance	20	1
Total	351	11

(Source: PIB Report No. 16, p. 10.)

The Board found that drivers earned more than conductors but this was due more to the longer hours they worked than to higher basic rates. Men conductors earned only 6 per cent less than drivers, while women conductors earned 8 per cent less than men conductors, although the women still earned far more than most women manual workers in industry.

Drivers in London earned more than drivers elsewhere, but this was due mainly to a difference in the basic rate as the London bus drivers worked shorter hours. London rosters were based on the forty-hour week in 1966, while over half of the municipal undertakings had rotas of forty-five hours weekly and some of over fifty hours. Municipal bus drivers, in turn, earned more than drivers in the bus companies.

Giving examples, the Board wrote: 'It will be seen that over the two years October 1963 to October 1965, the earnings of London busmen increased faster than those of provincial busmen and of other workers. This is because by October 1964, the recommendations of the Phelps Brown report for raising the pay of London had been put into effect' (ibid., pp. 12–13).

It was pointed out that the increases mentioned above had been due mainly to the formula produced by the Phelps Brown Committee, which, although it had laid down links between pay and productivity, also gave the busmen the impression that there was a correct relationship between their pay and that of some outside industries. The Board complained that the formula produced by the London Public Transport Board (LPTB) and the TGWU was based on a misunderstanding of the Phelps Brown formula.

London Transport had based their justification of the proposed 6·6 per cent pay increase on their acute shortage of manpower. In greater and lesser degrees, the municipal undertakings and the bus companies followed this line of argument. The evidence offered was that of the ratios of vacancies to establishment in the particular case. Over the three sectors the shortage of labour ranged from 12½ per cent to 15 per cent. The Board countered this argument by saying: 'How is a labour shortage best met? The White Paper on Prices and Incomes Policy states that labour shortage can justify an exceptional pay increase only if such an increase would be both "necessary and effective" for the purpose of redistributing manpower. In an area of general labour shortage a pay increase has to be very large if it is to be effective. And a very large increase in pay in a labour intensive industry such as the bus industry, without an equivalent increase in productivity, would hasten its contraction' (ibid., p. 17).

The Board then gave its verdict, on which most of the subsequent arguments were to turn: 'The most effective remedy for an undertaking suffering from a shortage of labour in an area of general manpower shortage is to make better use of the labour which it already has' (ibid., p. 17).

The Board also looked at the relationship between the three sectors of the bus industry, as they had all asked for a uniform increase of 6·6 per cent in rates. The Board disagreed with this claim, saying that more efficient undertakings who could raise their men's earnings would soon be followed by the less efficient arguing comparability. This was an attempt to separate the three sectors from a 'follow my leader' policy which had led to a series of leapfrogging claims in the past.

Having refused comparability between the sectors of the bus industry, and rejected formulas for comparing busmen's rates and earnings with those of other industries, the Board examined the case of the London busmen, and criticised their claim as follows: 'The formula gives great weight to the pay of London Transport Underground motormen, which is closely linked with that of the footplate staff of British Railways. There is no good reason why railway footplate staff pay should occupy a unique position in determining the remuneration of London busmen. . . . The use of engineering earnings in the formula is also open to objection' (ibid., p. 24).

Another objection was that the claim excluded voluntary overtime: 'Incomes and costs, however, are determined by gross pay including overtime earnings. A comparison which neglects them entirely is inadequate' (ibid., p. 24).

This argument was bound to be unpopular with the busmen who pointed out that their basic rate is low and that their earnings, which compare favourably with industrial averages, depend on excessive overtime.

The PIB, having put forward the doctrine that there is no labour shortage where labour is not being efficiently used, put forward its own proposals for doing this: cut down on non-productive paid time and on unnecessary limits on vehicle speeds; instigate more flexible times of working to meet the peak demands, interchange of staff between jobs, the transfer of drivers to conductors' duties and vice versa; increase the number of standing passengers, etc. Warming to its task, the Board then suggested the greater use of part-time temporary staff to meet peak demands and do week-end work. This could be coupled with a major switch to one-man operated buses (OMO). Some progress had already been made in some areas, but much more could be done by following Scandinavian example: 'In Copenhagen and Stockholm, for example, buses are operated by the driver alone at all times, including peak hours, and in dense traffic areas. All Stockholm buses have been one-man operated since 1960; 20 per cent of the drivers are women who drive double decker buses' (ibid., p. 20).

The PIB followed these suggestions, most of which have little chance of acceptance for some years, with more detailed proposals about productivity in Report No. 50 (Cmnd 3498), 'Productivity Agreements in the Bus Industry', some eighteen months later. Although Report No. 16 had agreed with the figure of 6·6 per cent offered to the London busmen, it had recommended that the municipal busmen and the company busmen should be kept to an increase in basic rates of 3–3½ per cent, unless there were improvements in the use of manpower. Some negotiations and agreements on productivity and OMO took place and the Board were asked to look at these in Report No. 50. This time they received full co-operation from all the unions in the bus industry.

The report noted that there were still complaints about shortages of staff, especially drivers and conductors, in spite of the fact that unemployment had risen from about 1·2 per cent at the time of Report No. 16 to 2·5 per cent at the time of the present report some eighteen months later. There were fewer shortages in London Transport, which of course had had a larger pay increase over the same period. Figures were given to show that the shortages were greater in the larger provincial cities, though the report said: 'it should be noted here that shortages are defined by reference to existing schedules and that in the provinces recruitment is sometimes deliberately limited by joint agreement between employers and unions as a means of providing additional overtime and thereby more acceptable take-home pay for platform staff' (op. cit., p. 4).

The heart of the problem, and the need for a change-over to OMO, can be seen from the following: 'Roughly 70 per cent of the industry's total costs are attributable to staff wages and about 50 per cent to the wages of drivers and conductors alone. London Transport, which is now subsidised from the Exchequer, was approximately £1 million in net deficit in 1965 and £6 million in 1966. . . . Some municipal authorities subsidise their bus fleets or aim to "break even" as a matter of policy; in the financial year 1966–67, 42 out of 92 undertakings showed a trading loss, as compared with 29 in the previous year' (ibid.). The bus companies were in a healthier position, because of contract work and express services amongst other factors.

Progress and prospects of OMO

The economic logic of the case for the move to OMO is that it would reduce labour costs considerably. The services of a conductor are not necessary on a great many routes, and he spends the greater part of his time in collecting the money out of which his wages will be paid. Given the two peaks of demand for bus transport, the conductor spends most of his working day riding around on a mainly empty bus on many routes. But the men see it more as an employment and redundancy problem, as well as one of real or imagined extra strain involved in OMO for the driver who would now be performing a variety of tasks (although American bus drivers in the main streets of New York seem to cope with conditions which might seem overwhelming at first to a London bus driver, collect fares, operate doors, and occasionally shout out the stopping places).

Progress to OMO has been slow in Britain, and though some two-thirds of municipal authorities have OMO, this only accounts for 5 per cent of the busmen or platform staff. The union objection is not based on 'luddism', as some claim, but on the extra payment for OMO, though there is also the fear of redundancy and of the tensions caused by unequal earnings between OMO men and the others during the possibly lengthy transition period. The Board summed up: 'In each main section of the industry, therefore, industrial relations are at present a major bar to future change . . .' (ibid., p. 6).

A number of advantages of OMO were listed, along with a number of possible difficulties, such as the fare-collecting machinery, but it was felt that an early introduction of OMO was necessary. The change-over was to be assisted by the government, making grants towards the capital costs of purchasing new buses (£5m yearly). Grants on other items, such as petrol and new bus depots, etc., were proposed. On the other hand the government, in the White Paper on public transport and traffic, also proposed legislation putting legal limits on actual driving time per day. These were criticised in the bus industry, as being bound to raise costs. But the Board insisted that only the more effective use of manpower could lower costs and raise the level of pay.

In July 1967 the difference in basic rates of pay between London and the provinces was £3 10s 8d or 27·7 per cent greater than the company driver's, whereas the difference between the municipal and the company drivers was only 2s 2d. The difference in gross earnings was not so great, as the municipal and company busmen worked longer hours than the London men; the working week being 54·5 hours, 55·7 hours and 47·4 hours respectively. This meant that although there were considerable differences between the hourly rates of pay, e.g. London Central 9s 11d, municipal 8s 2d, company 8s 1d, there was not a large gap in average gross weekly earnings, with London Central highest with £23 11s 10d, and the municipal figure at £22 6s 5d.

There are other factors in busmen's pay which led to differences between the three sectors and between different authorities. London Transport had 'efficiency payments' and 'safety allowances' (averaging out at about 18s for the first and 2s 6d for the second). Some municipal undertakings paid 'deviation bonuses' of up to £1. (The NJIC allows deviation from the national rate up to this amount to meet labour shortages, but some authorities have paid more and have left the NJIC to do so. The argument about national rates and local rates became acute in the disputes in the latter part of 1968.) Most municipalities paid 'service pay' related to length of service, averaging out at some 16s weekly.

The large gap between the basic rates of the London busmen and the provinces was the main theme of the unions in their mid-1967 pay claim, together with labour shortages and comparative earnings. These arguments were put at length in 'The Busmen's Charter', which appeared in the TGWU union journal, June 1967. It asked for a basic rate of £15 weekly, more pay for OMO, longer holidays, the closed shop, and other changes in time worked and payments made for such time, which would increase total earnings considerably.

The Board pointed out that the effect of the Charter would be to raise labour costs considerably as 'Neither the Charter nor the two claims deal at any point with productivity; and the provisions of both would considerably increase rostered additions to earnings, as well as basic rates' (Report No. 50, p. 13).

The claim of the busmen for comparable rates with other workers was also rejected. The Board said that the weekly earnings of the men compared well with other groups, and returned to their main thesis, that earnings could only be raised through greater efficiency in use of manpower. With this aim in mind, the Board examined the current payments in the bus industry for OMO, and found that they varied considerably as some authorities had left or been expelled from the Employers' Association for paying higher rates than permitted. They had reached local agreements with their employees. The percentage addition to basic rate for OMO varied from 10 to 20 per cent as shown by Table 6.

The Board also found a number of working practices which they held to be mainly restrictive, such as 'signing on' and 'signing off' allowances which were often unjustified. Also the following: 'opposition to the use of part-time labour, an opposition which is widespread; refusal to accept alternative work when otherwise unoccupied; and opposition to the curtailment and diversion of buses to meet traffic congestion' (Report No. 50, p. 17). Schedules were often based on slow speeds which were no longer justified. The PIB said that all these practices raised labour costs, which made more urgent the need to use manpower more effectively.

The PIB also suggested that the two negotiating bodies for municipal undertakings and the companies, the NJIC and the

Table 6 *Percentage addition to basic rate for OMO, 1967*

Sector or undertaking	Addition to base rate (%)	Remarks
Company sector (NCOI)	15	Subject to enhancement,[1] Sundays, rest-days and public holidays
Municipal sector (NJIC)	15	Seat capacity Up to 61 ⎫
	16	61–70 ⎬ Flat rate
	17	71–80 ⎪
	18	81–90 ⎭
London Transport Country	10	Up to 26 seats ⎫ Subject to full
	15	Over 26 seats ⎭ enhancement[2]
London Transport Central	15	Conventional ⎫ Subject to full
	5	'Red Arrow' ⎭ enhancement[2]
Manchester	20	Single-deckers ⎫ On NJIC flat rates
	25	Double-deckers ⎭
Birmingham	20	Subject to enhancement. Base rates include service pay increments
Coventry	17	Flat rate on basic of £18
Reading	15	Plus £1 extra flexibility bonus Flat on NJIC base rate

[1] See paragraph 49, which indicates the principles on which enhancement is based.
[2] In London Transport the OMO driver also receives extra 'efficiency pay' above that of the crew driver.
(Source: PIB Report No. 50, p. 16.)

National Council for the Omnibus Industry (NCOI), should be merged into one single body. London Transport was to remain on its own. There should also be a shift towards local productivity agreements, although progress had been slow here and there had been opposition from the busmen. There could be a national framework for the local bargaining with the limits and rewards for various allowances laid down, and a code drawn up for the employment of part-time labour, and perhaps the ratio of part-time to full-time staff. The normal rules for productivity agreements as laid down in Report No. 36 should be followed.

Industrial disputes in the bus industry, 1967–8

As the report 'Productivity Agreements in the Bus Industry' had pointed out: 'In each main section of the industry, therefore, industrial relations are at present a major bar to future change' (Report No. 50, p. 16). This comment bore fruit in the middle of 1967 and subsequently. On 16 June the union side of the NJIC for the Road Passenger Transport Industry (the negotiating body for municipal transport) gave notice to end the National Agreement. They put forward alternative proposals based on the 'Busmen's Charter' which has already been summarised. The Federation of Municipal Passenger Transport Employers (FMPTE) refused to negotiate on this, and subsequent meetings produced little change in the situation. On 12 October 1967, the union side gave notice at the NJIC that the National Agreement had expired with the three months notice given in June. They announced that their members were now free to negotiate local agreements.

A number of local claims were made which were backed up by sanctions. Here we will trace the attempt to move from a well-established system of national agreements to local negotiation.

Local negotiations in Cardiff

Examples will be taken from several municipal authorities. The main case study is Cardiff, which had some 1,400 employees in its municipal undertaking. As in other authorities, the transport system is run by the city council, which delegates most of the detailed work to the transport committee, which in turn leaves the day-to-day administration to the transport department under the transport manager and his staff.

Cardiff City Council had seventy-eight members: nineteen aldermen and fifty-nine councillors, who met as a general council once monthly. The transport committee, which was one of the standing committees of the council, had seventeen members. The city council seldom discussed municipal transport unless there was interference with the transport service, either for technical reasons or alleged organisational inefficiency, or through industrial action by the employees. As indicated above, most of the discussion took place in the transport committee.

As the transport undertaking was the only large commercial enterprise run by the city council, and cost some £2 million to run, with a revenue only equal to, or less, than this amount, it might have been expected that the transport committee had been chosen for its knowledge of, or interest in, the efficiency of municipal transport. And municipal transport illustrates admirably all aspects of Professor Dunlop's industrial relations system, the state of technology, the market or budgetary controls and the locus of power (J. Dunlop, *Industrial Relations Systems*, Holt, Rinehart and Winston, New York, 1958). The transport committee, which represented the lay management control of municipal transport was a committee made up, to a large extent, of junior councillors, or less experienced councillors. Council committees were in a descending order of importance and status, e.g. there was competition to serve on the finance, public works and planning, parliamentary, watch and civic receptions committees. There were good reasons for this: Finance is the most important committee as it controls the expenditure, and therefore to a large extent, the policy, of the other committees of the council. Its prestige is high, both in the eyes of the council and also of the public. The watch committee controls the police force and has high status, shown by the large number of senior councillors on the Committee. Public Works and Town Planning is also a high-status committee in the eyes of the council and of some of the public, especially if large plans are afoot for town planning changes with their effect on property development. Even small structural changes sometimes require planning consent and for this, and other reasons, members of the public works and town planning committee are regarded as being as important and prestigious as the members of the finance committee.

One of the peculiar paradoxes of a large council like Cardiff, among others, is that the transport committee had only one alderman in its seventeen members, whereas finance had eight out of seventeen, and civic receptions ten out of ten, proving that banquets are more important than buses. It is easy to see why Transport was one of the unpopular committees, as most municipal transport had become increasingly slow and late due to mounting traffic congestion. The committee was therefore on the receiving end of a great deal of public criticism, much of it funnelled through the correspondence columns of the local newspapers. Another paradox was that the lay managers of the public transport system seldom used it, and knew little about its running and service standards. Probably less than 10 per cent of the average council used the municipal transport service and in Cardiff, only about four members of the transport committee used the city buses.

This was one of the reasons why the market pressures were comparatively ineffective when strikes and sanctions were applied by the busmen. The effect on most councillors was marginal, although public complaints were relayed to the transport department. Budgetary restraints were far more effective in the minds of the council. The municipal transport authority is required by statute to be self-sufficient with no subsidy from the rates. This leads to a demand that the costs of the undertaking must be kept within limits rather than that the efficiency be increased. The most

important council debate of the year is that in which the annual
rate is fixed. As this provides the keynote for the annual council
election, most councillors in the country, and particularly in
Cardiff, would rather have the rate stable than have an efficient
transport service. This is abundantly demonstrated by the mani-
festoes in the local government elections.

For these reasons any councillor who attempts to point out that
output is a function of cost is given short shrift by the council and
by the Press, which reasons correctly that the public is more
interested in money costs than in technical details of transport.

The question of social costs is also regarded as a time-wasting
and academic curiosity. Although Cardiff did commission a
Buchanan Plan, and paid some £300,000 for it, they were unwilling
to face the implications of the social-cost approach to traffic
problems. This had been developing in London for some years,
and the Select Committee on London Transport (1964) argued that
the full self-financing principle for transport should be relaxed and
that the board (LTB) 'should not be required to meet its capital
costs where wider social benefits could be shown'. The article
reporting this underlined the average councillor's dilemma, when
it pointed out that before long, most municipal transport will
'be in the red. Any suggestion that this trend is inevitable induces
apoplexy among the devotees of the commercial transport. They
say that if people want public transport they should pay for it;
subsidised transport results in the uneconomic diversion of
resources to an activity for which there is not a genuine demand'
(*The Times*, 1 February 1965). The Cardiff city council favoured
the strict commercial approach to the financing of their bus
services, and advocates of the social-cost approach were attacked
as advocates of 3s to 4s on the rates.

It has already been shown that labour costs are a high proportion
of the total costs of bus operation. A rise in wages leads to a
deficit in the operating budget of the undertaking, or a subsidy
from the rates, or a rise in fares. Applications for fares increases
have to be made to the Traffic Commissioners, which often results
in a delay in the proposed increases, which are sometimes refused.
Although members of the public can appear and give evidence or
present complaints or criticisms to the Commissioners, little is
done to encourage this. A citizen can lose a day's time and work at
a fares application hearing, while the city council may spend a good
deal on legal fees, although legal representation does not appear
to be necessary.

Market and budgetary constraints

The 1966 Annual Report of the general manager showed the relationship between wage increases and fare increases: 'There are at present wage increase applications under consideration for all employees and the small surplus will be quite inadequate to meet the resulting increased costs. I consider it therefore inevitable that in the near future arrangements must be made to increase our revenue, and at the present time this means an application for fare increases. Sooner or later there will have to be a new look at the method of financing public transport. The main difficulty is the large measure of unremunerative operation for social service.' The manager pointed out that if the Sunday services were discontinued there would be a net saving of £35,000 per year.

The statistical tables showed the continuing fall in passenger miles without any corresponding fall in staff employed. The undertaking carried 105,278,307 passengers in 1948/9, 90,382,683 in 1952/3, and 70,113,748 in 1965/6. Yet the numbers of staff employed fell very slightly, from 1,568 in 1948/9 to 1,407 in 1952/3, and 1,404 in 1965/6. There had been no change in staff numbers over fourteen years while the number of passengers had fallen in the same period by some 22 per cent, and was continuing to fall.

As the undertaking is constrained in the wages it can offer by the tight budgetary constraints imposed on it by statute, by the falling public demand for public transport, and by the difficulties in the way of speedy modernisation, it finds it difficult to recruit and keep staff. In the summer of 1965, the shortage of platform staff 'reached a record peak of 113 drivers and 37 conductors and there was very little improvement until November and December' (ibid., p. 7). The platform staff wastage for the year was over half the total of platform staff (518 against 980). There were 432 resignations and 60 dismissals.

The department has been short of suitable staff for some years and claims that not only are the numbers of applicants lower than they wish, but the quality is also poor. The reasons for the unpopularity of platform work in the bus industry have already been mentioned; apart from the relatively low wages, the hours are inconvenient and a bar to normal social and married life. The necessity to work long hours of overtime to improve the basic wage cuts further into the normal working week. Conditions of work are also poor: the drivers face traffic congestion and numerous stoppages upsetting the work-scheduled times, the conductors have to cope with an increasingly irritated public, fretting because of higher fares, slower buses and poorer service. Morale in municipal transport is low for the reasons stated, and the older employees seem to feel that the quality of staff entrants has fallen, although 'lower quality' might be a euphemism for their attitude to 'immigrant' workers. Relative wages have also fallen sharply, as has the relative security of the employment. In the 1920s and 1930s the transport undertaking was a sought-after job due to the low average wage in industry and the general insecurity and unemployment of the inter-war years. H. A. Clegg wrote that London busmen were earning up to 50 per cent 'above the average for adult males through most of the inter-war period. But not even their well-deserved reputation for militancy has prevented a decline (associated with the rise of private motoring) to well below the national average today' (H. A. Clegg, 'The Purpose of Trade Unions', *Listener*, 4 October 1962, p. 499). The busmen are caught in a declining industry, hemmed in by constraints of technology (the spread of private car ownership, changing social habits, traffic congestion), the budgetary and market constraints (the statutory control of costs and transport finance) and the power context (lay management on the local councils and the lack of interest among councillors in the efficiency of municipal transport).

Industrial action in Cardiff

The regional secretary of the TGWU in Cardiff told the writer that industrial relations in the industry had deteriorated badly from the early 1960s, and this was most noticeable on the NJC for municipal transport. There had been a growing gap between the London busmen and the municipal busmen, a differential that had been widening over the years. The PIB Report of 1966 had recommended 6·6 per cent for London busmen and 3½ per cent for the provinces. The TGWU had opposed this report. Then there had been the freeze of 1966 which had stopped the provincial busmen's increase. This had led to industrial action in some areas. The TGWU were now (July 1967) putting forward the 'Busmen's Charter' with its demand for a union shop, £15 weekly for forty hours work, a greater sharing of savings from OMO, overtime agreements and three weeks holiday on average earnings.

The low morale in the transport undertaking in Cardiff and the surrounding areas, symptomatic of the country as a whole, was evident earlier in the year. The most outstanding issue was that of pay, as the period of severe restraint in the first part of 1967 meant that the 3½ per cent increase gained on 20 January after months of negotiation, to be paid on 1 March, was under government order not to be paid before 1 July. Mr Cousins, General Secretary of the TGWU, who had resigned as a cabinet minister some eight months previously, was prepared to take up the challenge on behalf of his busmen. The settlement of 20 January 1967 had only been reached after threats of one-day strikes and continued attempts by the employers to have many alleged restrictive practices eliminated.

The mood of the busmen in 1967 was therefore bitter. The evidence for this can be found in their behaviour at work and attitudes towards the public. In the neighbouring town of Newport, with some 100 vehicles and a staff of 500, there had been complaints over several months about the bus service, and a lengthy correspondence in the local newspaper. In February 1967 a Committee of Inquiry was set up into relations within the Newport passenger undertaking, and was chaired by Dr G. F. Thomason. The committee listed the main points of complaint by the public against the bus service as being: (1) lateness of buses; (2) infrequency of buses on particular routes; (3) 'lack of consideration, discourtesy and rudeness', in relations with the public; (4) bad time-keeping by the bus crews due to prolonged breaks (card-playing at the terminal) and time-wasting (Report of Committee of Inquiry, pp. 17–18). The men's representatives agreed with a number of the complaints but said they were mainly due to traffic congestion, and that people naturally became bad-tempered when they had to wait half an hour for a bus. The committee made a number of recommendations which need to be read in their entirety, but the main points for reform of an unsatisfactory situation were that the disciplinary procedures and the negotiating machinery should be improved, and steps should be taken towards a productivity agreement. Significantly, the committee said that the formal union structure was weak and that little effective authority was exercised by the union over the men.

Cardiff also found its transport service criticised in February 1967, less by the public through the newspapers, as by the examiners of the South Wales Traffic Commissioners. They listed 195 faults or irregularities in the bus service, which was forty-nine more than they had found at Newport, which they had checked the previous month. Some of the criticisms listed included: no service route numbers or destination indicators, or incorrect ones displayed; services leaving the terminus late or early, or failing to operate; lack of consideration by bus crews, failure to set passengers down near the kerb; bus crews smoking on service, not wearing badges. There was also a lack of supervision and an

G

absence of inspectors. The Cardiff transport manager said that he would issue a 'pull up your socks' directive, and an alderman promised strong action (*Western Mail*, 11 February 1967).

The busmen's representatives met the transport committee on 21 February and replied to the charges made against them. One of their main points was that the quality of personnel had deteriorated compared with the longer-serving busmen. This was due to the transport committee refusing to pay sufficient incentive bonuses. The chairman said that they could only engage men who were willing to offer their services. There had to be a tightening-up, and the regulations had to be obeyed. Throughout the meeting there was no real attempt by the committee to meet the argument of the men that if the wage or earnings were raised this would lead to an improvement in the quality or performance of the recruits and staff.

Local bargaining and national negotiations

This deterioration in industrial relations at the local level mirrored what was happening at the national level. At the National Joint Industrial Council of 16 June 1967 the trade union side gave three months' notice of termination of the national agreement under Clause 10, which said that the agreement could be terminated on three months' written notice on either side. The reasons advanced by the trade unions included a general 'feeling of frustration' due partly to the terms offered by the employers on OMO—an added rate of 15 per cent. The trade union side felt that this was too low, and needed further negotiation. There were also complaints about 'scheduling, speed regulation, and the interpretation of rates of pay under the agreement' (Report of the General Manager of City of Cardiff Transport, 11 July 1967).

It was reported to the transport committee that the trade union side had objected to part of the 1965 national agreement, quoted below:

(1) That the National Council recognises that a national incentive bonus scheme based upon traffic receipts and/or carrying capacity could not be sufficiently elastic to meet the variety of conditions of operation encountered by the individual Municipal Undertakings.

(2) That the National Council accepts the need to adopt measures which would lead to maximum efficiency so that economies can be effected to meet rising costs which could

thus be absorbed without necessarily increasing fares.

(3) That as from today's date the terms of the settlement set out in Document '2' attached to these Minutes shall become part of the Conditions of Service Agreement dated 19th November, 1965.

Document 2 laid down the conditions for additional payment for drivers and conductors (known as service payments) which were related to length of service, starting at 10s weekly after six months service and rising to 30s weekly after twenty years service. The grades were based on an extra 2s 6d up to 20s for five years service. This was paid at six-monthly periods.

The controversial clause in the agreement, which later became known as a 'penal clause' and was similar to that in the Ford agreement of early 1969, stated that the service payments could be forfeited for any absence other than certified sickness or authorised leave of absence. This applied to individuals and the union did not make an issue of this. However, the clause continued: 'If the absence is collective on the part of a number of employees, the current six-monthly payment shall be automatically withheld from them. . . .' The union also objected to the rate for OMO, and the general manager reported that he felt that this was the main reason for the trade union side leaving the national agreement. The men wanted an extra percentage for driving double-decker buses as compared to single-decker ones. The employers insisted that there was no difference in difficulty between the two types of vehicles (although later PIB reports on the bus industry awarded a higher rate on OMO for double-decker operation).

On 17 October the general manager reported on the breakdown of the national agreement. The trade union side had presented the employers' side with a proposal for a new national agreement, and the employers had passed this on to the Wages Committee. The committee reported to the employers that there was no reason why the existing national agreement should not be continued, and that the trade union side should make an application for an increase in the basic rates of pay as 'it was general practice at this time of the year' for them to do so. The unions said they would submit a claim if the employers agreed to pay any increase negotiated, even if the government decreed that it should not be paid. The employers argued that this would mean that they were acting illegally. The trade union side then returned to the submission of the new national agreement, which the employers rejected. There were no minutes of the discussion at the Wages Committee on the new proposals, as the unions refused to agree to them. The report said that the main new proposal had been for the cancellation of the 'penal clause', on the grounds that it was being used by managements up and down the country to intimidate employees. The employers had replied that they had taken 'into account wage increases in other sections of local authority service, nationalised industries, etc., and then given the Craftsmen about one-fifth of what they had asked for. Following the ending of the NJIC, the Employers Federation advised their members to deal with their employees as if the national agreement were still valid. All employees should be given a copy of "Particulars of Terms of Employment".'

The report to the transport committee ended with the statement which led to several months of sanctions and strikes up and down Britain, from Southend to Aberdeen. This was over the attempt by the unions to persuade the local authorities to enter into local negotiations instead of the national agreements. The employers' case was stated as follows: 'The Executive Committee of the Employers' Federation urge most strongly all its members not to enter into any negotiations locally which would normally be dealt with at national level, and not to concede any issues which would normally be matters of National consideration. They ask that any threats or approaches from the Trade Unions should be reported immediately to them, so that appropriate advice may be given, and point out that in the circumstances outlined the Federation's strength will lie in unity among its members and all members are asked to give their utmost loyalty at this time.'

At a time when there had been evidence of a shift away from national negotiations towards local or plant bargaining, noted by the Donovan Commission in its analysis of the 'two systems of industrial relations', the bus industry had insisted on the strict application of national rates and conditions. As the labour market situation varied from area to area this had led to strains and to several cities leaving the National Federation. Cities such as Birmingham, Coventry, Manchester, Reading, with low unemployment and labour shortages in a high-wage area, had to devise special rates and bonuses to attract recruits, and hold existing staff. Some variations from the national agreement were allowed and this was done in some local authorities, e.g. in Nottingham, with a 32 per cent shortage of drivers and a 21 per cent shortage of conductors, the undertaking paid premiums 25 per cent above the nationally agreed rate for spread-over duties, and 10s weekly for an attendance and good-conduct bonus (PIB Report No. 63, p. 30).

The labour shortage of drivers in Nottingham was above the national average of 17·1 per cent, but the shortage of conductors was below the average. The driver shortage is partly explained by the fact that recruitment of conductors was unrestricted while the unions had placed barriers to driver recruitment by insisting that they should be recruited from conductors, and in cases such as Nottingham, from senior conductors.

Cardiff was a representative transport undertaking as it adhered closely to the national agreement. One variation was that the spread-over duties were slightly better, but this only affected a small range of work. There was also pay for meal breaks on 65 per cent of the duties, and 35 per cent of platform staff were paid eight and a half hours for eight hours work while on split duties. As indicated, there was a shortage of staff relative to establishment, but one view was that this increased the amount of overtime available for other staff and raised their pay to a level comparable with industry. The Board found this to be common, as Report No. 63 showed (p. 9): 'Our recent inquiries have borne out that establishments are not necessarily a true reflection of need. Not only have we encountered recruitment limited by agreement with the staff, but in some areas it has been managerial policy not to attempt to recruit up to full strength, in order to maintain earnings at acceptable levels.' This was borne out in the same report, where it was shown that 19·3 per cent of bus drivers in two-man crews were clocking from sixty to seventy hours weekly. Some 40 per cent were working a range of hours from fifty-five hours weekly upwards.

Sanctions and stalemate

As the national agreement had been ended on 12 October, the Cardiff transport committee agreed to follow the advice of the Employers' Federation. The transport manager read a letter from the regional passenger group secretary of the TGWU asking for a meeting to negotiate a new local agreement. He added that the union intended to ban standing passengers on buses, and voluntary overtime, and were not to co-operate on the introduction of OMO. The transport committee resolved to continue to treat the matter as a national issue, not a local one. The transport manager reported that he had spoken to the Secretary of the Federation of Municipal Passenger Transport Employers (FMPTE) who had advised him not to negotiate locally, that pressure was being put on other local authorities and sanctions were already being used by busmen in

Stockport and Belfast, and that a statement was being sent to all municipal undertakings, for circulation to the employees.

The employers' case

The statement by the employers regretted the withdrawal of the unions from the National Council, which had functioned successfully since 1919. There were now no agreements, no forty-hour week, no overtime rates or other provisions. The sanctions the busmen were asked to follow by their unions were a breach of their conditions of service. The forty-hour week was introduced in November 1965, along with the service bonus which gave a half-year payment between £13 and £39 according to length of service. The unions, for their part, had agreed to look at the whole question of productivity, but had instead presented the 'Busmen's Charter' (see above). The employers replied that the proposals were 'ideals and objectives of the trades unions but they are not proposals for productivity'. They had suggested to the unions that they should look again at the national agreement, and had invited them to submit another pay claim. The unions refused and asked for the agreement to be revised. A further meeting on 29 September 1967, brought out the objection by the unions to the 'penal clause' in the service bonus. The employers pointed out that in the two years of the agreement, there had only been three cases referred to the National Council: the first case had the penalty reduced from six months' loss of service payment to one month; the other two cases arose from withdrawals of labour arising out of assaults on bus crews. It was agreed that there should be no forfeiture on these cases. The employers said that the clause was not a 'penal' one and 'no man carrying out his work in a normal way has anything to fear or to lose because of it'.

The phrase 'work in a normal way' referred to the possibility of the busmen engaging in sanctions or unofficial strikes. This had been made explicit in the first part of the notice, where it said that sanctions were a breach of the conditions of service: 'If the bargain is broken, Management will have no option but to revert to the position which existed before the bargain was made, i.e. if the capacity of vehicles is deliberately reduced by the non-carriage of standing passengers or if the introduction or extension of one-man operation is impeded or unreasonably withheld, the Management will have to withhold the payment of service bonus pay. Likewise, if the services to the public are reduced by the collective banning of VOLUNTARY overtime—voluntary meaning it is up to the

INDIVIDUAL EMPLOYEE TO DECIDE not the Union nationally or locally—the Management will have no option but to make every effort to recruit up to the full establishment and/or employ part-time labour to provide the necessary services.' Management said they hoped that this would not happen, but a bargain or agreement had been made and if broken, it was broken on both sides.

The declaration was quite specific that there should be no sanctions, or even refusals to co-operate in the manning and running of one-man buses. The threat for non-compliance was the loss of the service bonus and of alternative labour being engaged. As the men knew the staff shortage position in the bus industry it is hardly likely they were dismayed by this statement of the employers' intentions. The trade union side replied immediately.

The union case

The national secretary of the TGWU passenger group replied that their action was forced on them by the 'lack of initiative' of the employers. He had sent out a circular to passenger group secretaries on 12 October 1967, on the imposition of a ban on standing passengers and voluntary overtime, along with a ban on the implementation or extension of OMO. This ban was being observed up and down the country. The advice of management to withhold service bonus pay, he said, could have serious consequences and lead to further sanctions by the men. The decision to ban voluntary overtime had been taken in a democratic manner by members of the union throughout the country. As part-time labour had never been any part of any industrial agreement in the industry, any attempt to do this now could lead to further action by the men. The 'Busmen's Charter' had been dismissed summarily by the management, who had refused to discuss it clause by clause. The management invitation to the union side to submit a wage claim was meaningless. The union had asked them what offer was in their minds and the answer had been 'that there was nothing on offer at all'. The union side had asked that the 'penal clause' be dropped from the agreement. The employers had refused. The union side saw that the employers had no desire to negotiate, and 'had no alternative but to terminate the national agreement of the National Council as such'.

The passenger group Secretary said that the NJIC had been breaking up since 1960, when the employers had walked out of negotiations. Since then, basic rates and working conditions had declined to the point where the staffing shortage was acute. 'No-one apparently wants to be a Bus Driver nowadays, and who can blame them?'

The documents from the employers' side were circulated to the transport committee, along with details of the 'Busmen's Charter', but little attempt was made to meet and hear the union case from the local union. A group of councillors from the minority group on the council met the regional passenger group secretary. He said that industrial relations on the NJIC had been deteriorating for some years. There was an atmosphere of distrust, as agreements were explained by the Federation secretary to the employers' side, but not to the union side. The 1965 Agreement had not been a good one due to the change-over of national secretaries at the time. The 'penal clause' had been raised in July 1967 but the employers had refused to discuss it: therefore they were responsible for breaking the agreement.

The discussion showed that the councillors knew that if the council negotiated locally and made an offer to the busmen this could be vetoed by the government. The passenger secretary agreed, but said that this would shift the negotiation from the council to the government and other steps and pressures could be taken. He said that contracts of employment should be agreed and not imposed. Cardiff had imposed conditions and made two threats: (1) to stop the service bonus, (2) to recruit more labour, either part-time or full-time. Conditions of work were disagreeable, the pay was poor, the hours were bad and anti-social, leaving bus crews little social life. This explained the 12 per cent shortage of platform staff, even though Cardiff had 4,000 unemployed.

Questions were asked about union restrictions on the employment of bus drivers, which the transport manager had complained about. This was denied, as the union had waived their rule of six months' service before an employee could qualify as a driver. It had frequently been shortened to a few days. There was no disagreement in principle about the employment of women drivers but it was likely to lead to a number of difficulties and was not a practical proposal at the present time. Part-time drivers were a possibility, although the employment of shift-workers, or others, was not as easy as it appeared. The union had sixty-year-old members who might do this part-time. The relationship between wages, costs, fares and rates was discussed. One of the points made was that the LPTB was subsidised to a certain extent, as were the railways. The passenger secretary said that this might be the long-term solution to the problem. The short-term answer was to open negotiations locally with the busmen for a new agreement and press for improvements in productivity to cover the costs as far as possible.

This informal discussion yielded far more information and proposals than any meeting of the transport committee or the city council had done, or was to do. One of the difficulties of lay management, in the elected and unpaid political context, was that declamation became more common than discussion. Another difficulty was that there was virtually no room for negotiation when the National Federation had forbidden members to negotiate locally.

At the beginning of November, the national chairman and the secretary of the National Federation toured the country addressing meetings of regional groups of local authorities. The group for South-East Wales met in Cardiff on 1 November. The meeting was private and no minutes were issued. The national chairman stressed the need to refuse local negotiations and to stand by the Federation and its agreements. The phrase was used by some of the members 'negotiate locally, and they'll have us over a barrel and play us off against each other'. Each municipal undertaking had representatives, although there was no distinction in voting power between municipalities; one small undertaking with six buses had several delegates. The chief anxiety of the delegates was that if fares rose then the rates would have to rise or a subsidy would have to be arranged. One delegate accused the manager of a largish undertaking of having begun negotiations, and thus staved off the use of sanctions. The manager said that he was negotiating, but it was simply a subterfuge, as he did not intend to make any agreement. This pleased some delegates and annoyed a few. One delegate argued that as the national agreement had been terminated locally, local bargaining should begin. He added that the function of public transport was to transport the public. The chairman summed up by appealing for loyalty to the Federation. This was agreed by most of the delegates.

Later in November the FMPTE issued a document to local authorities recommending non-payment of service pay on two grounds: clause 1(f) stated that 'if the absence is individual and caused through the Employee's own action, the service payment shall be forfeited by that employee for one week. If the absence is collective on the part of a number of employees the current six-monthly payment shall be automatically withheld from them.' Under 2(c) of the agreement which introduced service payments, the management claimed that there were no restrictions outside legal ones limiting the number of passengers to be carried: 'Thus, an employee has no right to reduce the carrying capacity of any vehicle as authorised by statute and to do so means that he is failing to comply with his contract of employment.' Management were not obliged to pay the service bonus under this breach of the agreement. The transport manager recommended that the guidance of the FMPTE be accepted, and that the employees be informed of the decision.

The Cardiff transport committee discussed the Municipal Passenger Transport Association (MPTA) circular interpreting the clause, and recommending action against the busmen as they were in breach of contract. A minority point of view was that the clause said 'may' be carried, not 'will' be carried. The transport manager agreed with this, but said later that 'may' usually meant 'will' and that standing passengers were carried. The vice-chairman, a lawyer, argued that the legal interpretation of the clause was that it pertained to the carrying capacity of buses, and that they must carry up to ninety persons where this is the capacity. An agreement was produced by the transport department, which they said showed the men were committed to carry standing passengers. But then they added that it had been superseded by another which was not produced, and the matter was not pressed. It was suggested that there was some doubt about the interpretation of the clause, and that it should be referred to the town clerk for his view. The chairman (a lawyer) said that the clause was clear enough. He did not explain why it was necessary for the MPTA to send round an interpretation one month after the dispute had begun. A suggestion that the clause should be sent to the Ministry of Labour locally for their interpretation on industrial relations lines, and not from a legal point of view, was defeated. The clause was sent to the town clerk for a legal interpretation.

The preoccupation of the committee with the narrow cost issue came out strongly when they discussed the government White Paper on transport policy, arising from a circular of the MPTA which was strongly against the government's proposals. One councillor criticised the circular, pointing out that its main point was that a central authority would raise wages all round to compare with the highest rates paid, whereas the committee had just refused to negotiate other than centrally on the grounds that national centralised negotiations were the most effective in keeping down the level of local wage rates The transport committee refused to discuss the issue of social costs in transport and its relation to the present dispute.

The nature of sanctions

A number of busmen were interviewed at the time of the sanctions and denied that they were working to rule. They said they were simply applying some of the rules: (1) They refused to halt at bus stops if there were cars parked in front of them (a universal practice in Cardiff although the areas are clearly marked as 'no parking') and they claimed that the instructions had in the past come from inspectors; (2) There were so many rules about road safety and vehicle checks that if they were all observed, the buses would be continually late.

The transport department* said that the disruption of services had been worsened by the sharp rise in the sickness rate, with 130 sick instead of the eighty or so before the sanctions began. Their view was that some of the men were avoiding duty and the angry public at the same time. They claimed that some of the men were making some of the vehicles mechanically unsound by small alterations in the garage, e.g. a speedometer could be pushed in with a shoe making the vehicle legally unsafe. Bus crews had also refused to work other than their normal duties, and with so many regular buses late and off their usual routes, this made the re-programming of buses very difficult. They said in addition that many of the sanctions used were outside trade union approval: one driver had refused to take out four buses in succession, although the fitters had said they were in good mechanical order; another driver had driven a bus onto an unauthorised route and disrupted timetables.

Notices had been put up warning busmen of this kind of behaviour. There was some divergence of view on managerial authority when these incidents were put before the transport committee. The transport manager said that the management wanted to avoid provocation and that disciplinary action might precipitate a strike at that point. Some members insisted that authority should be imposed on those guilty of flagrant breaches of ordinary working rules.

---

* One councillor (a member of the transport committee) went to see the transport manager to find out more about the nature and effect of the dispute. An appointment had been made, but the transport manager began by reading out Clause 41(a) of the standing orders of the council. He said that he had been speaking to the Town Clerk, and that he had been instructed to read the clause which forbade councillors to visit heads of department during a dispute. The councillor said that if this was the interpretation of the clause, then he could submit a number of questions in writing and expect written answers as soon as possible. This illustrates the difficulties of lay management bodies with council officials working under council rules, while operating a large public transport undertaking.

Public pressure on the transport committee

Nationally the firm front of the FMPTE had begun to break up and a number of local authorities had begun to negotiate with their local union. This news added to the pressures upon Cardiff to meet their men locally. There was also a deputation from the Chamber of Commerce, who argued that the sanctions had forced many shoppers to stay at home and trade had been badly affected. Matters could become worse if a speedy solution could not be found, as it would soon be the Christmas season.

The Cardiff city council met at its monthly meeting, no special meeting having been called, and discussed the bus dispute among other issues. The ban on overtime had been in operation for two weeks. The debate lasted over an hour, and the chief issue for the majority was the cost of local bargaining. The vice-chairman argued: 'If the full charter (the "Busmen's Charter") was implemented, who would bear the cost of something like £300,000?—the travelling public, of course. They would be hit by much higher bus fares and we would find ourselves paying more each year. We could be picked off like cherries once we decided to negotiate locally. We stand to lose the balance, the power, and the fairness of collective bargaining.' The chairman agreed with this point of view, and said that the opinion of the FMPTE was that 'to abandon national negotiation in favour of local negotiation would, in the long run, be disastrous for all parties'. Local bargaining would lead to frequent negotiations, with the trade unions trying to get the best parts of local agreements into all the agreements. He pointed out that the mines and the railways bargained nationally and said it would be foolish for the council to agree to local bargaining for the Cardiff busmen. He intended to meet the union leaders later to discuss the two-week-old sanctions, but he was not negotiating, and neither was the transport committee. One of the critics pointed out that the first principle of industrial negotiation was to meet your employees. The council voted to support the transport committee chairman.

At no point in the debate did the majority of the council discuss productivity and the possible effect on future industrial relations of a refusal to negotiate. Nor was there any discussion of the relative merits of national versus local collective bargaining, and an attempt to put this was ignored.

The *South Wales Echo* spoke up for talks with the busmen. In an editorial, 'Why Must the Misery go on?', the newspaper argued that 'although there is some resentment against the crews, the deeper feeling is that this conflict has been mishandled from the start by the transport committee. Passengers point out that in Newport, Aberdare and West Monmouthshire no sanctions have been applied because the authorities agreed to talk to the union— to talk, not to negotiate.' The editorial asked why the committee had waited so long before meeting the union leaders: 'Perhaps it was thought that the busmen would crack. Perhaps the committee failed to visualise how effective, and painful, the sanctions would be. Perhaps the committee members are all car owners and have forgotten what it is like to wait for hours in a winter bus queue.' The last comment was largely true; the editorial could have added that there were no financial or personal reasons to involve the councillors in local negotiations when the employers' side of their Federation had decided against it. There was also the clinching factor that higher wages would raise fares, and might affect the rates. The councillors probably feared that to give way would lead to a spiral of rising wages in the bus industry.

The councillors began to realise that sanctions were causing as much criticism now of the transport committee and the council as they were of the bus crews. While both the council and the transport committee refused to meet a deputation from the Trades Council, they began to receive petitions and letters from bodies they acknowledged as influential, like the Chamber of Commerce, who pointed out that sanctions were causing great losses to trades in the city centre. The chairman told the delegation that the refusal to negotiate was 'a matter of principle'. The delegation said that women were the main sufferers, as most homes did not have two cars. The chairman said that there were two schools of thought: (1) stand firm and uphold the national agreement; or (2) give them anything they ask for. One of the council minority group objected to this and said that this was not the situation: negotiations could lead to productivity concessions and a more efficient and cost-conscious service. The delegation asked for an independent arbitrator, but a Conservative member said the dispute and the sanctions were political. Labour objected to this and said the issue was economic: whether the council should bargain locally instead of nationally, as many firms already did in many industries. This point was not discussed.

The town clerk appeared before the transport committee with his opinion on the controversial clause in the contract of employment. He asked what conditions of service had been broken, and was shown Paragraphs 2a, 2b, 2c (relating to the carrying capacity of a bus being up to ninety passengers) as these were the conditions served on the employees under the Contract of Employment Act. The town clerk said that the document was obscure as to meaning. A committee member (a lawyer) suggested that a legal opinion should be obtained. This was criticised on the grounds that it would take weeks, and also that the document was not a legal one but simply interpreted the spirit of the work bargain. It was argued that if a legal opinion were obtained, it would not get the men working normally, and if the legal opinion went in favour of the union this would give their case great support. The transport manager said that the agreement to carry standing passengers had been a condition of employment since 1949. It had not been a written agreement but a verbal one of long standing. He also circulated details of the up-to-date position throughout the country.*

A member moved that the bonus be not paid for the period during which the busmen had used sanctions. This was criticised on the grounds that it would probably lead to a strike. The voting for the motion was five for, six against. It was agreed that 'the service payment be made for the period during which sanctions have been in force' (Minutes, Special Transport Committee, 28 November 1967). A discussion followed about the possible counter sanctions that the city council might use. The transport department view was: 'Employers are being kicked around. It is time we started kicking back.'

The effect of sanctions

The TGWU had instructed its 77,000 busmen to ban standing passengers and refuse voluntary overtime on 12 October. Coincidentally, the post office workers accepted a 7 per cent increase in pay the same day. Sanctions began in Cardiff on 23 October and it was forecast by the union that 50 per cent of the services in the city would be withdrawn. Eight other local authorities in South Wales faced the same threat of sanctions unless they began local negotiations. These were Newport, Merthyr, Caerphilly, Pontypridd, Aberdare, Gelligaer, Bedwas and Machen and the West Monmouthshire Omnibus Board. All nine local authorities were members of the South Wales area of the MPTA. Cardiff transport committee had refused to negotiate locally with the union on 20 October, the chairman saying, 'We have rejected this ultimatum', and the passenger secretary stating, 'Now the sanctions will be

* In South Wales, with nine municipal transport undertakings, two were on strike, two were working normally, four had 'normal' sanctions. Cardiff had more extensive sanctions. No negotiations were reported.

applied and will remain until such time as the committee changes its mind' (*South Wales Echo*, 21 October 1967). The Cardiff transport department said that the services would be seriously affected, though the extent of this depended on how the men interpreted voluntary overtime.

The threat of a complete stoppage of public transport grew as the goods and passenger trains in the South Wales valleys were disrupted by railway guards as they followed a union ruling and refused to take second-man duties. This move prevented hundreds of commuters in the area from reaching their daily jobs (*South Wales Echo*, 19 October 1967).

The refusal of the Cardiff transport committee to negotiate led to demands by some of the busmen for a strike. The refusal was described as 'provocative' and the passenger secretary referred to resentment at the proposal to refer the dispute to the NJIC, which no longer existed. There was also some ambiguity over the statement by the South Wales Secretary of the FMPTE, that the nine South Wales local authorities with passenger undertakings had a unanimous policy to deal with the threat of sanctions. The passenger secretary said that as Newport and West Monmouthshire had agreed to open negotiations on new local agreements, the sanctions did not apply in their cases. He asked whether it could be said that the nine undertakings had a common employer attitude as two of them were now ready to open negotiations. As we saw by the description of the employers' meeting, it did not seem that the negotiations were intended to bear fruit, but simply to avoid sanctions.

The sanctions began on 23 October with the transport manager admitting to 25 per cent of the buses being off the road and the union claiming a higher figure would be reached that evening.

By the fourth day of the dispute, the transport manager was advising people to shop early and not use the buses during peak periods. About 30 per cent of the buses were now affected by sanctions. A few miles from Cardiff, the busmen at Gelligaer, who were operating the overtime ban, went on strike on 25 October because of the action of the local manager in taking out a one-man bus. The men argued that the national work to rule had banned an increase in the number of one-man buses in operation. The strike was called off later in the day. The transport branch secretary in Cardiff objected to the 'Statement of Facts' issued by the FMPTE which ended with the words: 'These are the facts—now you must work out for yourself whether you will benefit by disrupting our industry. The future is in your hands.'

The disruption of the bus service grew worse and queues waited up to an hour in the evening in bad weather. The AA and the RAC issued 'free lift' stickers to motorists, but this had only a minimal effect on the situation. The chairman of the Cardiff transport committee said that they would not negotiate locally, and told the local press that there was no prospect of a special council meeting to discuss this, and the next meeting of the council was in two weeks time. The passenger secretary affirmed that they would call off the sanctions as soon as they were told that there would be negotiations. The busmen were working without a pay agreement and without agreed condition of employment. He added: 'The transport committee do not seem to realise the days when management could impose their terms on the workers are ended' (*South Wales Echo*, 25 October 1967). The transport committee chairman said that the suffering of the travelling public was caused by the decision of the men to impose sanctions.

The public, who were obviously suffering a good deal during the cold rainy weather from the sanctions, which had the effect of making the buses very late, or absent, were angry both with the busmen and with the council. Letters were published in the local press criticising both in fierce terms, though some pointed out the low wages of the busmen and the difficult conditions under which they had to work. Some suggested that the whole municipal transport undertaking should be sold to a private company, a point of view which was also held by some councillors. Newspaper interviews affirmed that while some wanted the transport committee to open negotiations with the men, the majority criticised the bus crews. Examples were given of old women in their eighties who had to wait over an hour in heavy rain. Other examples were of a twenty-minute journey taking four hours due to non-appearance of the buses. (The writer can confirm this, as he was using bus transport at times in this period. When interviewing busmen at the terminus, angry women who had been waiting a long time for a bus which did not appear, started shouting that the busmen 'should be sent to Siberia'.) Talks at national level had been arranged in London, but these proved abortive, and early in November sanctions were still being imposed in Cardiff and three other nearby undertakings. The South Wales passenger secretary said that this showed that the employers were not prepared to negotiate either locally or nationally. He accused the council of being indifferent: 'As far as Cardiff Council is concerned they are not the least bit bothered about sanctions. . . . They are saving money on overtime, and the public is still getting to work.' He predicted that the travelling public would soon lose patience and exercise pressure on the transport undertaking to negotiate (*South Wales Echo*, 4 November 1967).

The dispute was interesting in the three-cornered play of forces: union, lay management, and travelling public. The union policy was to demand local negotiations as a substitute for national ones, although the counter-accusation of the NFMPE members was that this was simply an attempt to lever up wages by using the more prosperous undertakings as a fulcrum. It was argued that while the local authorities were negotiating separately, the union was asking to be informed of all local negotiations and terms. The lay management was under little pressure. It has been pointed out that few of them used the buses; there was no financial motive for them to seek a better performance, and for a number, time given to the problems of the undertaking detracted from the time they could give to their own work; as the undertaking was losing money, there was some truth in the allegation of the union official. This became clearer later, when the men went on strike and several senior council members told the writer that every day of the strike saved the council money. The most constant theme of the 'no-negotiation' group was that the council could not afford to pay higher wages, as this would mean higher fares (which would be unpopular at election time) or higher rates (which would be more unpopular still). The discussions of the lay management centred far more around the costs of the transport service than about suggestions for improving its productivity. Although the National Federation had narrowed the area of negotiation locally to marginal issues, some negotiations could have been begun.

By 23 November it was reported that the busmen had widened the range of sanctions: no bus was to leave the depot unless it was fully manned; each bus must have its list of running instructions 'showing in detail the job the crew have to do. Busmen will not do any journeys that have not already been designated. They will not change from one route to another to make administration easier for the Transport Department. They will not allow any defective bus to leave the depot. Drivers who arrive early for work will not accept early turns as "favours". Crews will not take buses with defective speedometers on to the roads' (*South Wales Echo*, 23 November 1967). As already noted, the bus crews refused to halt the buses at stops which had cars parked in front of them. Appeals were made by some citizens for motorists to pay regard to this situation.

Councils in the South Wales area were concerned also with the

H

problem of exercising authority in the midst of sanctions. Newport, which had avoided sanctions by talking with the local union, discussed the lack of progress in introducing OMO. The public works and services committee recommended that Newport council should tell the busmen that 'they will have to seriously consider stopping bonus payments from next January until the one-man system comes into operation'. The Newport transport manager 'warned the Committee that if the Council refused to pay the bonus there would be a strike' (*South Wales Echo*, 7 November 1967).

Caerphilly had two walk-outs by the busmen in a week over the issue of 'legitimate' instructions from management. Busmen refused to pair incomplete crews. Notices were posted informing bus crews that they must follow proper orders. The Caerphilly transport committee chairman said that his committee thought that 'a state of indiscipline has been reached among the busmen which can no longer be tolerated as it makes the task of management completely impossible and produces chaotic conditions' (*South Wales Echo*, 16 November 1967).

Cardiff transport committee had met the national passenger group secretary of the TGWU on 15 November. He had told them that other local authorities were negotiating and that unless they negotiated there would be new sanctions introduced by the busmen. He told the committee that it was not the FMPTE which employed the local busmen, but the Cardiff city council. The committee decided to take no decision as there was to be a meeting of the FMPTE in London two days later. A move by the Labour group on the committee to have the Press admitted to the meeting was turned down.

The nation-wide dispute moved to the Minister of Labour. In a letter circulated to all local authorities in the Federation, the FMPTE said:*

The Minister assured the Federation of the importance which the Ministry attached to effective national negotiating machinery, and emphasised that any agreement which might be reached by individual undertakings would be subject to scrutiny in the light of the requirements of the Prices and Incomes Policy and should be reported to the Ministry under the early warning procedure . . . In the light of what the Minister said and his recognition of the importance of

* Letter from the FMPTE to general managers of member undertakings, 23 November 1967.

effective *national* negotiating machinery, it will be even more
evident to you that there is an absolute need for continuing
to support the resolution carried at the special meeting of the
membership held on Friday last, 17th November.

The Minister of Labour was to see the unions on Tuesday, 28
November. He was also under pressure from the shopkeepers of
Cardiff. The Chamber of Trade sent a telegram to Mr Gunter:
'Retail trade in Cardiff is declining and the bus dispute is bringing
business to a halt. We urge immediate action to settle this dispute.
Only early settlement will prevent a ruinous Christmas.'

The Cardiff transport committee were also in constant communication with other local authorities to find out what the situation
was. They had been told in their meeting with Mr Alan Thomson,
National Passenger Group Secretary, that negotiations were pro-
ceeding with Aberdeen, Halifax, Sheffield, Leeds, Lincoln,
Newcastle and Darlington. The Cardiff transport manager
produced a report on the situation in those undertakings which
stated that Aberdeen was negotiating 'under great pressure';
Halifax 'negotiating only on general lines, which apply any time of
the year. Nothing special'; Sheffield 'negotiating, but nothing
has been definitely offered'; Leeds 'not negotiating. If there is no
hope of settling at national level before the 31st December, 1967,
prepared to negotiate after that date. Men have agreed to normal
working.' This was in agreement with the FMPTE. Lincoln and
Grimsby were negotiating on productivity, and the sanctions were
being lifted at Lincoln. Newcastle was operating under sanctions
and a strike was threatened. The Newcastle transport committee
had offered the men a 23s per week increase on the basic rate (this
was the TGWU demand) or £1 on the basic rate plus better rates for
Saturday overtime. This was subject to ratification from the city
council and the Ministry of Labour. Darlington: 'Not strictly
negotiating . . . sticking to National Agreement' (Report at Meeting,
21 November 1967).

Managerial authority and the strike

The transport manager submitted to his committee a document
which he was issuing to the busmen. It stated that the demand by
the busmen for local bargaining had begun with two sanctions.
After 31 November, six more sanctions were introduced, one later
being withdrawn (this was the refusal to set passengers down at
stops encumbered by cars). He said that individual busmen were

also introducing their own sanctions. Management now intended to apply disciplinary action for the following actions by employees: '(1) Spare men refusing to work allocated duty where work content plus time from signing on to commencement of late duty does not exceed eight hours. (2) Crews running on unauthorised routes without instructions. (3) Use of physical force in imposing sanctions. (4) Unjustifiable delay in effecting reliefs. (5) Failure to complete scheduled duty. (7) Refusal to pair up where alternative duty is within compass of own duty. (8) Failure to inquire if relief crew or vehicle is available. (9) Defecting vehicles for unjustifiable causes.' A list followed which stated that out of ninety-two undertakings, a possible six were negotiating, about twelve were on strike. Six were negotiating normally. Finally he added that any settlement would be scrutinised by the Ministry of Labour (notice to drivers and conductors—sanctions, 28 November 1967).

The transport committee authorised the transport manager to issue the warning and to take any necessary action. This led to a strike three days later when an employee was dismissed. The union claimed that the management were fully aware that if they dismissed a man for finishing his work at the proper time this would bring the rest of the men out. The transport committee chairman denied this, and said that the man had refused to work and had been dismissed. He told the Press that there were no plans to meet the union and begin local bargaining. In this deadlock an important intervention took place from the Chamber of Trade, who issued a statement in which they said they were convinced that relations in the industry had deteriorated in the last two years: 'There has been much muddled thinking and intolerance on both sides and it is tragic that the city is brought to a standstill on one of the busiest Saturdays of the year, by the foolish dismissal of a man for carrying out a sanction which for three weeks had been in being.' The statement continued by saying that the busmen 'had a sound case for an immediate improvement in pay and conditions'. A three-point plan was put forward which said that the busmen should return to work immediately, that the Minister of Labour should act urgently to get a new national agreement or set up new negotiating machinery. A time limit of one month to be imposed. If no agreement had been reached by 3 January, then local negotiations should commence in Cardiff (*South Wales Echo*, 2 November 1967).

The effect of sanctions, culminating in a strike, the obvious disruption of office work (Cardiff is a large administrative centre) and central area shopping in the busy pre-Christmas period, added weight to the Chamber of Trade statement. At the next council meeting, on 4 December, it was evident that the discussion about the buses was no longer divided along political lines as it had been before, with most of the minority Labour group arguing for meetings and talks to be held with the busmen and the majority Conservative group opposing this. There was now a majority view for conciliation and the need to get the transport undertaking working again in the cold and bitter December weather. There had been a good deal of pressure on councillors from many citizens, and the intervention of the Chamber of Trade helped to point the need for action. It was decided that the dismissed busman would be reinstated as a diplomatic move. Labour members asked for this decision to be linked with a promise to pay the busmen their six months bonus. The chairman of the transport committee argued that this should not be done. There was no wish on the part of the committee to avoid making the payment, but the position arising from the strike had to be examined. He was warned that this would lead to a continuation of the strike. But the matter was not pushed to a vote as it was argued that the council would almost certainly vote not to commit themselves to paying the bonus and difficulties of procedure would arise. The lord mayor told members that they would not have to wait until the next meeting in January, as a special meeting would be called if necessary to deal with the situation. In addition to the disruption of trade and work, car drivers reported a great deal of traffic congestion, with journeys taking twice as long as usual.

The busmen refused to return to work until the city council gave an undertaking to pay the six months bonus, which had been due on the day after they went on strike. They also intended to return to work with sanctions, as before, or until the council negotiated a new agreement.

A special meeting of the transport committee was called the day after the busmen's decision to continue the strike. The meeting was unusual in that the proceedings began with a deputation of inspectors who demanded that the council support them in putting an end to 'the trying times of a critical public and rebellious staff. An end is needed to this madness, as it is impossible to enforce discipline with the operation of sanctions.' The decision to reinstate the conductor had been wrong. As this was the first time the transport committee had met any of its employees, apart from union officials, it seemed strange that this intervention came just as a move was being made by the lay management to adopt a conciliatory pose and end the strike. It was agreed that the transport manager had the full backing of the transport committee in disciplinary matters, although what this meant was unclear, as the committee did not want further 'incidents'. Letters were received from citizens and groups urging negotiations. A letter was received from an industrial consultant offering to examine the city transport system. The letters were noted, although some were highly critical of the committee.

The transport manager reported a meeting between the regional TGWU secretary, the Editor of the *South Wales Echo* and himself. The question as to whether the service bonus should be paid was discussed at length. It was reported that the regional secretary had asked for the strike to be made official. The transport manager said that an unofficial strike could not be made official retrospectively in order to qualify for service bonus. Extracts from the Minutes of the NJIC relating to the Birkenhead unofficial strike were produced in which the union side had given an assurance that 'there would be no further instance of declaring strikes official as had happened in the case of Birkenhead' (NJIC Minutes, London, 19 May 1966). A councillor asked if it would be legal to pay and if not, what could be done? The deputy town clerk interpreted the agreement in the fact of the decision by the trade unions that it was no longer valid. As there was no collective bargaining machinery, the council could decide to pay the service bonus without the question of surcharge of illegality being raised in a court action. The treasurer's department reported that the total cost of paying the bonus would be £15,000. The chairman said that other authorities had suspended payment. Some councillors argued that the council should stand up and fight the busmen. One said: 'Every trade union official in the country would wish that he had this weak-kneed transport committee to deal with. If you buy peace you will go on buying peace.' A lawyer spoke of the legal implications if the busmen were in accidents while operating sanctions. A motion was tabled 'That the Service Payment for the period up to and including December 2nd, 1967, be paid in full on the understanding that the recommendation to return to work is accepted by the employees.' An amendment was moved 'That the bonus be not paid until the men return to work.' The chairman asked the transport manager if he wished to comment. The manager criticised the busmen strongly and asked for a 'tough no-nonsense line' to end the indiscipline. He was asked if his statement meant that the strike should continue. He replied that he was not making any suggestions. The transport committee voted for the service bonus to be paid by ten votes to five. It then discussed the Chamber of

Trade letter suggesting that local negotiations be begun if there were no national settlement by January. It was agreed that the date, 18 January 1968, be the starting point for local negotiations if no result had been reached by then.

The following day there was a special meeting of the Cardiff city council (General Purposes Committee) to discuss the recommendations of the transport committee. Copies of the Chamber of Trade letter were circulated to members, and references were made to letters from individual traders in the city. A deputation from the Chamber of Trade was present and had also sent a telegram. The transport committee chairman reported that Mr Gunter might convene a meeting of the employers and the union side and start national negotiations arising out of the PIB report on municipal transport which was due to be published shortly. There was an urgent need for an early settlement of the dispute due to the bad weather and the Christmas season. He said that the regional secretary had recommended to the men that they return to work if the conductor was reinstated. Following a mass meeting of the busmen the following resolution had been sent to him by the men:

Recommendation of Committee of 4/115 Branch to Members
That having regard to the decision of the Cardiff City Council to withhold bonus payments due to be paid on December 8th, which decision we consider to be a further deliberate act of provocation we do not agree to resume work at this time. We urge the Cardiff City Council to reconsider their attitude and agree that the bonus will be paid. Immediately this decision is reached we would recommend an immediate resumption of work.

The transport committee chairman said that it was never the intention of the council not to pay the bonus but they had to look first at the legal implications of the strike. A discussion took place as to whether 'return to work' meant 'return to normal work'. A councillor moved 'No payment without a return to full work.' He mentioned the deputation of inspectors, their plea for a return to industrial discipline and that there should be no appeasement and no buying of peace. In reply it was argued by an alderman that the NJIC no longer existed and that the council should keep its earlier bargain to pay the service bonus, without making any conditions. This would create an atmosphere which might lead to better relations. This was agreed to by a large majority.

It is doubtful if this would have been the view of the transport department, as the advice circulated to members giving the facts of the situation included the statement:

> It may be that because of the provocative attitude of our bus crews the Committee may wish to harden its attitude. If this be so, a suitable action would be to send written termination of employment to each person concerned, on the basis of termination of employment becoming effective three days following notice unless a return to normal work took place, together with the offer of consideration of re-employment as a new employee upon individual application. This would mean that all employees dismissed would lose existing holiday entitlements, sick pay entitlements and accrued service pay entitlements, this because service pay starts following six months service and increases progressively. . . .

The intention of the advice offered may have been to show the transport committee the range of options before them. But the dismissal and re-engagement of staff on a large-scale basis would not have been practicable in view of the constant difficulty in obtaining and retaining staff.

The following day the busmen went back to full normal working, in spite of snowy weather. The Chamber of Trade received praise from both sides to the dispute for its plan which, according to the *South Wales Echo* (9 December 1967) 'decided the issue'. Although the Chamber of Trade had suggested that local negotiations should begin on 3 January if no national settlement had been reached, they were in favour of national bargaining as 'There is so much difference in the size of the transport undertakings and their pay claims that national level negotiations would be much better' (ibid.). Here again the emphasis is on the cost aspect, rather than on the possible yield in productivity.

While Cardiff went back to work, Pontypridd busmen voted to stage a number of strikes on Saturdays, until the council agreed to negotiate with them at a local level. Caerphilly, also a few miles from Cardiff, had been on strike for a month. The council there offered them local negotiations on 22 January, if national talks had not started by then. The transport committee of Caerphilly council voted against local talks by the casting vote of the Labour chairman, but the special meeting of the council voted to have local talks in January in spite of the warnings that they were being held to ransom. Those for negotiations and an end to the strike argued that children were struggling through the snow and old people could not shop. One councillor said: 'Our loyalty should be to the people of the community, not to a federation of municipal employers against local talks but split' (*South Wales Echo*, 12 December 1967). The voting showed a reversal of political roles compared with Cardiff. There the voting had shown that the Conservatives were against local negotiations, and the Labour group for. In Caerphilly, thirteen Ratepayer and Independent members voted for local negotiations and nine Labour councillors against. It was alleged during the debate that some busmen had been working for local firms during the dispute, but this was denied by the busmen's shop steward who said that if he were given any names and proof of the allegations then the men concerned would be taken before the branch committee.

The Cardiff transport committee were told on 19 December by the transport manager that a five-hour meeting on 14 December between the FMPTE and the unions had reached agreement. The proposals were: £1 increase per week in basic rate; the 'penal clause' to be re-examined; the £2 per week supplement to holiday pay to be re-examined; service pay to be forfeited only for the period of actual withdrawal of labour; the NJIC to be re-constituted forthwith. The unions had asked for national rates to be minimum ones, but the employers had not agreed as they had instructions from their members not to accept minimum rates. However, a special general meeting would be held in the future to decide this issue. The transport manager was not in favour of national rates being minimum ones but thought a refusal on this might lead to more industrial unrest. He favoured a compromise, which would suggest 'no rate of pay above the minimum is to exceed the minimum rate of pay plus 8 per cent, or some other agreed percentage'. He said that there might be some move away from a common national rate and quoted the White Paper on public transport and traffic (Cmnd 3481, para. 46), which said:

> The principle of common conditions for those engaged on comparable work is obviously right. But it may well be thought that the conditions of work for bus staff are by no means identical throughout the whole of a Passenger Transport Area, and it may be that there will be a case for paying premium rates in certain parts of the Area where conditions of work are most trying and consequently it is particularly difficult to obtain enough staff.

The cost of the sanctions and strike in Cardiff were also put before the transport committee. The city treasurer said that there would be a £50,000 loss in revenue from the buses in 1967 and a deficit of £100,000 in 1968 unless fares were raised. The transport manager was instructed to prepare an application for a fares increase to be put to the traffic commissioners. The city treasurer was interviewed the following day and said that the increased fares ought to bring in another £150,000 in revenue. He referred to the £1 a week increase in basic pay, and pointed out that the cost of such an agreement to Cardiff would be in the region of £81,000. He added that the transport undertaking would have broken even but for the dispute.

The Prices and Incomes Board, however, found that the £1 a week increase given to the municipal busmen was 'not in accord' with government policy. The rise in basic rates meant that there would be an increase in average earnings of approximately 7½ per cent. The report, 'Productivity Agreements in the Bus Industry' (Cmnd 3498), suggested a 10s per week bonus for all drivers and conductors in garages where firm agreement could be reached on the introduction of OMO and special bonus payments of between 15 per cent and 22½ per cent for OMO operators. Local productivity deals were to be encouraged.

The TGWU's reaction was that there might be industrial action, that the report was 'pious and pitiful' and that it was foolish to imagine that the co-operation of the men in the introduction of OMO could be bought for 10s a week (*Guardian*, 22 December 1967). The mood in Cardiff was similar and there was talk of a national stoppage if the rise were delayed. The chairman of the passenger transport branch said that the PIB was set up to look after the lowest-paid workers, 'and if we are not low paid I don't know who is' (*South Wales Echo*, 22 December 1967). The feelings on the employers' side was that they had carried out their part of the bargain and the matter now rested with the government. This was the view of the Cardiff transport committee as voiced by the chairman. The chairman of the FMPTE, Alderman Harris, said: 'It was a shotgun wedding—I told the Minister so today. But we had every intention of implementing it although we said it was subject to ministerial clearance.' Alderman Harris had been extremely critical of the unions throughout the dispute and had issued a statement on 13 November saying that the unions' demands amounted to over £2 weekly and that it was wrong of them to say that the employers would not move beyond 20s weekly, on which issue the talks broke down. He said: 'This is a monstrous and cynical lie and typical of the obvious insincerity and hypocrisy of the union throughout the talks' (FMPTE Press Statement, 13 November 1967).

Pressure was put on the Cardiff transport committee by the TGWU to pay the increase. The committee was told at a special meeting on 29 January 1968 that a letter had been received from the regional passenger group secretary to this effect, referring to the NJIC ratification of the award on 11 January 1968, and demanding that the matter be treated as urgent. The committee were also given a letter from the joint secretary of the employers' side of the NJIC. He referred to a meeting with the Minister for Labour and the Chancellor of the Duchy of Lancaster (Mr Fred Lee) and ministry officials on 17 January. The Minister had been given full details of the negotiations. The unions had pressed for the payment of their award, especially the £1 per week. The employers' side had said that as they had signed the agreement of 14 December, 'whatever the circumstances might have been at the time, they felt there now existed an obligation to pay'.

The Minister had told both sides that the government felt that the award was not justified under the criteria of incomes policy. He advised them to start negotiations on productivity in municipal transport as suggested in Report No. 50. He warned the NJIC that if the award were paid the government would use their powers.

The transport manager said that he had sent a letter (28 January 1968) to the local TGWU branch of the busmen, telling them that the undertaking had been in a healthy financial state in July 1967, and a small surplus for the year had been possible. This had now disappeared with the sanctions and many passengers had been lost. He gave details of the losses amounting to £18,000 per month, and said that further industrial unrest would result in the loss of more passengers and revenue. He had ended the letter:

I repeat my verbal offer of increases within the National Board for Prices and Incomes' Report on Productivity Agreements in the Bus Industry. Among the recommendations were a 10s per week bonus straight away to all garages which gave a firm agreement to the introduction and/or extension of one-man operated buses, and the added rate for one-man operation is recommended in urban areas to be 20 per cent for single-deck buses and 22½ per cent for double-deck buses. There are other aspects of increased productivity upon which, if agreement could be reached, an increased weekly sum could be paid and I do hope that on the basis that 'half a loaf is better than no bread' careful consideration will be given to this matter.

Labour costs and passenger losses

Before the end of 1967 a number of local authorities in South Wales were planning to raise fares in the New Year in order to meet the cost of the £1 a week award as well as to recoup the losses from the long period of sanctions. Every member undertaking of the FMPTE in South-East Wales declared that it would present an application for a fares increase as early as possible. The authorities said they had very little room for manoeuvre as the only options were (a) a rise in fares, (b) an increase in the rates to subsidise the bus service, internal economies and a decrease in services. It should be noted that none of the authorities saw OMO as a short term answer to their difficulties. Cardiff made an estimate of the undertaking's losses at the end of January. It was reported that Cardiff Corporation had lost 720,000 passenger fares during the first month of normal working in January. This meant that the city transport lost £18,000 or some 10 per cent of the monthly fare income. This was the loss for January 1968. The figures for the two months of sanctions and the strike, November and December 1967, were put at £25,000. January figures were estimated to be the equivalent of 1,200 fewer passengers per day. The chairman of the transport committee said that he was sure that people had found alternative ways of travelling during the dispute. The transport committee agreed to put forward an application for a fares increase which would bring in an extra £150,000 a year. The estimate appears to have compared January 1968 with January 1967, without making an allowance for the yearly decline in passengers which had gone on every year. Nonetheless, there had been a substantial falling-off in the numbers of passengers carried. This was to continue as the busmen, although back to normal working, now developed a higher rate of sickness, which meant that many buses were late or did not run at all. Consequently, numbers of people changed to other modes of travel throughout 1968, including the suburban railway lines.

Newport, among other local authorities, complained that absence from work was reaching 'alarming proportions'. The Newport transport committee were told that on one Saturday in December, two days before Christmas Day, there were 33·1 per cent of the total driving staff absent, and 44·5 per cent of the conductors. Another large group, both drivers and conductors, were off sick. The Newport transport manager said that the sick pay scheme was open to abuse. In Newport, unlike some other undertakings, men were paid from the first day of sickness. The union were informed about the absenteeism and promised to co-operate (*South Wales Echo*, 29 December 1967).

The most interesting reversal of political roles was the proposal of Gelligaer Labour Party to cut down the deficit on municipal transport by selling their bus service to a private operator. Their main grounds appeared to be the long-term rising costs of a public service and the fears that there might be a revival of sanctions. The secretary of the Gelligaer Labour Party said in a letter to the Urban Council, 'A return to the chaotic conditions which the public have been subjected to would be intolerable' (*South Wales Echo*, 10 January 1968).

At the same time, the decision of the government to refer the busmen's pay increase to the PIB cut away the main argument for a fares increase. Most municipal undertakings in the Cardiff area were gloomy about their financial prospects but decided to wait for the final decision about the pay rise before making application to the Traffic Commissioners.

The union reaction to the PIB

The first demand for strike action came from the annual conference of the Scottish busmen on 28 December, where the conference voted for 'positive action' defined later as a national bus strike. This was followed by the representatives of the London busmen, who described Report No. 50 as a 'gross impertinence and inter- ference with collective bargaining' (*Guardian*, 9 January 1968). They intended to continue with their claim for higher basic rates and improved productivity pay.

Mr Ray Gunter, Minister of Labour, announced that he would use his powers to impose a six-month pause on the municipal busmen's pay award, unless they agreed to forgo the award volun- tarily (union officials could be fined up to £500 for organising strikes or action to enforce payment during the 'freeze'). The employers, who had also met Mr Gunter, said they would not pay the increase, but had asked him to support them by invoking the Prices and Incomes Act (*Guardian*, 10 January 1968).

In South Wales, the regional passenger group secretary said that there was much resentment about the refusal to allow the pay award and that the men would support any action decided by the union nationally. The local branch secretary agreed with this view, as did the union representatives in Newport and other areas nearby.

The delegate conference met in London on 18 January and Mr Cousins went through the range of options open to them. There were five main points: a national strike, selective stoppages of short duration, work to rule, local disputes to get the award from employers who had agreed to pay, and last, an acceptance of the advice of the government to re-open negotiations at a national level.

One authority, Nottingham, decided to pay the award locally. They asked other municipal undertakings to follow their example, although Nottingham's main reason for paying was the acute staff shortage. The town clerk had advised them that the payment could not be stopped under the present Prices and Incomes Act until an order was made prohibiting the payment. After that, the council could be liable to a penalty.

The TGWU busmen decided on 25 January not to strike, but to take legal action, on the advice of Mr Frank Cousins, against the refusal of local authorities to pay. The employers could be brought to court for a breach of the individual contracts of employment. Mr Cousins said: 'We shall take the step of advising employers that they are illegally withholding money which rightly and properly belongs to their employees' (*Guardian*, 26 January 1968). The government countered this move by the TGWU by referring the increase to the Prices and Incomes Board. The reference meant that the award could be delayed for three months, possibly six months or longer, under Part II of the Act. This also made it illegal for the employers to pay the £1 a week increase. In order to pay the ninety-seven local authorities concerned would have to decide to break the law and risk an unspecified but costly fine. The busmen had pressed to the point of conflict, and the government had refused to pay.

The decision to take legal action was criticised by the industrial correspondent of the *New Statesman*, who dismissed the lawsuits as 'propaganda' and quoted Mr Cousins' left-wing critics as asking why militant industrial action was not taken instead of a 'feeble' civil law action. He also mentioned the trade union leaders opposed to a legal framework for industrial relations and fearful that Mr Cousins might open the door to legal intervention by his appeal to the courts (*New Statesman*, 2 February 1968, p. 133). It was also noted, correctly, that the long-drawn-out sanctions and strikes had left the busmen in no mood for a national bus strike, and that the main effect of the standstill order would be 'Services will continue to become even more erratic and unreliable because of chronic staff shortages.' This is, in fact, what happened in Cardiff during the year of the standstill. To 'staff shortages' could have been added 'absenteeism and sickness'.

Cardiff transport committee voted seven to five on a decision to start negotiations with their employees on a local productivity bonus agreement. They were advised not to do this for legal reasons by the chairman, who argued, as a lawyer, that the matter of payment was now before the courts and therefore *sub judice*. He also argued that, as the award had been referred to the PIB, the whole agreement was at a standstill. This was yet another example of the damaging effect of the dispute between the Board and the TGWU on productivity negotiations.

Jack Jones, then the assistant executive secretary of the TGWU, made a vigorous attack on the government's decision to freeze the £1 increase for the busmen and refer the increase to the PIB. He complained that this was a breach of the contract reached between the unions and the FMPTE. In other words, it was an infringement of free collective bargaining. He quoted the basic pay which the busmen received, and added that it was below the TUC's minimum earnings figure for forty hours. Although the busmen's earnings had been higher than this, they had only been achieved by working a considerable amount of overtime, with a fifty-five-hour week being common. He criticised the 'hurried and ill-thought-out intervention by the Prices and Incomes Board' and said that industrial relations in the industry were at their lowest point. Municipal busmen 'who are paid fewer shillings each week than Aubrey Jones is paid pounds' were not, in the eyes of the Board, low-paid workers. Did this mean, he asked, that the differentials between clerical, service and industrial workers should always remain the same? Trade unions should be allowed to push for higher rates for their low-paid workers. The Board had not studied the agreement and did not understand it.

The £1 increase was to have been part of a new approach to collective bargaining in the bus industry. Item 4 of the agreement had said that in future the basic rate would become the minimum rate instead of the standard rate which had been imposed by the NJIC in 1951 and had prevented the unions from negotiating local productivity and efficiency deals. Jack Jones said that the move away from the standard rate would have improved productivity bargaining in the industry, and blamed the PIB for preventing this by freezing the £1 increase and thereby worsening industrial relations in the municipal transport (*Tribune*, 2 February 1968).

The busmen and the PIB, 1968

The lengthy struggle of the busmen, beginning with their announcement of a withdrawal from the NJIC on 16 June 1967, continuing with sanctions and strikes from October to December, and ending in a settlement on 14 December 1967, was notified in a letter to the Ministry of Labour. The letter, dated 19 December, gave the details of the settlement in full, the main point being the £1 per week increase for a forty-hour week; that national minimum rates be adopted instead of the existing standard rates; that the NJIC be re-convened immediately; that the service payment would be forfeited only for the weeks in which strikes had occurred; that normal working would be resumed. This was referred to the Prices and Incomes Board by the Secretary of State for Economic Affairs and the Ministers of Labour and Transport. The notice appeared in the *London Gazette*, 27 January 1968 under the heading 'Prices and Incomes Acts 1966 and 1967'. The object of the reference, apart from putting the agreement under the scrutiny of the Board, was to apply a standstill under Section 15 of the Prices and Incomes Act 1966, until the publication of the Board's report.

As indicated above, Section 15 resulted in a standstill on the Agreement of 14 December 1967, the standstill being referred back to that date, and in the case of the Nottingham Agreement, back to 22 January 1968.

The Board then had three months in which to produce a report on the settlement in municipal transport. It must be assumed that the Board spent the first few weeks in collecting the available statistics and information, and in deciding the form which the inquiry should take. It appears, from conversations and interviews with some trade union officials, that a questionnaire on earnings was sent round a number of municipal undertakings, which was in sufficient detail to provide a comprehensive picture of earnings and hours. This is confirmed by pages 41 to 53 of Report No. 63, which, in twelve tables, sets out the Board's findings. Appendix E states that the Board had asked for information from twenty-eight federated municipal undertakings, chosen as a sample in 'terms of size, character and region'. All the authorities co-operated in the survey, unlike some of the other industries surveyed by the Board. There was also full co-operation from the unions concerned, the TGWU and the NUGMW.*

There was also a survey of staff shortages from ninety-two undertakings, which supplemented the July 1967 survey from seventy-nine undertakings.

In addition to these statistical surveys, the Board sent out their own investigators, who conducted on the spot interviews and

* 'In the course of our enquiries we had numerous contacts with union officials at all levels' (ibid., p. 23, para. 88).

assessments. The Board also appear to have used industrial consultants (ibid., p. 57, para. 9).

The White Paper criteria and the busmen

The Board considered the busmen's claim under the heading 'The Case for an Exceptional Pay Increase'. They estimated that the net effect would be to raise labour costs by 7 per cent, and the pay of platform staff by $7\frac{1}{2}$ per cent, due to their overtime and other premium payments: 'an increase of £1 on the basic rate produces an average increase on platform staff earnings of about 31 shillings' (ibid., p. 5). Local authorities estimated that this would require a fares increase of 6·5 per cent, bringing in 4·5 per cent more revenue 'after allowing for the decrease in passenger demand resulting from these fare increases' (ibid., p. 5).

The Board considered the three criteria for exceptional pay increases, having dismissed the productivity claim until the unions produced more evidence than a willingness to talk about it. They considered the manpower question at length, as it was one of the staple factors in the busmen's argument. They found that shortages of drivers ran at about 10·8 per cent—more in the larger undertakings—although the point was made that the figures of intake had been limited by local agreement in order to raise overtime earnings. It was shown that 'Average shortages of drivers therefore rose from 10·8 per cent to 17·1 per cent between July 1967 and January 1968, although there have been fluctuations in the totals. This 6·3 per cent increase in shortages,' said the Board, 'we attribute primarily to the unrest which prevailed in most municipal undertakings in the last quarter of 1967: this unrest lowered overtime earnings, discouraged recruitment, caused some staff losses, and hampered or prevented the training of further conductors as drivers' (ibid., p. 7). This analysis shows the Board costing the wage increase in terms of the rise in fares due to increased labour costs, but there is no attempt to cost the loss in revenue or disruption of services through sanctions or strikes. Admittedly this would have been difficult, but a survey of the change in revenue of undertakings during this period could have been calculated and adjustments made. This would have given the public a clearer idea of the actual costs of the industrial action.

The figures for turnover of platform staff were given and conductors were higher than drivers with a rate of 48·4 per cent for them as against 26·1 per cent for drivers. This was explained by the fact that most drivers were recruited from conductors on seniority,

I

and therefore tended to be the more stable element from an employment point of view. The retention rate was considered to be more important than the turnover figure. This showed the numbers who remained throughout the year measured. The Board concluded that the retention figure shows a high stable element in municipal transport and pointed out that the turnover figure is higher in other service industries. On this point the Board might have looked at the numbers of women employed in other service industries, as well as at the wage level before they advanced this argument. Another factor is that the stable element in municipal transport might be a declining proportion as the conditions of the work deteriorate in comparison with other work.

The conclusion was that there was no serious manpower shortage in the municipal transport sector, especially as there were local agreements with the unions 'which prohibited the direct recruitment of qualified drivers. We regard this as a restrictive practice which makes the shortage of staff much greater than it otherwise would be. It may also discourage qualified drivers from applying for busmen's jobs because of the need to serve for some time as conductors' (ibid., p. 9).

Table 7 *Platform staff earnings*

Category of employee	No. in survey	Average weekly earnings £ s d	Range(s) of lowest weekly earnings £	No. of employees in the lowest ranges	% of total in category	Range of hours worked for lowest earnings
Driver-operators	493	25 13 8	16–18	1	0·2	42½–45
Drivers (two man crew)	10,136	22 5 9	14–15	25	0·2	40–42½
Conductors	10,494	20 9 6	(a)13–14	20	0·2	40–42½
			(b)14–15	255	2·4	Under 40–50

(Source: PIB Survey, February 1968, Report No. 63, p. 11.)

The low pay criteria

The criteria for low pay allows increases 'where there is general recognition that existing wage and salary levels are too low to maintain a reasonable standard of living'. The Board's earnings and hours survey was designed to find out how many busmen were in the low pay (undefined) category. Table 7 shows the range and average of earnings and hours.

The conclusions drawn by the Board were that 'even where their working week does not exceed $42\frac{1}{2}$ hours, there are no platform staff earning only the basic rate'. People who earned least had high leisure preferences or low commitments, or other wage earners in the family. There was the suggestion that some had part-time jobs, although no evidence was produced to support this. The summing-up on the low wage argument appeared to be that if the men worked longer hours they could earn more: the 'low pay' argument of the busmen was dismissed; they did not come under the low pay criteria of the White Paper and there was 'no evidence of "low pay" which would warrant special adjustments of the basic rates' (ibid., p. 12).

Comparability

The busmen argued that their earnings were behind those of London and behind those of other industries. The comparison with the busmen of Central London was rejected. The Board found 'exceptionally difficult working conditions' there and noted a considerable difference between the work of busmen in the provinces as compared with London. The comparison with other industries was also rejected, on the same grounds as those advanced in Report No. 50, which found that the earnings of busmen 'compared reasonably well with other workers while their hourly earnings were significantly lower' for a 52·6-hour week, while semi-skilled in engineering averaged 8s 7d for a week of 45·3 hours.

It is difficult to see how the Board could argue that busmen's earnings compared 'reasonably well' with those of time-workers in engineering, when the busmen were working 52·6 hours and the engineers 43·6 hours. On the specific point of the lower hourly rate, the Board argued that this related to the recent past rather than the future, and mentioned the recommendations they had made to raise hourly earnings. How far this prophecy proved true may be seen from the critical speech made by Jack Jones, by now General Secretary of the TGWU, at the October 1969 Labour Party Conference, some eighteen months after the publication of Report No. 63, where he repeated most of the points made in the *Tribune* article of February 1968 in criticising Mr Aubrey Jones and the Prices and Incomes Board.

Summing-up on the municipal busmen's award, we find that the Board had tried the award on the grounds of productivity, manpower shortage, low wages, and comparability, and had found it wanting in all respects. The busmen were advised instead to seek higher earnings through greater productivity.

Productivity

A number of suggestions for improving productivity were made. The chief suggestion, which had been made by a number of people for some twenty or thirty years and had been done efficiently in many countries for the same period, was that buses could be operated by one man instead of two. The savings in labour costs would be considerable, and as labour costs come to some 60 per cent of the total cost of operation, this shift of manpower to OMO would offer a more hopeful future for municipal transport. Some of the advantages and difficulties were discussed in Report No. 50 and were also briefly mentioned in Report No. 63. In this there were, apart from OMO, suggestions about operational efficiency, based on the techniques of Operational Research and reflecting the work done for the Board by their outside consultants. Crew scheduling was also dealt with; this is the problem of the twin peaks, morning and evening peak hours, which mean that 'as much as a quarter of the total buses and their crews is not actually required from about 9.30 a.m. to 4.00 p.m.' (p. 17). This creates problems of work-allotment involving split duties or spread-overs. Local restrictions on spread-over duties meant that more staff might have to be employed than are actually needed.

The main change that could be made here was to persuade the busmen to exercise greater 'flexibility', particularly if numbers of men could be trained as 'driver/conductor/handyman' with a higher hourly rate. Suggestions were made about the use of part-time labour, although this is strongly resisted by the unions and would involve changes in the present national agreement. The employment of women as part-time conductors, part-time labour at peak times, and the use of women as bus drivers, are other points which were made, although on this last issue the Board underestimated considerably the feeling in the bus industry against the employment of women as drivers. This may be due to the suspicion that the practice of employing part-time women drivers might spread. One transport manager said to the writer, only half in jest, that 'the long-term solution to the rising diseconomies of municipal transport is the employment of part-time women drivers, half of them taking the morning peak, and half the evening peak, with a small number of full-time male staff. . . . In other words,' he continued, 'one-man buses run by half women.'

Management

The Board devoted a section to the problem of management. This was meant in two senses: the influence of the lay management over the professional full-time management, which the Board tended to regard as a hindrance to efficiency rather than as an aid to the citizen, and the professional management, which the Board regarded as unequipped to deal with modern business methods: 'Our consultants have commented on the conservative attitudes of many managers. . . .' There was little information given on this point, and possibly important points were lost due to the brevity of the treatment. We were told that industrial relations should be dealt with by the manager and not by the committee. Yet from a study of the strikes in some areas, it is arguable that it was the influence of the transport committees, and especially of the councils, which brought the strikes to an end rather than the attitude of some of the professional managers who saw the strikes as a challenge to authority and were looking more to the possible long-term consequences of this than the councillors, who wanted to make an important public service operational again. There is some evidence that the professional managers may use the transport committee as a lightning conductor against the criticisms of the men. The writer talked to some busmen who blamed the lay management for their difficulties when the unreported facts of the committee meeting would have shown them in error.

The problem of management is not so much, as the Board suggested, due to faults of management structure, as to the unimportance of the transport committee on the average council. A number of councillors are able enough, and experienced enough, to contribute to the more effective running of municipal transport, but they usually seek more important committees. The reform of local government, bringing in more full-time councillors, or payment for part-time work, would give some incentive to spend the time necessary for the running of this important public service.

The local agreements and the Board

During and after the period of industrial conflict, a number of local authorities had reached local agreements with their municipal busmen. Yet nowhere in their reports on the bus industry do the Board seriously consider the merits of national bargaining as opposed to local bargaining, although this was one of the main issues in the dispute of 1967. It is true that Reports Nos. 50 and 63 both make suggestions for local productivity bargaining, especially as this would result in productivity bonuses which could later be consolidated into basic rates and reduce the gap between wage rates and earnings. It was argued that productivity bargains are necessary to offset the loss of working hours when the hours of driving are curtailed. Few specific examples were given of productivity gains which could be followed by other undertakings and it may be that the Board was optimistic when it stated: 'We generally found acceptance of the need for change towards one-man operation, readiness to negotiate local productivity agreements, and considerable confidence that there was scope for doing this.' This underestimates considerably the union reaction towards the freeze of the £1 a week increase, which discouraged some promising attitudes to productivity changes. We can, however, look at the reports of the Board on a number of local agreements and examine the criteria by which they were judged.

The most important of the reports was No. 69 on Belfast, Glasgow and Liverpool ('Pay and Conditions of Busmen employed by the Corporation of Belfast, Glasgow and Liverpool', Cmnd 3646). The local agreements reached in the three cities were not under a Standstill Order: 'they were concluded subject to Government approval in terms of Incomes Policy, reported to the Government under the "early warning" procedures, and referred to us on 1st March, 1968 with the voluntary assent of the undertakings concerned' (ibid., p. 1). The agreements were reached in November 1967, before the national agreement had been reached. Each agreement specified pay increases: 18s 4d in Liverpool, 15s in Glasgow, £1 in Belfast. There were also a number of minor concessions; higher premium rates for Saturday afternoon and evening in Liverpool and Glasgow. None of the agreements made any noticeable provisions for productivity changes. The national agreement of 14 December superseded the local agreements in Glasgow and Liverpool, as previously arranged, but not in Belfast.

The union embargo of 27 March on OMO developments was followed in Glasgow and Belfast. Liverpool went further in direct action and started on a two-month strike on 11 March which was still continuing when the report was published. This militancy, and the considerable discomfort suffered by the citizens and industrial workers in an area which has many export industries, seems to have influenced the findings of the Board.

Liverpool

The Liverpool claim was considered under the four criteria of productivity, manpower, earnings (low pay), and comparability. The conclusion was that the productivity provisions were of a minor order. Management had suggested eleven proposals to improve working practices and the men had agreed to three. It was thought that the three concessions might pave the way to a better productivity agreement, but nevertheless the report said, 'The Liverpool Agreement cannot be justified in productivity terms.'

The claim based on manpower shortage was also dismissed. The overall shortage of drivers and conductors, at 18·4 per cent, was not markedly different from other municipalities. The two-month unofficial strike led to a further loss of manpower, but the report dismissed this as untypical. There were also union restrictions on recruitment, some of them agreed with management. Platform staff were kept at 94 per cent of establishment, and no women conductors were recruited between the years 1956 and 1966. Even now the numbers were far less than they were in cities of comparable size. There was no part-time labour, as this was opposed by the unions. The Board argued that, as there would be a fall in the demand for bus travel as a result of the strike, this would answer some of the staff shortage problems, while a speedy change to OMO would also make a better use of existing staff.

The claim based on low earnings was also dismissed. The analysis showed that 'the average weekly earnings of drivers in January–February 1968 were £22 19s 8d and those of conductors £21 5s 4d for working weeks of about 53½ and 52½ hours respectively. No Liverpool drivers earned less than £16; only 3·8 per cent earned less than £18; and 30·8 per cent earned more than £25.' The conductors earned amounts a little less.

The Board turned to the criteria of comparability. This was the breach through which the Liverpool busmen were to pour. The report gave three measures of comparability: (1) with other industries; (2) with large cities (non-federated) such as Manchester and Birmingham; (3) the Board made a concession which was unusual for a body which had pronounced so long against comparability; it was argued that hourly rates in Manchester, Birmingham and London were all more favourable to the busmen, and that the Liverpool men were at a disadvantage here. The conclusion was that 'pay is considerably out of line with that for similar work in at least some other large provincial cities' (Report No. 69, p. 10).

Glasgow

The Glasgow agreement of 19 November 1967, was for a 15s increase in basic rates. There were no provisions for productivity. The survey found that there was no great shortage of manpower and the figure was lower than the national level, at 11·7 for drivers and 10·0 for conductors (national average, 17·3 per cent). Although there was a high turnover of labour among the recruits, there was a stable core of long-service staff. The Board found no important restrictions on recruitment, apart from the observation already made about other municipal undertakings, that part-time staff could be employed as well as women drivers.

The level of earnings was looked at; it was found that 'the average weekly earnings for Glasgow are higher than those for all the other undertakings we have surveyed. The lowest average range of earnings for Glasgow's drivers is £16–£18 . . . 24 per cent of Glasgow's drivers and 16 per cent of conductors earned over £25 per week as against corresponding figures for other undertakings of £21 and 10 per cent' (ibid., p. 17). The report concluded that the earnings level was not low.

The analysis of comparability followed the same lines as in the case of the Liverpool busmen: comparability with other industries, with 'other non-federated undertakings of similar size', and with London. Earnings compared well with industrial earnings, although the hourly rate was lower. Although Glasgow busmen had the highest average earnings of any undertaking surveyed, they were still lower than those of Birmingham and Manchester. In the case of Liverpool, the Board had argued the close proximity of these two cities. For Glasgow, the Board returned to their theme that there might be a system of tiers, with the large cities on the top tier of the pay structure. These tiers would be based on 'effort and strain', and Glasgow and Liverpool, on the Board's estimates, qualified for an exceptional pay increase because of these factors. The finding in the report was that 'pay is considerably out of line with that for similar work in at least some other large provincial cities' (ibid., p. 19). Suggestions were made about improving productivity and operational efficiency, and changing working practices.

Belfast

Belfast, by any definition, is a large provincial city, with some 500 motor buses; but it was not large enough to satisfy the Board's criteria. The agreement of 21 November 1967 had been for an increase in the basic rate for platform staff of £1 per week. Here, as in other undertakings, the labour costs were 60 per cent of total expenditure and 'a rise in revenue of about 6 per cent would be necessary to cover the additional cost occasioned by the wage award' (ibid., p. 25). There had been some concessions to productivity in the agreement; there was a cut in services, which reduced the number of vehicle miles by 1¼m, with further reductions of 200,000 miles of services to follow. The Board criticised a bonus of about 15s linked to the number of passengers carried. They pointed out that, if services were cut further, the earnings based on passengers carried would rise. There were also concessions on single manning, although this required a change in the Construction and Use Regulations in Northern Ireland, which required two-men crews for double-deckers. However, the finding was that these concessions did not represent a significant advance in productivity.

The shortage of staff, as in Glasgow, was below the national average, with rates of 12·7 per cent for drivers and 10·8 per cent for conductors. Another finding was that conductors stayed longer than they did in other municipalities, and there was a 'hard core' of about 80 per cent long-service employees. Significantly, in view of the troubles of 1969–71 in the city, Belfast did not recruit from all men who apply for jobs, reflecting the policy of the Northern Ireland Government 'which limits the employment of non-Ulstermen throughout the Northern Ireland economy, and also at present precludes the employment of women on public service vehicles' (ibid., p. 27). The undertaking did not employ seasonal labour, as was done in many other cities, and opposed part-time employment. The report did not go into the peculiar circumstances of manpower in Northern Ireland. The object of the ban on non-Ulstermen was primarily to keep out the Irish, or many Catholics. This had the effect of making jobs available for the Northern Irish, or Protestant group. The non-employment of women was partly related to the high unemployment of the area, which was ignored by the Board. Unemployment in Northern Ireland was treble that of the average for the United Kingdom, which went a long way to explaining the relatively satisfactory manpower position. The Board rejected the application for an 'exceptional pay increase on manpower grounds, particularly as only a relatively small amount of overtime is worked'. The report did not mention the unemployment figures for the three cities. In March 1968, the Midland Region had 2·2 per cent unemployed, Scotland 4·0 per cent, and Northern Ireland 7·1 per cent (Source: Department of Employment and Productivity).

The survey found that the average earnings for Belfast drivers and conductors were £18 11s 1d and £17 7s 5d respectively, as compared with figures from £3 10s to nearly £4 higher for all municipalities. The Board discounted this differential as the Belfast busmen worked fewer hours than elsewhere—drivers nearly five hours less and conductors three hours less. As the survey showed ways in which earnings could be increased, mainly through OMO, the conclusion was that the busmen are not low paid workers.

The argument on comparability followed the lines of the other two cities above, the important difference being that comparability with other industries was confined to Northern Ireland where the earnings were lower than in Great Britain. The Board did not do this in the case of Glasgow, where industrial earnings were lower than in England. Belfast drivers were only 6s less than the average for all industrial earnings, and conductors some 10s behind. The point was made that such comparisons show busmen behind on hourly rates, as elsewhere, although busmen are paid for spreadover time when they are not actually working.

The conclusion was that Belfast did not qualify for the top tier as Glasgow and Liverpool did. It was agreed that the 'effort and strain' of work in a large city is greater than in smaller municipalities, but the 10s acceptance bonus, the negotiated increase of £1 per week, was not supported by the Board. Reference was also made to the 'untypically short working week in Belfast'. Suggestions were made for higher productivity, efficiency and OMO.

Report No. 69 was casuistical in some of its arguments. While it was sensible to recognise that work in the great cities involves more effort and strain than in smaller cities, as it does in London, no satisfactory measure of this was produced. Nor was the argument for comparability dealt with in a satisfactory way. Glasgow and Liverpool busmen were found to suffer from comparability, while Belfast busmen did not. Yet Glasgow's comparability was related to Great Britain and not to Southern Scotland, while Belfast was compared to Northern Ireland, not Great Britain. It would be realistic to assume that the Board, faced with a two-month strike in Liverpool, found reasons for giving the busmen a rise, which they would not have got had they not gone on strike. Glasgow had the same disruptive strike potential and received a high increase on the same grounds of comparability which the Board had rejected in other reports. Liverpool, in fact, had had restrictions on the employment of direct entry drivers until 1964 when they were relaxed in exchange for a bonus payment of 10s per week (ibid., p. 44).

Smaller undertakings

The Board also examined the agreements negotiated by a number of smaller undertakings: Rochdale, Dundee, Wigan and Great Yarmouth. The Rochdale agreement, made on 1 May 1968, provided for a 'productivity bonus of 15s per week to weekly paid platform staff and depot grades'. The Dundee agreement, made on 15 July 1968, provided for: (a) the introduction of a local efficiency payment, and (b) an increase of £1 per week of 40 hours in rates of pay, with effect from the first full pay period following 14 December 1967.

The Wigan agreement, made on 13 August 1968, provided for (a) an increase in basic wages of 10s per week as and from the first full pay period following 14 December 1967, and (b) payment, as soon as legally possible, of a further increase in basic wages of 10s per week as and from the first full pay period following 14 December 1967.

The Great Yarmouth agreement dealt with a 'bonus payment of 10s per week . . . in connection with the extension of one-man operation during the 1968 summer season'. The agreement had a stormy passage, as the first one of 26 May, on OMO, had been withdrawn on 12 August. The busmen had then discovered that they would not be eligible for the 10s acceptance bonus, suggested at national level, and had gone on unofficial strike. The Great Yarmouth Corporation then agreed to pay the 10s award which was referred to the Board. The recommendation was that although the agreement did not satisfy the White Paper criteria, the Board would be satisfied if the two parties went back to the agreement of 26 May 1968, which broadly satisfied productivity requirements. However the Board insisted, as they had done in the case of Dundee, that busmen could not be paid 10s twice for accepting OMO.

Nottingham was dealt with in Report No. 63. The £1 per week increase, awarded on 22 January 1968 by the Nottingham City Council in an attempt to implement the NJIC agreement of 14

December 1967, was referred to the Prices and Incomes Board. The findings were that the award should not be paid; there were shortages of drivers greater than the national average, but recruitment was confined to senior conductors and highly restrictive. The shortages of platform staff lessened in 1968. Although the earnings spread was wide, there was no 'low pay'. Productivity could be improved considerably. No mention was made of comparability.

Results of the PIB surveys

We see from the analysis of the above reports that none of the agreements under examination satisfied the requirements of the Board as laid down in Report No. 50. This appeared to the municipal busmen to be a more exacting standard than that applied by many firms to the earnings and work of their employees. Industrial relations in the industry continued to be bad and flared up again in the summer of 1968.

The Prices and Incomes Act 1968 became law on 10 July, and gave the government the power to delay the municipal busmen's award until 26 December. This presented the TGWU with the choice of negotiating on the basis of productivity or, by refusing, of having their £1 per week increase of 14 December 1967, stopped for twelve months.

The new standstill led to angry speeches and threats of industrial action up and down the country, and promises of stoppages of the kind that had caused disruption in October and November of the previous year. The new factor in the situation was that any industrial action to make the municipal councils pay the award might lead to a fine of £100 on summary conviction, or up to £500 on indictment. The legal difficulties which faced those who might have to enforce the legislation were that the busmen worked for many different municipalities, and a number of scattered legal actions up and down the country would be extremely unpopular with the Labour movement. The TGWU argued that the employers were in breach of their pledge to pay the award. Some government spokesmen argued that the busmen should accept the 10s bonus offered for acceptance of OMO and 10s on the basic rate by meeting officials of the DEP and drawing up the guidelines for productivity bargaining. However, under the 1968 Act, the power to delay the £1 increase could only last for twelve months, and the government would be unable to prevent the retrospective payment of the award after that date.

The reaction in South Wales was as hostile as elsewhere, and the regional passenger group secretary said that it would be difficult to keep the men at work, as they would be very angry at the decision. The secretary of the Cardiff busmen's branch said: 'The attitude of the Cardiff busmen is very militant.... At the moment there is a 50–50 chance of strike action' (*South Wales Echo*, 11 July 1968).

The new dispute between the TGWU and Mrs Barbara Castle was over the conditions to be attached to a pay increase. Mrs Castle insisted that the payment of £1 weekly could not be made until there was agreement over OMO. The union wanted the agreed award to be paid without strings. On 11 July they informed the employers that they wanted the £1 to be paid and also a further 10s locally as soon as OMO was introduced (*Guardian*, 12 July 1968). There were short stoppages and some sanctions in Southampton, Wolverhampton and Wigan. In spite of this action by the local branches and the leadership of the TGWU, it was suggested that the threat of fines up to £500 would have a dampening effect on militancy. In Glasgow, a large representative conference of busmen voted to start an overtime ban on midnight, Sunday 4 August. A London meeting was advised by Mr Frank Cousins to make the stoppages local instead of national, and thus avoid a direct violation of the standstill order. The delegates voted to strike by a majority of two to one (*Guardian*, 18 July 1968). The Dundee busmen were on strike, and at Grimsby there was a one-day stoppage with more trouble promised. Great Yarmouth had a two-day strike. By 26 July the TGWU national executive had decided to give instructions to its thirteen regions for a national bus strike involving 77,000 municipal busmen on 12 August. The Secretary for Employment and Productivity said that she would confirm the order stopping the payment of the £1 per week increase for the third time since December 1967. This brought a confrontation in the newspapers between Mr Frank Cousins and Mrs Castle, with the former quoted as saying: 'If the law takes its course . . . I shall have to face it', while Mrs Castle said that it was 'still open to the union to reverse its destructive decision and to accept the settlement that we have offered them' (*Guardian*, 26 July 1968). The offer made to the busmen was that of 10s on the basic rate for following productivity guidelines and 10s bonus for the acceptance of OMO. The DEP view of the issue was that they had to pay in advance for promised productivity changes. As the busmen had not agreed to OMO until 13 June, the DEP were not willing to backdate the 10s to the previous December.

A number of moves now took place which avoided the confrontation which might have put Mr Cousins, if not some of his top officials, in prison. In Scotland it was reported that 'Glasgow, Edinburgh, Dundee and Aberdeen corporations are to be approached by the union to see if they cannot follow Manchester's lead and agree to a £1 pay award if the strike is called off.' The Scottish Regional Secretary of the TGWU pointed out that this did not break the law as the Act only had delaying powers over wages and could not prevent wage rises being backdated, once the legal time limit had lapsed (*Guardian*, 2 August 1968). An example of the type of agreement reached was that of Cardiff, which issued a statement unanimously agreed by the transport committee. 'The Committee recommends that a written undertaking be given to the trades union representatives that the Council will pay the agreed sum of £1 per week basic pay to the staff of the transport undertaking governed by the National Joint Industrial Council for the Road Passenger Transport Industry for the full pay period following 14 December 1967.' This money would be paid 'if and when it becomes legal to do so' or until a new national agreement was reached (*South Wales Echo*, 6 August 1968). The busmen's delegate conference in London decided to call off the national strike by forty-six votes to fourteen on 9 August. The meeting was told of the large number of authorities employing nearly half the municipal busmen, who had agreed to pay the £1 increase as soon as it was legally possible and to backdate this to the date of the award of the previous December. Pressure at local level was to be put on other undertakings who had not agreed to this.

An example of the local pressures which led to a strike and to a change of policy by the municipal authority can be seen by tracing the sequence of events in Pontypridd. This is a market town lying at the foot of the Rhondda valley, with some fifty buses. Nearly half of the buses serve the Treforest Trading Estate some miles away, so that a bus strike would have a considerable effect on the many factories there. The bus undertaking came under the close scrutiny of the council, which stuck closely to the rulings and agreements negotiated by the FMPTE. Due to the rapidly growing numbers of cars owned by workers and the increasing congestion and rising costs, the undertaking had been showing a deficit in 1967 and 1968 of some £20,000 to £30,000. The rateable cost of the deficit came to nearly 8*d* in the pound. There was little support by the council for the introduction of OMO, and the busmen were opposed to it because of the narrow streets and reversing problems in the town. Redundancy was also mentioned as a factor.

When local pressures were applied in September 1968, they

began with a passenger group secretary urging a special transport committee meeting on 4 September, to give a written assurance to the busmen that the council would pay the £1 increase on a back-dated basis to the previous December, as soon as it was legally possible to do so. He argued that 40,000 busmen had received such a promise, including the large neighbouring authorities of Cardiff and Newport. The decision of the local transport committee was to tell the TGWU that if they did not want to wait for a national settlement then they could negotiate a local pact on the lines laid down by the FMPTE. This was based on a 10s payment retrospective to 14 December 1967, and a further 10s paid from 14 June 1968. The local passenger transport branch of the TGWU decided that unless written assurance was received from the council, there would be a strike on the following Saturday, 7 September. The strike took place, and a few days later the chairman of the transport committee said they were prepared to give the busmen a verbal promise of payment but not a written one. By the tenth day of the strike the Pontypridd Chamber of Trade was appealing for action to end the strike. The president said: 'I have heard in some instances of traders losing 50 per cent of their business and others 20 per cent.' He added that the position was serious and called for a special meeting. The busmen marched through the centre of the town and handed out leaflets to explain their action to the public and enlist their sympathy. The leaflet said: 'If you feel that the attitude of the Council is unreasonable we would be grateful for any pressures that you are able to exert to persuade the Council to adopt a more reasonable attitude in line with that taken by most other municipalities' (*South Wales Echo*, 16 September 1968). The chairman of the transport committee denied that the council had refused to pay the £1 pay rise retrospectively. He said that the council had been following the instructions of the FMPTE not to give the written assurance, and were still ready to negotiate on pay and productivity. The council finally agreed to pay the £1 rise retrospectively on 24 September, although the busmen did not go back to work until a few days later.

The results of the twelve-months standstill

The municipal busmen received their £1 per week increase in December 1968, paid retrospectively to 14 December 1967. Some newspapers referred to it as 'Mr Cousins' Busmen's Holiday Fund', and drew the moral that if the union were determined enough, they could find their way through the White Paper on Incomes Policy.

This was the view of the busmen. At the TGWU Conference in 1969, the chairman said in his address that they had 'driven a bus through the government's Prices and Incomes Policy'. At the most the government had achieved a year's delay of the pay rise to 77,000 municipal busmen and possibly prevented other groups from basing pay claims on comparability with this. It might also be said that the busmen's claim was halted at a critical time for the British economy, and may have given the government a small success to show in their fight against wage inflation.

On the debit side, the losses, though unmeasureable, were probably far greater than any success the standstill order may have had. Many towns and cities suffered sanctions and strikes, and thousands of workers suffered hours of delay and frustration waiting for buses and arriving late, with consequent losses for industry. Some statistics of the disruption suffered in a short period are available in Cardiff, where on Saturday, 28 December, only eighty buses out of a total 152 were operating. On New Year's Day, forty-three buses were missing, while on some other days nearly one-third of the buses were not running. This, on a lesser scale, had been the pattern during the several weeks of sanctions. The whole year of the standstill saw many buses missing at different times on routes. (The writer lives on a bus route where inquiries showed that his regular bus did not run on 500 occasions in the year.)

A large number of employees were lost to the undertaking during the year, and recruitment fell owing to the standstill. The transport manager reported that one disturbing factor was the 'very large increase in the number of employees claiming exemption from working overtime and rest days. One week commencing 22 December 1968 the average per day exempting themselves was 75·5 employees . . . 38·3 on the following week' (City Council Meeting, 6 January 1969).

Costs of the Cardiff dispute

The Cardiff transport undertaking was in deficit before the 1967 dispute began with a deficit of £77,505 in 1966/7, due to the delay in increasing fares. This was met in various ways, such as 'raiding' the reserve fund of the undertaking, by not contributing to the vehicle repair fund, and by £8,139 from the rates. In 1967/8 there would have been a deficit of £78,142, but this was helped by a reduction in insurance cover of over £20,000. The net loss to rates was £17,979, plus a rate fund contribution of £38,026 for concessional fares to old age pensioners. This put the rate support to the transport undertaking at £56,005, or a penny rate. As fares were increased in July 1967, it was expected that the undertaking would break even, but the city treasurer reported that the 'work to rule' and the week's strike caused a disruption of seven weeks in all. He reported a loss of £100,000 during this period, offset by savings of £46,000. Losses continued after full working was resumed. It was expected that the £1 increase, when awarded, would lead to a further application for a fares increase. The number of passengers carried fell by seven million over the previous year, and the mileage by nearly half a million (Report of the City Treasurer and Controller, Cardiff Corporation, 22 July 1968).

Manpower costs

There was also a number of working days lost through sickness and absenteeism (the words being used interchangeably, as in many cases the man not wishing to work collected a certificate stating that he had had a cold or headache or stomach ache). Absenteeism (absence without permission or medical certificate) in the last half of 1968 (before Christmas) averaged from 10 to 11 per cent for drivers and conductors. Conductresses had a slightly higher absence rate. No figures are available for this on a national level, but 10 per cent is frequently found in some industries in South Wales. Absenteeism in the mines in the South Wales area has been as high as 30 per cent in some pits and over 20 per cent for whole areas. It is frequently said by industrialists in the area that this high absenteeism is endemic in South Wales and stems from the high incidence of, and history of, mining in the area.

Discontent, low morale and low earnings would also be reflected in the shortage of staff up and down the country, although this is sometimes influenced by agreements between management and the local union to limit recruitment in order to increase the overtime earnings. The staff shortage varies according to the labour market situation in different regions and tells us a good deal about wage rates and employment in the area. The figures for all platform staff in municipal undertakings showed a shortage of 17·3 per cent, with towns having more than 500 drivers being slightly higher. Comparisons between the regions showed some striking differences: Liverpool had a platform staff shortage of 18·4 per cent; Glasgow was much lower than this with 10·8 per cent; Belfast was only slightly higher than Glasgow, with 11·8 per cent. It is significant that Scotland and Northern Ireland, with unemployment rates

K

standing at two and three times the figure for Great Britain respectively had shortages of only 12·8 per cent (see Report No. 69 for the three above cities) against the national average of 17·3 per cent. From these figures it is hardly necessary to guess at the relative earnings and conditions of municipal transport compared to surrounding industries and job opportunities. Clearly the busmen's job was regarded as better in Belfast than it was in Liverpool.

Labour turnover

The turnover for all municipal undertakings was 37·2 per cent, while Liverpool was 36·6 per cent and Glasgow 62·4 per cent (Glasgow has a very high turnover of short-term staff). Belfast was 27·9 per cent, mainly owing to a low figure for conductors. Figures in South Wales vary, but 40–50 per cent labour turnover is not unusual. Most of the turnover is from short-service staff, who are highly mobile. Liverpool's figures showed that 96 drivers and 378 conductors left before one year of service, out of 911 leavers. Drivers generally show a higher retention rate (length of service with the undertaking) than conductors, although Belfast, with a relatively low turnover, finds that its conductors are close to the drivers' figure.

The implication from these figures is that a move to OMO will also reduce labour turnover, and the higher earnings improve recruitment.

National versus local bargaining

The lengthy dispute in the municipal transport system began in July 1967 when the union side withdrew from the NJIC for the Road Passenger Transport Industry. From October they were attempting, through various forms of industrial action and pressures, chiefly sanctions and strikes, to persuade local authorities to negotiate locally. This was resisted by the employers' side of the NJIC, whose chairman and secretary toured the country appealing to the local authorities to 'stand firm', 'be loyal', 'resist all pressures'. Most local authorities did this, until the pressure on the public led to pressures being put on local councillors (as reported above) to negotiate locally with the busmen if no moves towards a national settlement were possible.

Few authorities debated the pros and cons of local and national bargaining. This underlines the comment of the Donovan Commission, who wrote: 'Many of those who conduct industrial relations in Britain are content with things as they are, because the arrangements are comfortable and flexible and provide a very high degree of self government.' In the meetings of the Cardiff transport committee, the case for local bargaining was put, with reference to the recommendations of the Donovan Commission and the new emphasis of the PIB on productivity and bargaining. There was little response to this; the counter argument was that the FMPTE had not advised them to do this, but to await developments; that if the local undertakings bargained separately, the TGWU officials had been advised to submit all agreements reached to Head Office for advice; that a favourable bargain reached by the men with one local authority would soon be used as a lever with others; that the railways and the mines negotiated nationally and that there would be great confusion if the municipal undertakings departed from tradition; finally, it was said that local bargaining would be certain to raise wages, and therefore the rates would rise to cover the deficit and councillors would be voted out of office or fares would increase with the same effect (the last two arguments proved to be the most effective in providing large majority votes for no change in bargaining procedures).

Strangely enough, the PIB did not deal with this whole question, which had been one of the central factors in the disputes which lasted over eighteen months. In the end, it was the local pressures of bargaining of the busmen which forced the hand of many municipal undertakings and led to the backdating of the £1 per week increase and the virtual defeat of the PIB so far as the busmen were concerned. The Board did achieve some success in making municipal undertakings more conscious of possibilities of raising productivity and reducing costs, but their main suggestion for change in the present structure of negotiations was to suggest a 'tier' system, with the largest cities having higher rates. There are limits to the extent to which local bargaining is possible in municipal transport. While it would, if taken seriously by the employers and the men, along with advice to both parties from their respective national offices, lead to more efficiency and cost-consciousness, there are certain dangers. One is the view that quite a few of the problems of municipal transport would be solved with more part-time or women drivers to get over the problem of the morning and afternoon peak user times. This might make the busmen resist change unless they were told that all such important changes would be fully discussed and negotiated with them. Another difficulty is that local bargaining, as recommended by the

Donovan Commission, takes place in the context of the commercial enterprise, which is usually self-financing. Public transport will, in the future, run at a loss, unless there are considerable technological and social changes. (Large cities on the continent and in Scandinavia have already recognised this: 'In 1966, 20 per cent of Stockholm's rates were applied to local transport; in Rotterdam the amount was 2½ millions; in Copenhagen £3½ million and Brussels receives a considerable sum from Government sources. In all these cities, fares are still responsible for the bulk of the revenue' (*Guardian*, 30 May 1969). As public transport will not be self-financing, wage increases may be related to the amount of subsidy the undertaking will receive, or the extent to which the rates can be raised. (The latter would be the more equitable from the national point of view, but the more difficult from the local councillor's view. It has been truly said: 'Taxes are paid in sorrow, but rates are paid in anger.')

In spite of these objections, it will be necessary to use social cost/benefit analysis on municipal transport and bus services in the future in order to make our cities habitable and reduce traffic congestion. The busmen will have to be paid a reasonable wage. As this is unlikely to be met from local transport undertaking funds, the development of Passenger Transport Areas and larger, more efficiently run groupings, will make possible the most effective use of transport resources and provide and channel the funds necessary for capital investment and for better wages and working conditions for the busmen.

Breaking the wages dam

By late 1969 the busmen, as with some other groups in the public services, were beginning to break through the incomes policy barrier. From an increase in June 1969 they followed with an increase of 9·7 per cent in January 1970, thus shortening the time-period between increases considerably. Eight months later the municipal busmen received a further 9·2 per cent, an increase of 19 per cent in eight months. This illustrates that the attempt by the Labour Government and the PIB to keep the busmen near the incomes policy 'norm' for three years, at the cost of 'go-slows', 'work to rule', strikes, and great inconvenience to the lower-income groups who use buses, as well as delays of many months in the introduction of OMO, eventually broke down. It might be argued that the government battle with the busmen held the flood of comparable wage claims in the public sector back at strategic times. In view of the increase in pay claims in 1969–70 it could also be argued that the effect of the downward pressure on pay was in fact to give an added stimulus to demands, like a spring being coiled and then released.

This latter view is held by R. G. Lipsey and J. M. Parkin, who argue that incomes policy was not only 'ineffective' but raised 'the rate of inflation above what it otherwise would have been. This perverse effect is very noticeable in the most recent periods of "restraint" since 1966' (Lipsey and Parkin, 'Incomes Policy: A Reappraisal', unpublished paper, University of Essex, August 1969, p. 2).

4

Local government

Local government employees are part of the rapidly expanding service sector, with 1,425 local authorities, employing nearly a million people. Their growing numbers reflect the rising national expenditure on social welfare, housing, health and education. This development is found in all industrialised countries, irrespective of the political system; e.g. the number of Federal, State and Local employees in the USA increased by 20·5 and 76·3 per cent respectively from 1947 to 1961, and 20·9 and 49·2 per cent from 1961 to 1969.

Along with this quantitative change has come a qualitative change in attitudes in the public employment sector. Traditionally in Britain, as in most other industrialised countries, public employees have been quiescent compared with the more unionised areas of private industry. The public sector had always recruited employees who were interested in security of employment, relatively good wages, and a pension. While these were the attractions for the first fifty years of this century, they were eroded from 1945 onwards by full employment, state pensions and inflation.

These changes, along with the greater numbers in the public sector, made it more difficult for employees to raise their wages without resistance from the government and local authorities. This, in turn, led to a greater spread of trade union membership than was the case in private industry. Professor G. S. Bain, after estimating that the rise in the numbers of white-collar employees will lead to their outnumbering manual workers by the 1980s, says: 'While roughly eight out of ten white collar employees in public employment belong to a trade union, only one out of ten are members in private manufacturing industry.'*

The nature of inflation in Britain has meant that industry and commerce have been able to pass on price increases to the con-

---

* G. S. Bain, 'The Growth of White Collar Trade Unionism in Great Britain', *British Journal of Industrial Relations*, November 1966.

sumer with relatively little resistance from either the customer or the government. In this way most firms have been able to meet the wage demands of their employees by passing on the cost to the public. This is a more difficult process for local authorities, and especially for local government.

Local government is a service industry, financed partly by rates and partly by funds and grants from the government, as well as by borrowing and rents. One estimate is that local authorities get one-third of their income from rates, although this is a general average which conceals the differences between the various authorities; e.g. one large city drew nearly half of its income from government grants in recent years (this will be looked at in more detail below). Local government has some trading services, such as municipal transport, markets, abattoirs and water, but these are frequently in deficit and contribute little to the finances of towns and cities. This means that the citizen and the councillor see local government as being financed chiefly by rates, and government grants are looked upon as being largely outside local control.

The preoccupation of councillors with the level of rates shows a healthy concern with their political survival, but the major result of this attitude is that the level of rates becomes an election issue, rather than the standard and efficiency of the services provided for the citizens. This forms the background in which industrial relations takes place. It explains why wages and salaries in local government are lower than those in comparable industries and why councils accept lower standards of productivity and performance if the alternative is to raise wages. When wages and salaries are raised, this is due to the effect of higher wages in the economy as a whole reacting on the local authorities' sector, as the latter have rarely, if ever, led the field in awarding increases.

Wages and salaries in the local authorities' sector have been subject to the cycles of boom and restraint in the economy and the attitude of the government to fiscal and monetary measures. The 'pay pause' of Mr Selwyn Lloyd in 1961 was the precursor of a number of pressures on local authorities to restrain increases to their employees and led to increasing militancy on their part. Mr Wilson, then Leader of the Opposition, moved a motion which 'deplores the Government's action in breaking agreements governing the pay of government employees, in interfering with established negotiating machinery in respect of teacher's salaries. . . .' He continued later in his speech: 'conditions in the public service should not be less good than in private industry. The Government's attitude is that the public sector, being under their control, must be the whipping boy' (House of Commons Debate, 23 October 1961). These were prophetic words, frequently quoted against the Labour government of 1964–70, as well as underlining the declared policy of the 1970 Conservative government. Mr Lloyd denied that he had been unfair and advanced three arguments which were to become received writ in government circles, irrespective of party, throughout the 1960s; defence of the pound, 'due regard to the Government interest as a provider of funds, as well as the national interest' (House of Commons Debate, 21 October 1961).

This policy was rousing the normally quiet public service unions to action. The day following Mr Lloyd's speech the staff side of the Health Service (Whitley Council) saw Mr Enoch Powell, Minister of Health, and protested about the pay pause. Mr Powell explained why the pay pause 'had to be applied to the Health Service in common with other public services'. The National Association of Local Government Officers (NALGO), in their 1962 Annual Report, referred to the 1962 Conference which produced 'an emergency motion submitted by the National Economic Council (NEC) and supported by a number of district councils and branches'. This 'endorsed the action taken by your Council in opposing the Government's wages policy which discriminates against the public service officer . . .' (*Guardian*, 26 October 1961).

The teachers were also campaigning against the restraint on their salaries. They were officially employed by the local authorities, who paid them but did not determine the level of their salaries. This was fixed by the Burnham Committee, over which the government attempted to exercise its influence during the 1960s, and finally did by changing the composition of the committee. The growing numbers of teachers and the strategic effect of increases in the educational sector upon the public sector salaries made the government increasingly restive and demands were made that the public (the government interest) should be represented earlier in pay negotiations. Successive Ministers of Education had complained that they could only accept or reject, and not influence, an award of many millions of pounds of which they had to find over half from government funds. The Burnham Committee was finally reconstituted in 1965, with the government having a direct voice in the size and distribution of salary awards. This was one of the ways in which the government of the day was gradually extending its influence over pay in the public sector.

Local government authorities were critical of the fact that, although they were the biggest single organisation in the country, and were employing nearly two million employees, 'Yet, as employers, we do not figure in discussions on incomes policies . . . at all.'*

The trade unions and the associations in local authority service would have agreed with this assessment of government pressure on public pay. The NALGO historian described Selwyn Lloyd's pay pause as 'the gravest threat that any government had made to collective bargaining, and the first time any had interfered with industrial arbitration'.† NALGO had welcomed NIC, whose aim they saw as being to protect 'people with less bargaining power, swamped by the crude application of a general average'.‡

NALGO had not wanted a yearly scramble for higher pay in which they had less effective bargaining power than many manual workers' unions. They welcomed their three-year agreement, signed in 1963, as giving them time for a thorough salary review. The three-year pact meant a three per cent pay increase yearly, and the NALGO newspaper reported that it was the first of 'the new style of long term settlements based on the Government's "guiding light"' to be negotiated for any major group of white-collar workers. 'The staff side has agreed to submit no further claims during its three year period, but has reserved the right to seek a review should exceptional circumstances arise.'§ The disputable terms here were 'exceptional circumstances', and later events were to show that local authorities and government circles did not see inflation as an unusual occurrence in a long-term agreement. NALGO members grew restive under rising prices, and in March 1965 put pressure on their executive to open salary negotiations in spite of the fact that the three-year agreement did not expire until the following year. The National Joint Council rejected the claim; though there was talk of strikes and sanctions, these came to nothing, as the militants knew that they had little support. One speaker put the matter bluntly when he told delegates that Ernest Bevin knew that if he lifted his little finger the dockers would follow him to Hell, but if the signal were given to the local government officers, the bolt holes would be jammed with people trying to escape.

There was a fall in local government salaries in 1964–5. Their gross salary increases between August 1964 and August 1965 ranged from 2·8 per cent to 3·2 per cent for the Administrative,

---

* T. Dan Smith, Association of Municipal Authorities' Annual Conference, 1965.
† A. Spoor, *White Collar Union: History of Local Government Officers*, Heinemann, London, 1967.
‡ *Ibid.*, p. 298.
§ *Public Service*, September 1963.

Professional, Technical and Clerical (APTC) grades, and between 2·6 per cent to 2·7 per cent for the clerical grades. This meant that their real income fell somewhere between 1·5 per cent and 2·1 per cent over this period. This fall in real income made NALGO suspicious of incomes policy from the start and they had little confidence that a policy of marking time would restore their differentials to a just level. The general secretary of NALGO summed up their positions over the twenty years 1948–67: 'Between 1948 and 1952, the purchasing power of most local government officers fell by 10 per cent or more. It remained at that low pitch until around 1960, when a little of the lost ground was recovered. Today, in terms of what their money will buy, the incomes of the lower ranks are broadly the same as they were twenty years ago, whilst those of their seniors are—excluding promotion—still some way below the 1947 levels. In the same period, the purchasing power of industrial workers has increased, on average, by around 50 per cent.'* He claimed that other sectors of the public service, in which NALGO negotiated, such as gas, electricity and the National Health Service, were in a comparable position.

The manual workers' side of the local authorities had also had a three-year agreement, as had the ancillary staff (Whitley Council) side of the National Health Service. However, in 1965–6, the local authority manual workers, county council roadmen, river authorities and National Health Service ancillary staffs, all had increases around the 'norm' on top of the rates in their three-year agreement, in order to catch up with the sharp rise in the cost of living.

We can say that in the first fourteen months of incomes policy, from April 1965 to the middle of 1966, the norm of 3–3½ per cent for wage increases was frequently exceeded. But the public sector had a number of cases where the settlement was around the norm, showing that the government could put pressure on the negotiations through their control of the public purse. On the other hand, the local authority sector was not disposed to be used as a dam against the inflationary river. The number of employees affected came into the region of two million, with a large group of 600,000 or so manual workers in local authorities, nearly 270,000 ancillary staffs in the National Health Service, as well as some 340,000 nurses and midwives. This group began to agitate in a manner that had not been done previously and the nurses in particular made effective use of television to air their grievances over pay and conditions. In this action they received much newspaper support

* W. C. Anderson, *Public Administration*, Autumn 1967, p. 266.

and public sympathy, and ultimately achieved a considerable success. In July 1965 they had an 11 per cent increase over a two-year agreement ending in June 1967, and in October 1967 some 4 per cent backdated on the annual salary scale. Stage I of a new agreement gave a 9–14 per cent increase* with a new salary structure to come in January 1969 in Stage II of the agreement.

One of the ways in which the new militancy of local authority white-collar workers was showing itself was the move to affiliate NALGO to the TUC. For most of its history the white-collar staff in various authorities had regarded themselves as in a different category from manual workers and had abhorred the thought of strikes or other industrial action. The recognition that the government was to intervene more directly in wage and salary negotiation brought a change of heart. But the initial suspicion and the grudging support given to the TUC on incomes policy changed when the July 'freeze' stopped a 7 per cent award to local government officers, which had been virtually agreed a few days before the 'freeze' was made law. This angered NALGO, and at the next TUC conference in September 1966, they found themselves part of the left-wing opposition to incomes policy. Walter Anderson seconded a motion proposed by Frank Cousins of the Transport and General Workers' Union, and the move against incomes policy failed only by some 4 million votes to 5 million.

The internal salary structure

While the national salary awards are the major method by which the pay of a local authority officer rises, many also have hopes or expectations of a promotion or a re-grading. NALGO emphasise this in their union literature: 'the individual officer who thinks he is not getting a square deal in pay and conditions of service has certain rights of appeal under the Whitley machinery and NALGO will help him, if he is a member, to prepare and present his appeal. Half of the appeals committee which will hear his case will be of staff representatives.'

There is a careers ladder in local government which is climbed by various types of training and examination. In a large city such as Cardiff, with fourteen-and-a-half thousand employees, there is a post-entry training, which involves about 300 staff, some in day or block release courses at technical colleges which lead to specific local government qualifications such as IMTA and DMA. There are practical and scientific courses for technicians and others. There

* Recommendation in PIB Report No. 60.

are a number of external courses provided for administrative professional officers. Professional and technical qualifications are important in career advancement, as the normal tests of business organisations are less available.

This can be seen from the 'Local Authority Staffs Appeal Form' which is presented to the joint consultative committee which hears appeals against decisions not to re-grade. The information presented includes age, qualifications, post occupied, department, date of appointment to post, present grade, date from when present grade has applied, grade claimed, up to questions on additional duties or responsibilities undertaken since the last salary revision. This was the major ground for many appeals heard by the writer when he was a member of the establishment sub-committee and of the joint consultative committee.

The establishment sub-committee and the JCC are advised by the local government equivalent of a labour personnel officer, under the title of Establishment Officer (EO). This officer appeared comparatively late on the stage of managerial development in local authorities. Warren, in his book *The Local Government Service*, writes: 'Many of the larger authorities have appointed establishment officers, under whom much, if not all of the work at official level can be consolidated, and who can make the necessary study and analysis of questions which arise for determination by the Council and its committees, and who can give specialised advice in regard to some classes of employees. Specialised appointments of this type are thoroughly justified. . . .'*

The EO plays an important role in collective bargaining. This can be looked at in two ways, the external wage structure and the internal. The first is the national rate which is negotiated through the appropriate bodies. In the case of Cardiff this is the Glamorgan and Monmouthshire Joint Wages Board, which follows the national awards closely.

In a sense, the internal collective bargaining shows the EO in his main role. Every employee has the opportunity of applying for re-grading to a higher paid post, and in times of incomes restraint, this has become a more common procedure. Chief officers from the applicant's department give their opinions about the application to the establishment committee, and they may be questioned by councillors. The chief officers and the staff side then withdraw and the EO is left with the councillors and will give them guidance on the merits of the application and, more importantly, the possible effect on salary or wage structure in particular departments. Of the

* J. H. Warren, *The Local Government Service*, Allen & Unwin, London, 1952, pp. 161-2.

two main issues before the committee, the merits of the case and the possible effect on relative salaries, the latter can often be a more clinching argument. But the expansion of local government in some areas, notably in the field of planning, has meant that authorities have to pay more to planners in order to attract and retain them, at the expense of other departments. An example of this was when two equally qualified employees in two different departments, one in transport and the other in planning, had a 50 per cent difference in salary at the age of twenty-six years. There was a shortage of planners and an abundance of development or 'Buchanan' type plans, which meant that young men could move quickly to high salaries by pushing for promotion or re-grading internally, or by moving to another authority. An issue of this nature sometimes sees the EO and the councillors on different sides as the councillors will argue that they must have planners to develop the city, while the EO argues that the high differentials paid in one department will cause resentment throughout the authority.

A typical batch of grading appeals analysed at one meeting showed seven applicants in Cardiff in a batch of forty to be over forty years of age, four of them in their fifties. This shows that far more members of staff apply for re-grading than can hope to achieve it, and that once a claim cannot be supported by new or improved qualifications based on examinations, then the claim goes forward on added experience, effort, or responsibilities. One applicant in 1968 had passed his last examination thirty-two years previously, and argued that some other towns and cities were paying his grade higher rates, that his professional association (most of whose members were not in local government) had issued figures showing that men with similar qualifications were earning more. He added a list of the new parliamentary Acts relating to his work which he implied would give him added work or responsibility, though no figures relating to his increased duties were given.

An applicant in the motor taxation section of the City Hall argued that the increase in motor vehicles on the roads had increased his work by 'mammoth proportions', that new Acts had increased his responsibilities and that new traffic offences had made his work more difficult. Another applicant, in the weights and measures department, wrote: 'The shortage of qualified staff in this Department is due, in my opinion, to the salaries' policy. . . . Until the establishment is filled, the present staff carry out their duties in an atmosphere of great strain and frustration, to the detriment of traders and the public alike.' Applicants from the rates department pointed out that the rent rebate scheme had meant increased work in spite of increased staff, while the new staff taken on to assist needed supervision which, in itself, was an added reason for re-grading. An added argument which frequently occurred was that the city had enlarged its boundaries two years before to embrace another 20,000 people.

Given the relatively modest yearly increase in local government pay, the successful applicant for re-grading can usually achieve an increase in pay from 10 per cent upwards, and also has succeeded in moving on to a new pay ladder.

No figures are available for the numbers who are re-graded yearly, although local authorities do have to publish additional payments which have not been allowed for in the annual estimates. Unless detailed figures are kept, it is difficult to separate the pay due to re-grading from the pay increases which are given after negotiation and whose amount cannot always be foreseen. A senior NALGO official said that if they succeeded with 10 per cent of their grading applications, they would think the figure quite good, but the percentage had been falling since incomes policy, and especially since July 1966. Apart from the arguments previously put forward in support of re-grading, the main argument used by the union side was the rate in comparable jobs elsewhere for local authorities. Union officials said that they had a dozen or so authorities around the 300,000 population size, from which they received information which helped to build a structure of salary scales and changes. An effective argument was to tell a local authority that they were 'paying under the rate'. The union view was that employers had access to more information as they could simply write to town clerks or establishment officers.

The practical effects of widespread re-grading on incomes policy are clear. It might represent a method by which the authority concerned could observe the restraints on the national rates while giving increases to some staff by moving them up, or above, their particular grade. The government were aware of this possibility and mentioned it in their post-July 1966 circular to local authorities.

The National Joint Council for Local Authorities (APTC), faced with the government clamp-down on the staff side award of August 1966, considered the effect of the incomes policy 'freeze' on the appeals machinery. They pointed out that most appeals were raised under paragraph 80 of the 'Scheme of Conditions of Service', which states:*

---

* Letter to Clerks of Local Authorities, 26 September 1966.

The particular duties and responsibilities attached to posts are of necessity and in many cases somewhat difficult of detailed definition, and may vary from time to time without changing the general character of the duties of the level of responsibility entailed. Such variations are a common occurrence and cannot of themselves justify reconsideration of the grading. In cases, however, where there has been a substantial change in the duties and responsibilities of the post going beyond variations of the kind referred to, then if the grading is not altered or the officer concerned is dissatisfied with the decision as to the grading taken by the employing authority, he has a right of appeal to the Provincial Council under this paragraph.

This interpretation was in line with the relevant paragraph in the White Paper 'Incomes and Prices Standstill' (Cmnd 3073), which allowed 'increases in pay genuinely resulting from promotion to work at a higher level, whether with the same or with a different employer'. The NJC warned local authorities that re-grading must not be used to defeat the intention of the standstill in incomes which would occur if, to quote the White Paper, 'Employers were to re-grade posts as a concealed method of increasing rates of pay.' The NJC told local councils and provincial councils to watch out for any large increase in the number of grading appeals.

Some local authorities may have allowed some re-grading as a disguised pay increase, but the majority of councils in the 1966–9 period had their aversion to raising the rates buttressed by the cuts in public expenditure in 1968/9. Industrial relations were placed under increasing strain as local authorities could plead that they were under government orders to limit the numbers re-graded. For example, the Cardiff city council quoted the White Paper 'Public Expenditure in 1968–69 and 1969–70' as saying that there would be no Rate Support Grant Increase Order during 1968–9 and that local authorities were expected to absorb any unavoidable increase in costs by savings elsewhere. As the wage and salary bill for Cardiff was 50 per cent of total cost, or £12½m as against £24m, the effect of a 10 per cent rise on the rate, even with the government paying some 50 per cent, can be seen (though the Rate Support Grant had in the past two years helped to cushion the pay increases).

In the economic straitjacket in which local authorities found themselves, the possible release suggested by the government and the PIB was through greater productivity. Report No. 29 of the Prices and Incomes Board, although it dealt with manual workers, would probably have reached the same conclusions if it had looked at the staffing and performance of most local authorities with all grades of employees. The report said that 'there was ample scope (in local government) for increasing labour productivity'. Trade union criticisms were forestalled as the report was also critical of the low standard of management. As there is 'extensive under-utilisation' of labour, it is hardly surprising that the Board found that some incentive schemes had raised productivity by 20–40 per cent. The Board's conclusions were that the pay was low because productivity was low, and a number of suggestions were made to improve the training and education of workers, to re-organise, re-train, develop work-study and encourage consultancy.

The Board estimated that progress in this direction would be slow and that the full implementation of the programme to raise productivity, and thereby wages, would take several years. It was suggested that a beginning could be made by introducing incentive schemes as a short-term measure. This caused confusion in the minds of many councillors as they did not realise that incentive schemes merely speed up work done under the existing system and methods. Productivity bargaining demanded a new approach to the total work problem and most councillors have neither the training, the time, nor the inclination to make local authority management more efficient. The Maud Committee (Committee on the Management of Local Government) wrote in 1967: 'The country is not getting full value in terms of human happiness for the time spent and for the increasing current expenditure now standing at £3,000m (9 per cent of the gross national product) that they spend each year.'

The Maud Committee found that a fundamental weakness of local government was that it was held in low esteem by parliament, Ministers and the Whitehall departments, as well as by the local voters. Apart from giving local authorities more power to organise their own affairs, the committee saw the problem as one of improving the calibre of management by raising the level at which decisions were made by departmental heads and allowing them 'to exploit their powers of initiative and expert skill'. As for the calibre of the councillors, who are to the corporation as the board of directors are to the company, the findings of the Maud Committee merely underlined what most people knew already, that the calibre and expertise of councillors needs to be raised considerably. It will be extremely difficult to raise the standard of lay management as 'the principal members of a busy local authority may easily spend half their waking hours on council matters—meetings, discussions, visits to institutions, ceremonies and the like. And most of it demands heavy brain work.'* The writer might have added the many hours of work spent in reading the various reports and minutes, and finding out what decisions really have been taken and which have been quietly ignored. Most men and women, especially the younger and more able and ambitious, shun council work as being both time-consuming and yielding a small return for the time spent.

Given a management which has neither the expertise nor the time to interest itself in productivity bargaining in the way that an industrial management might do, and given the fact that pay is based on national rates, it is understandable that progress has been slow. By the middle of 1966, even before the July 'freeze', the restraints and coming shadows of incomes policy were producing warning noises from groups in local authority service, such as the police, firemen and manual workers. The chairman of the Police Federation, P.C. Webb, said at the 1966 annual conference of the Federation: 'If any attempt is made to fob off the police, at this time of crisis, with a diluted pay award in which they were sacrificial lambs on the altar of an incomes policy, no one on the National Executive Council of the Police Federation would be prepared to take responsibility for what would happen to the police of this country.' He asked whether, in view of the crime wave, the police or the criminal was to prevail, and said that the fact that the arbitration tribunal had told them that they were bound to take note of pay movements in other fields 'made the police wonder whether there was any real value in arbitration in the public service'.†

The president of the Fire Brigades' Union told his annual conference that 'the employers' proposals to link improvements in pay with the better use of manpower were unacceptable'. The employers were suggesting a forty-eight-hour week with various duties attached; the union wanted a forty-hour week without strings. He complained about the firemen's long hours of duty and said that they should be paid for.

The manual workers' side in local authorities presented a lengthy argument for a 9·5 per cent pay increase. They pointed out that while an all-industries index of earnings showed an increase in the

* W. Eric Jackson, *Local Government in England and Wales*, Penguin, Harmondsworth, 1969, p. 144.
† *News Summary: Local Government Pay and Conditions*, Local Authorities' Conditions of Service Advisory Board, London, July 1966, p. 6.

last twenty years of 243 per cent, that of local government workers only rose 225 per cent. 'Low rates, short overtime hours and few incentive schemes together explain the low earnings in local government.' In a number of cases the earnings were lower than a man with an average family would receive on National Assistance. The old attractions of local government, the provision of pensions, secure employment, sickness and redundancy pay, had lost the attraction they once had, as the state and private industry now provided much of this cover. The case was made that the increase was not inconsistent with the government's White Paper on Incomes and that the claim met the four criteria:

1   The unions were willing to negotiate on productivity.
2   It would help the local authorities to achieve the expansion in manpower forecast in the National Plan.
3   Present rates of pay were too low to maintain a reasonable standard of living.
4   The rates of pay had fallen seriously out of line with those of comparable groups of workers.

The NALGO conference of 1966 debated the use of sanctions in support of claims on pay and conditions. It was claimed by a speaker that they had been successful in the electricity industry, while a Health Service speaker was against them. The NEC said that they had been prepared to support strike action in a recent dispute, and agreed to investigate 'all aspects of the use of' sanctions.

The firemen pressed on with their claim for a forty-hour week, which the employers opposed as leading to inefficiency and higher costs. The employers were prepared to offer an increase greater than the norm of $3\frac{1}{2}$ per cent and to make a number of other concessions, but the firemen objected strongly and said that they would support their claim for shorter hours by withdrawing some voluntary services. Both sides were seen separately by the Home Secretary on 20 July, and told about the incomes standstill. The claim was submitted to the PIB to examine 'in the national interest'.

Another group of senior local government officers who had their pay claim stopped in July were the town and district clerks and chief officers. They had been in the course of negotiating a 7 per cent increase on the basic scale, with changes in the population grouping (which is related to salary scales) and an increase in the discretionary element of local authorities to raise salaries by 5 per cent on each salary range maximum. At the same time the government also referred to the Board the proposed salaries for senior officials of the GLC.

The ability of the Government to control pay increases in the local authority sector, even by referral to the PIB, was limited by the ability of the group concerned to influence the press or the public, or both. The police were in this category, and the government walked warily to avoid a confrontation. Mr Michael Stewart, First Secretary of State, announced in the House of Commons on 22 November 1966: 'The Government consider that the police, whose next pay review was originally to take effect from September 1966, are in a special position because of their importance in combating crime . . . the Home and Scottish Secretaries are, therefore, prepared to discuss in the Police Council an increase payable in July 1967, retrospective to March 1967' (House of Commons Debates). As the police pay negotiations took place every two years, the Police Council replied that there were special factors which should be considered in the case of the police: (a) that they had had no compensating rise in pay since August 1964; (b) the police were essential to the community and pay levels needed raising to prevent an adverse situation. It was pointed out that the government had themselves said, 'the guiding principle . . . must be that of national economic and social priorities'; (c) there were difficulties in measuring police productivity, which should not 'preclude (at an appropriate time in the future) an adjustment of pay in respect of more effective work actually performed, as may possibly follow operational and administrative changes arising from the current discussions in the Police Advisory Boards' (*News Summary*, December 1966, p. 4).

The irony of the situation is that Mr Stewart, a teacher of long standing, would hardly have said that the teachers were in 'a special position because of their importance in combating ignorance'. Yet the difference in the attitude of the government in assessing the relative importance of the two groups, the teachers and the police, illustrates the intrinsic difficulty of criteria in pay in the public sector, when the public would favour an increase for the police first. Employees in workshops for the blind also sought public support by striking in May 1966 and lobbying parliament.

The report of the Board on Fire Service pay (Cmnd 3287) appeared in May 1967. It pointed out that there was now more damage caused through fire, from £25m in 1956–8 to some £80m in 1966. New types of materials were involved and the work was now more complex and hazardous. Safety and fire prevention controls had multiplied, and more premises had to be inspected. Lastly, firemen had to cope with other types of emergencies as well as fires, from flooding to pollution, and the 'number of special services provided by Fire Brigades has nearly doubled in the 10 years since 1956' (p. 3).

In addition to the extra workload, the service was seriously under-manned; London had a manpower deficit of 24 per cent, four Brigades had deficits of more than 25 per cent, fourteen of the larger Brigades had deficits of some 15 per cent, and so on down the scale. Seventy-six of the smaller Brigades were relatively fully manned.

By 1965 the employers had decided the time had come for 'a long cool look at pay and duty systems'. A working party was set up and held a number of meetings. As fires happen on a random basis and fire brigades have to wait for such contingencies, the employers' problem was to increase the hours of availability of men, and thereby achieve economies in the use of manpower. The employers were prepared to offer more than the $3\frac{1}{2}$ per cent norm and made a comprehensive offer with a forty-eight-hour week as standard and some money allowances, including some increased overtime rates. The government were unhappy about the offer and told the employers that $3\frac{1}{2}$ per cent should not be exceeded and that 'their proposals that extra duty allowances and regular over-time should be made pensionable would have undesirable reper-cussions' (ibid., p. 9). The employers went ahead with their original offer. Both sides were near agreement on a $7\frac{1}{2}$ per cent increase with a new overtime rate and a bonus shift payment when the government told them of the 'freeze' on 20 July, the day before the NJC was to have met. This was the background of the reference to the Board for Prices and Incomes.

The Board agreed with the approach of the NJC towards a smaller and more efficient service. Productivity would be increased by extending the hours of availability. They agreed with the suggested $7\frac{1}{2}$ per cent increase, and added another eighteen shillings to the £4 bonus shift (which amounted to £170 in a year). The Board's recommendations added up to an increase of some 25 per cent in exchange for an availability over fifty-six hours instead of forty-eight hours. When this is contrasted with the attitude of the government to the original proposals of the NJC, it can be seen that the report was far better than the government would have approved of and was also an advance on the NJC offer. As the Board's recom-mendations were rather better than those for other sectors and industries, we must assume that they were strongly influenced by the shortage of manpower in a vital area, and impressed by the dangers involved in spraying water into flames from a 200 ft ladder.

The manual workers in local authorities, the National Health Service and gas and water supply, were dealt with in Report No. 29 (Cmnd 3230), March 1967. This pointed out that the pay movements of these groups had been closely related in the past. We shall concern ourselves mainly with manual workers in local authorities, who make up the largest group of the four and whose wages bill came to £341m out of £570m for the four groups. The report found that the workers surveyed were lowly-paid. The broad picture was that despite national wage rates that compared favourably with those negotiated elsewhere, the average weekly earnings of manual workers in water supply were below, and in the National Health Service and local government, far below the average for all industries; only in gas were weekly earnings near the average—primarily in consequence of the extensive overtime worked in the industry. In fact, in none of the 129 industries covered by the Ministry of Labour's list were earnings lower than in local government, and only in six were they lower than in the National Health Service.

Average weekly earnings were said to be low as both local government and the National Health Service have 'a lower proportion of skilled labour than is found in industry generally'. Another important reason was that less overtime is worked in local authorities than in the other three groups surveyed, and several hours less than in industries such as shipbuilding, construction and engineering. On the credit side, conditions of service, holidays, sick pay and pension schemes, were as good as, if not better, than in industry generally.

Labour productivity was said to be too low in local authorities and 'there is extensive under-utilisation of labour'. The greater use of work-study was suggested, as some 59 per cent of local authorities had over 40 per cent of workers on such schemes. Even so, 'less than half the workers receiving incentive bonuses were covered by schemes which had been set up following work study'. The picture drawn was of incentive schemes used as devices to increase earnings rather than to measure output and reward effort. The main blame for this state of affairs was placed on the backs of management and not, as some suggested, on the poor quality and higher age of council employees. The structure of local government, with its mixture of large and small authorities and lack of central direction and control on the part of management was also criticised. The findings of the Maud Committee would, it was hoped, improve the management side. As has already been noted: 'Another important factor is that local authorities and their departments are concerned more with overall expenditure than with unit costs and efficiency. Audit control is mainly concerned with keeping total expenditure within budgetary targets and too little attention is given to value for the money spent' (p. 23). This last remark gets to the root of the inefficiency of local authorities, where an elected and determinedly amateur lay management strives to keep the rate down at all costs and municipal transport and other services decline in manpower and efficiency.

The report also criticised the lack of attention to the personnel function, or the field of labour management, or even basic managerial skills. It followed from this that 'insufficient attention is given to equipping the officials concerned with the necessary managerial expertise and to encouraging cost consciousness. Although there is interest in the training of engineers in engineering, there is a lack of awareness of the need for formal training in management' (ibid., p. 24).

The organisation of the manual workers in the National Health Service (NHS) was as divided as it was in local government. Financial control related to budgets and not to unit costs. The survey found that there was a great deal of scope for work- and method-study, and said that the unions concerned had been protesting at the lack of incentive schemes.

The proposals made by Report No. 29 stated that higher pay could come mainly through increased productivity or better utilisation of labour and that the necessary progress was bound to take time. Local councils and employers in the NHS would have to be converted to the view that change is necessary. Short-term proposals suggested that productivity increments could be paid to manual workers in both groups when 'a pre-determined saving in manpower has been achieved'. This amount could be negotiated, but it was suggested that a 10 per cent reduction in total labour costs could result in a 10 per cent increase in basic wage rates. Incentive schemes based on work-study would have to be well designed, properly measured and costed, and warnings were given against the attempt to give increases based on 'phoney' criteria. The long-term proposals related to the need to raise the standards of management, and especially labour management. The pay and standard of supervision would have to be raised and in 'both local government and the National Health Service there is a need for work study in a much wider range of manual tasks'.

The Board's view that it would take time to convert local authorities to the value of work-study and incentive schemes was affirmed by the local government work-study group, some of whose members said that the chief barrier to incentive schemes was the attitude of the local authority, though some members questioned whether financial incentive schemes were the best way of getting the best results. Other groups interested in improving the efficiency of local authorities were the Royal Institute of Public Administration, who had set up an operational research unit, and the Local Authorities' Management Services and Computer Committee (LAMSAC), which was intended to organise research into the whole field of the committee and to extend the present training and development in these areas by and through a full-time staff.

The later union reaction to the report on manual workers was given by Lord Cooper, General Secretary of the General and Municipal Workers' Union, who told the third annual conference on productivity in local government (March 1968) that the unions wanted to see an extension of incentive bonus schemes as they could lead to higher pay and greater productivity without raising rates or taxes. He also wanted more flexibility between grades and changes in the spread of hours and manning scales. Local joint pay and productivity committees should be set up. At the same conference, Professor H. Clegg suggested the extension of productivity agreements in local government, and followed Lord Cooper in suggesting a national agreement fixing basic pay, with each local authority having discretion to set up its own work system and forms of saving on labour costs. These systems could be checked by central control.

These suggestions that local authorities should have greater freedom in local negotiations based on productivity were in tune with the recommendations of the Donovan Commission, which had pointed out that national negotiations were becoming less important in industrial relations and that collective bargaining was moving to the shop floor. However, the comprehensive system of national negotiations built up over the years by local authorities is not likely to be readily changed, and there is much resistance to paying higher rates locally. One of the reasons for this is the great variety of authorities, from the large to the small. Many of the smaller councils find difficulty in paying the national rate, and are anxious that higher earnings in the larger authorities should not be used as a lever to raise rates in the smaller authorities.

The NJC for manual workers engaged a firm of management consultants to examine the PIB's proposals for a productivity increment based on work-study. The increment was to result in increases of 10 per cent paid out in two stages of 5 per cent over two years or so. The consultants looked at several authorities and reported that some progress was being made. They measured the success of various schemes by assessing whether there had been a reduction in labour cost without a decline in output and examples were given of some of the methods used. The NJC arranged, with the support of LAMSAC, to examine schemes submitted, authorise payments and give advice to authorities. To calculate the bonus, norms have to be set, which involves the necessary setting up of work standards and the collecting of statistics. In these steps the NJC was supported by a number of advisory bodies, such as the Maud and Mallaby Committees, which both recommended the use of work study and organisation and methods techniques.

One of the criticisms that could be made of the development of incentive schemes is that these are not productivity bargaining or agreements, defined as: 'One in which workers agree to make a change or a number of changes in working practices that will lead in itself—leaving out any compensating pay increase—to more economical working; and in return the employer agrees to a higher level of pay and other benefits' (Report No. 36, 'Productivity Agreements'). Productivity agreements are more far-reaching than the programme put forward in 'Pay and Productivity' (Circular NM 190) issued by the NJC in late 1968.

The consultants reported in January 1969 that the labour savings could be made and the two increments of 5 per cent paid, in the authority studied, and that the scheme was relatively easy to operate without specialised staff. They said that it was important not to create redundancies, and also to start planning for longer-term schemes linking pay and productivity. Some of the difficulties found were: (a) the definition of a reduction in labour cost, which had to be done over a period; (b) efficient departments complained that the scheme favoured the inefficient department, which had far more scope for cost saving; (c) some local councils said that the scheme was certain to lead to redundancy; (d) there were complaints about communication and a need for a simple guide to the scheme, as well as meetings with workers, unions and management. The consultants said that none of the difficulties need hold up the wider use of incentive schemes based on work-study.

It is unlikely that this progress in greater labour efficiency would have been possible without the impetus provided by Report No. 29.

After the period of standstill and severe restraint, which lasted from July 1966 to 30 June 1967, some relaxation was permitted to local authorities in making pay awards, but the greatest emphasis was put on the need to link pay with better performance, on the guidelines laid down in Report No. 36 on productivity agreements. Throughout 1967 other groups besides manual workers received increases: the teachers in primary and secondary schools received 6–7 per cent from July, and Justices' clerks received an increase which tapered from 7 to 3 per cent. The aim of the Justices' clerks was to relate their pay more closely to that of barristers and solicitors in the public service (who, in turn, related their salaries to their colleagues in private employment, whose salaries are untrammelled by any government edict). In this way, outside salary comparisons feed into the public sector.

The police received an increase of 9 per cent in March 1967. The police and their serious undermanning with the resultant need for large pay increases to attract recruits and retain experienced men, represented another area of local authority pay where the incomes policy had little effect.

Report No. 45 dealt with chief officers and senior officers in local authorities. They received a tapered salary increase similar to that of the Justices' clerks, with some 7 per cent at the lower end of the scale (up to £3,000) up to 3 per cent at the £6,000 end. The report criticised anomalies in the salaries of officers with comparable responsibilities, and the tendency for some authorities to pay salaries near the top of a particular grade and thereby encourage 'salary drift'. Their final recommendation was for the salary structure to be based on job evaluation. Little came of this and the traditional criteria for assessing the salaries of chief and senior officers have remained relatively undisturbed (except for some job evaluation in the London area), underlining the comment of the cynic who pointed out that work-study is invariably for the lower-paid workers.

The white-collar side of the local authorities, represented mainly by NALGO, had strongly resented having their salary increase frozen in July 1966 and the report of their executive to the 1967 conference summed up their opposition to the prices and incomes standstill: (a) that comparability and cost of living movements must be recognised as criteria for wage and salary increases; (b) the importance of the need to maintain proper differentials for skill and responsibility.

NALGO also criticised the unsatisfactory criterion of increased productivity in non-manual and service industries (NALGO Annual Report 1967, p. 35). It was to be expected that white-collar workers would feel the effects of the rising earnings of manual workers as incentive schemes were introduced. One paradoxical result has been that while manual workers are demanding staff conditions and privileges, the staff workers have been asking for some of the manual workers' conditions, e.g. payment for overtime work and for additional work done, which was formerly required of them on a voluntary basis as part of their staff status.

At the 1968 TUC congress, NALGO submitted a motion noting that legislation on wages and salaries had hindered trade union activity, and proposing rejection of any legislation which would 'curtail basic trade union rights'. This was composited with motions of a similar kind and was carried. The executive council also pressed for comparability to be recognised as a basis for salary claims for the NALGO members. At the same time the national executive council accepted the principle of job evaluation 'providing there are proper safeguards and that there is joint participation and consultation between employers and the trade unions' (1968 Report, p. 37, cf. TUC Report). The NEC also objected to Whitley decisions being interfered with by the government and said that the criterion of comparability should be recognised in pay negotiations in the public sector. The growing militancy of the NALGO members was apparent in two decisions in the 1967 conference which voted to ask for the introduction of 'a complete trade union shop policy' and that union membership should be a condition of employees' agreements in collective bargaining. By 1969, the association had gone further, and in their salary claim they asked that the settlement should only apply to officers who were members of their appropriate trade union.

The 1969 claim, submitted in April, aimed to shorten the salary scales of clerical staff, following the lines suggested by the Mallaby Report; to keep the necessary differentials to give incentives to accept responsibility, to undertake training, and to keep staff in local government service. The claim followed the trend in other professional groups, such as teachers, to shorten the incremental scales and to loosen the bars between grades which could stop staff moving from one grade to another.

The claim considered the criteria in the government's White Paper (Cmnd 3590) on Incomes Policy. The criteria applied to lower-paid workers (wages 'too low to maintain a reasonable standard of living'), increasing productivity, manpower shortage and comparability (where pay . . . 'has fallen seriously out of line with (that) for similar work'). On the first criteria NALGO argued that a fair minimum wage is around £15 per week and that 'many adult workers in Local Government have not reached this minimum standard'. Examples were given of grades which were wholly or partly paid under this figure. On productivity it was argued that this is difficult to measure in the administrative, professional, technical and clerical sector, although the Association had always been in favour of the service being run as efficiently as possible and had co-operated in this by supporting measures for training, management conferences, and the re-organisation of local government.

The extent of the manpower shortage was pointed out, and several local government professional groups 'fall far short of the officers required' (*Review of Salaries*, April 1969, p. 2). The Mallaby Report had shown that such shortages were spread widely throughout the service. The employers' side were urged to consider the salary levels which would assist career prospects and job satisfaction in the service. The last part of the claim related to comparability and here it was said that while the government allowed comparability in the civil service it rejected the argument in local government; this had meant that the salary gap between the two services had widened against local government officers. The claim ended by saying that while wage rates had risen over 5 per cent from February 1968/9, and employees' earning by 8·3 per cent over the year ending January 1969, local government staff had only had 3½ per cent over the year, at a time when the retail price index had risen by 6·2 per cent in a similar period. The NALGO view that the manpower shortage needed drastic action was confirmed by a survey made by the Graduates Appointments Register into the attractiveness of various occupations to graduates. One company newsletter commented: 'The poor showing of local government in the survey (almost bottom of the poll) can leave no doubt in the minds of local authorities of the magnitude of the task facing them if they are to dispel the obstinately abiding popular image of dull, monotonous work, with limited horizons' (*News Summary*, January 1969, p. 13). By the beginning of 1969 the recommendations of Report No. 29 on pay and productivity for manual workers were slowly beginning to take shape. The NJC for Manual Workers received a report on 9 January from PA Management Consultants Ltd on their pilot schemes to test the practicability of the interim productivity scheme suggested in Report No. 29, and on the production of an 'implementation manual' to help local authorities with such schemes. Pilot schemes had been carried out in Farnborough, Leeds, Gloucestershire and Leigh. The object of the scheme was that a 5 per cent increase in pay would be made when there was a 5 per cent saving in labour costs and a further five when there was a total 10 per cent saving.

Among the difficulties encountered was the definition of a reduction in labour cost. This was best done over a period. Another criticism was that the most efficient units, with the least chance of making dramatic cuts in unit costs, would be penalised as against the authority with a lot of slack. The consultants said that they had found few examples of the efficient unit and that nearly all authorities would benefit from the proper use of work-study. Criticisms of redundancy and lack of communication were best left to local arrangements, but councils should do their best to avoid difficulties over both. The views of the different participants in the scheme, including management and consultants, appeared to be that it was 'transitional, limited, and it raises acutely some of the fundamentals of industrial relations' (p. 3). Shortly after this the NJC agreed that where savings of up to 10 per cent were made in labour costs, there could be a 10 per cent addition to pay without having to go through the 5 per cent stage first. Councils were asked to publicise the scheme by holding conferences.

The dustmen's strike of 1969

The negotiations on pay and productivity described above moved slowly through the cumbersome machinery of the many local authorities. One large local authority had a report submitted on manual workers' incentive bonus schemes by the city engineer, who criticised Circular NM 190 for suggesting the introduction of short-term productivity schemes as an alternative to work-study-based incentive bonus schemes: 'Neither of these proposals are, in my opinion, technically suitable for local government operations of the type reviewed in this report. Any short-term scheme would in all probability seriously embarrass any negotiations for a more permanent work-study-based scheme. Productivity agreements are more suited to factory and manufacturing operations than to the type of local government field which is the subject of the present feasibility surveys.' He went on to point out that there were a number of men who were not productive enough at the time to justify the standard rate of pay which they were receiving, and that they would have to be brought up to the minimum level.

However soundly based the objections to productivity schemes were, they reflected the general cautious approach of the local authorities towards adopting them, and explain why, after two years, less than one-fifth of authorities had moved to meet the complaints of low pay and low productivity noted by the PIB.

The dustmen were already restive over the way in which other industries and groups were outstripping the manual workers in local government; e.g. in September 1968 a DEP survey showed that one-third of them at that time earned less than £15 weekly. The award of that month gave them an extra 11s 8d. By July 1970 the men were claiming another 15s on the basic rate.

A new factor increased their militancy. This was the government award to their industrial employees of 8½ per cent, which was due to a new wage structure. This threw the local authorities into some confusion as they had been bargaining on the incomes norm of 3½ per cent. There were also other negotiations at this time for other workers in the public sector which were well above the norm. The network of comparability was affected by the fact that several unions overlapped most of the local authorities involved.

The significant fact which emerges here is that the union leaders of the NUGMW, the NUPE, and the TGWU, showed less militancy than numbers of their rank and file followers, who forced the issue. The Hackney (London) branch of NUPE demanded a £20 basic wage. This claim was backed by the Conservative majority council on the grounds that the men's take-home pay was too low, but other London boroughs decided to bargain as a group. The men eventually received an 8½ per cent increase instead of the 3½ per cent which was discussed.

An important point in support of the men was that most of the national press supported their claim for higher wages in principle. As the strike extended across London, other local authority workers, from grave diggers to lavatory attendants, came out along with the dustmen, and much inconvenience was caused to the public as the rubbish piled up in the streets.

Agreement was reached between the employers and the unions two weeks later, with increases from 15s to 35s, and dustmen getting 30s on their basic rate, an increase of 8½ per cent. The TGWU did not agree to the settlement at first and paid their members on strike £4 weekly, but accepted after a short period. The other two unions accepted the settlement, although they were now much more conscious of the militancy of the dustmen and other low-paid workers, and promised to display more militancy themselves in future negotiations.

This large increase, and the daily national coverage for the unofficial strikes, appeared to have some effect on other groups of workers, particularly the miners, who rejected the National Coal Board (NCB) acceptance of their full claim for the first time ever (in spite of the urging of their national executive) and large numbers went on unofficial strike. But it would be unfair to say that the dustmen were responsible for the rapid crumbling of incomes policy in late 1969. This would appear to have been achieved by the airline pilots several weeks earlier, who simply left their planes grounded at various airports overseas and were photographed sitting around swimming pools waving their glasses as they moved towards their target of £13,000 yearly for a jumbo jet pilot. The airline pilots' salary increases must have been the most dramatic of any group since World War II; in December 1969, the minimum salary for a senior captain was £6,750 for fifty-five flying hours; by March 1970 they were being offered £10,000 a year for flying jumbo jets; by May 1970 they were still arguing about an offer of £11,000.

By early 1970, large percentage increases in wages and salaries were being made across the whole of the public sector; Post Office workers received 12½ per cent, and nurses an average of 20 per cent. The armed forces got 15 per cent in two stages, while the police had 8½ per cent to follow their 9 per cent agreement of 1968 which had been intended to cover two years. The white-collar workers in NALGO were claiming around 10 per cent, as were the civil servants, with the teachers close behind with an 8½ per cent claim.

Besides the rapid rise in the size of wage claims, there was a growing atmosphere of militancy among groups in the public sector who had no history of strikes and who would have thought such action unthinkable several years ago, such as teachers, nurses and local authority white-collar workers. Much of this attitude stemmed from the well-publicised success of manual and skilled worker unions in private industry, in engineering, chemicals and especially in the car industry. While hourly wage rates in local authority work were comparable with the private sector, the latter gave its workers more chance of increasing earnings through overtime and productivity schemes.

Pressure on the public sector

The victory of the Conservative government in June 1970 brought a difference in the government attitude to the public sector. The Conservative manifesto had promised to attack the problem of inflation at the source by discouraging excessive wage demands. They developed this theme by saying they would take action against price rises in the public sector, while abolishing national agencies working in this area, such as the Prices and Incomes Board.*

They were soon put to the test by manual workers in local authorities. By September, pay talks had been deadlocked with the men demanding 55s weekly, plus an extra payment of 10 per cent on basic rates for those not on productivity or bonus schemes. The size of this claim was estimated at £90m, with the employers' side offering £60m. The unions claimed that since their 8½ per cent increase last year, there had been a 'wages explosion'.

The strike began at the end of September and various authorities were selected for strike action. Workers in several London boroughs were among the first to come out, this time on official strike. The unions said that some 80,000 workers would eventually be involved. As is now customary on such occasions, the union leaders were interviewed on press and television and stated that they regretted that the public were inconvenienced. Mr Fisher of the National Union of Public Employees (NUPE) said: 'One of the objects of the strike is to demonstrate to the public the value of the workers concerned. . . . We are not anxious in this exercise to put life in danger. We do not intend to hit the sick, the infirm or the aged. . . .' Mr R. E. Griffiths, representing the employers' side of the NJC replied: 'It will affect the sick. Who else uses ambulances?' (*The Times*, 28 October 1970).

Two weeks later, the local authorities raised their offer by 1 per cent and the government promised to indemnify them for any claims for damages resulting from the strike. This was necessary as there was much public concern over the pollution to rivers caused by sewage plants being closed by the strike and the crude sewage flowing untreated into rivers.

Public sympathy was again on the side of the dustmen, although *The Times* questioned the dirtiness of their job and said that a brewery had a more unpleasant smell than the modern sewage works. Mr Griffiths, the employers' Secretary, resented the criticism of the employers and the complaints about low wages; he stated that the average weekly wage, including bonus but excluding overtime, in the city of Coventry, was £22 10s and would become £24 6s under the new offer. The public attitude to

* This viewpoint was harshly dealt with by Mr Aubrey Jones, Chairman of the Prices and Incomes Board, in an article summing up his five years of incomes policy: 'Let me rule out one option straight away. That is the option that the Government, by sitting hard on prices and incomes in the public sector, will be followed in its shining example by the private sector. This is what Mr Selwyn Lloyd attempted in 1961–2. The private sector did not follow' (*Observer*, 1 November 1970). He might have added that pressure on the public sector by the government led to the first strikes by the traditionally peaceful groups, such as nurses and teachers.

the strike claim appeared in a characteristic letter to *The Times*: 'There are few of us who would be willing to do a sewerage worker's job at any wage, let alone the present rate at which this vital job is rewarded' (12 October 1970).*

The Conservative government refused, under the urging of the opposition and some newspapers, to allow the Department of Employment Conciliation Service to intervene, and described the local authorities' offer as 'generous'. A court of inquiry was set up under Sir Jack Scamp, which infuriated the government by awarding an increase of 50s to the strikers, 5s less than their full claim, but 10s more than the employers' offer. The award was nearly 15 per cent, and seemed to set a norm of 14 per cent for other wage claims.

The Scamp Report noted that the agreement of the previous year had added 8½ per cent to the wage bill. The trade union side put their claim under five headings. The first was basic rates, where they argued that these had just kept pace with the national increase for manual workers, that other industries were about to get higher rates, that the lowest-paid took home less than they would get on social security benefits, that basic rates were a higher proportion of total earnings than was the case in other industries, where men could earn on bonus or overtime. The employers' side countered by saying that the basic rate compared well with comparable labour, that the offer was a good one, that a large rise would make inflation worse and lead to cost push and 'leap-frogging' effects. On earnings the unions argued that the gas industry had had a substantial increase over the last year of 16·9 per cent. The employers said that the composition of the local authority labour force contained a large number of low-skilled and disabled, with little overtime, so that earnings were low. Their last offer was for a 45s weekly increase. On pay and productivity, the unions complained that there had been lack of progress on bonus or productivity schemes, that three years had passed since Report No. 29 recommended these; the employers argued that a good start had been made and that progress would be faster now. Under other factors, the case was put for a service supplement, holidays and shift rates. The fifth point (general economic considerations) was a wide-ranging discussion with reference to the local authority manual workers as a low-paid group, to the TUC campaign for a minimum basic rate

* This represents a considerable shift in public opinion over the years and reflects the moral factor in wage rates under full employment. It can be contrasted with the views expressed in Cardiff council in 1889 when, in reply to a criticism of the low rates, 3s to 3s 6d per day, paid to sewage workers, the reply was that these men had little skill and if they were not employed by the council they would be in the workhouse, and a charge on the community. The council was being benevolent in employing them.

of £16 10s for all workers, and lastly to the claim that the wage demand of the unions was being threatened by the political attitude of the government to an unheard-of degree. The employers 'recognised the difficulties of the low paid, but at the end of the day there was only so much to go round'. In their conclusions and recommendations, the committee said that the two main issues for them had been the special plea for the low-paid and the danger of cost-inflation. They conceded the low pay argument, and on inflation wrote the much quoted comment: 'Given the pace of inflation in the country as a whole, there is no chance that it can be arrested by a somewhat smaller pay increase for local authority employees. All that would achieve for certain would be a deterioration in their position without a significant benefit to the country as a whole.' The Prime Minister, Mr Heath, described this statement as 'scarcely believable' and implied that he thought little of the committee's findings. Most newspapers saw the result of the contest between the dustmen and the government as a win for the workers, and drew gloomy conclusions for the future of inflationary wage demands.

By early November 1970, the police were putting forward a basic claim of 35 per cent, as against an official offer of 10 per cent. The arguments for this large increase were the same as in past years: growing crisis conditions 'with premature wastage of staff and a deteriorating manpower situation'. Although the police had received an increase of $8\frac{1}{2}$ per cent in early 1970, this had not helped the situation. Other groups in the local authority sector were also pressing claims: firemen ('substantial'), teachers (37 per cent) and clerical staff, amongst others.

Most of those services mentioned are labour-intensive, and the effect of large wage increases would immediately show themselves in increases in the rates unless the government were to increase the size of the Exchequer Rate Support Grant. In 1970 the allocation for different government grants for rate support added up to some £1,900m. This amount raised doubts as to the support which the government would give, as they had stated their intention of damping down pay increases in the public sector. In fact, the government reduced the amount of the grant.

We have argued earlier that the reluctance of councillors to pay higher wages by raising rates tended to keep employees among the lower-paid groups and that this was partly caused by their lower productivity and in turn led to their adoption of a low work rate, which management accepted. But measures to increase productivity or efficiency will be forced on them by the fact that the

M

present rate of wage claims will raise rates sharply; e.g. a rise of some 19 per cent in manual worker wages (with a constant level of output) is equal to a rise of one shilling in the pound on rates. When we remember also that education takes the major part of local authority expenditure, and that this is labour-intensive, the future spiral of wages, salaries and rates can be clearly seen. While it is difficult to introduce work study or other aids for increasing productivity in schools, there is much scope for such methods in most sectors in local authorities.

Absenteeism: the problem of the missing men

While various groups, such as LAMSAC, have been set up to improve efficiency in local authorities and work study and other management services are beginning to spread, the main problem is to deal with the absentees. The output of work or services could certainly be stepped up, and this will be done in time, but in the short run a cheaper and effective way would be to cut down the number of people missing from work every day.

The numbers of missing men are largely unknown, although numbers of authorities are beginning to keep figures—without, however, having done much about the problem. Absenteeism means absence from work, either through deliberate absenteeism or non-existent sickness. Few men nowadays stay off work without covering themselves by a medical certificate (although the November 1970 changes in social security regulations state that there will be no payment for the first three days, making a saving of £20m).

The immense savings and output which would flow from better attendance at work can be calculated. Given an absentee rate of some 10 per cent among manual workers (it is higher in municipal transport) and that there are around 600,000 manual workers, this gives us a figure of 60,000 man-days lost per working day, or 300,000 in a week. Assuming that the men collect about £2 per day while sick, this comes to £600,000 weekly. With a working year of fifty weeks (no Saturday or Sunday working), this is around £30m. But the other side of the coin is that these employees, if working, would be producing at least £2 worth of services per day, or £30m. So the total cost to local councils of absenteeism is in the nature of £60m.

These figures cannot be accurate, as the number of absentees is not known. They also exaggerate the savings which can be made, as a certain number are long-term sick, and a small number may account for a large number of work days lost. There is also the number of genuine sick, though some managers estimate that their genuine sick are only 30 per cent of the absentees and that some 70 per cent have 'various other reasons'. But if this reduces the figure of £60m to some £30m, this would still represent a substantial saving for most authorities.

The extent of the problem can be seen by looking at municipal transport, which has an average absenteeism of over 10 per cent. This means that an authority with a platform staff of 1,000 has to carry 1,100 on the establishment or accept around 100 missing men per day, and provide more overtime all round. The evidence suggests that this is being done. One manager said that he did not keep the establishment at full strength, but around 92 per cent, so that the average earnings could be boosted by overtime. This is clearly inefficient and costly. The view of some transport managers is that, high as absenteeism is on the buses, it would be higher yet if they did not insist on a medical certificate for the first day of sickness.

Local authorities allow a worker to claim up to thirteen weeks sick pay after one year's service. Opinions are divided as to the extent to which this scheme is abused, and the association agreed to continue with it for a period, inviting councils to look at the way in which their sickness figures were developing. One local authority produced detailed figures over five years for its busmen which showed that the absenteeism figures had risen steadily over the years. There was an average of six and a half weeks' paid absence for sickness, but more significant was the smooth curve of absence over the work force. The actual working time, once a few spectacular absentees had been deleted from the figures, showed a consistent curve ranging from 70 per cent of working time (based on attendance at work) to 95 per cent. Around one-third of the labour force had less than 86 per cent of attendance, and the majority had less than 90 per cent.

It is statistically improbable that the 100 or so busmen could have had the uniform distribution of sickness which they showed. In a number of cases, the absentee figure was higher than that of the miners, which was around 22 per cent in the area. The advantage of frequent days off for busmen was that it increased the total amount of overtime and therefore earnings of those who wished to work overtime, while giving others the benefit of five days' pay for four days' work. It appeared that paid absence from work had become one of the 'perks' of the job, and was recognised as such.

Another large rural council in the same region complained that continued absenteeism was leading to a breakdown in the public health service. The council was told that the absentee rate for its fifty employees in refuse disposal was running between 25 and 35 per cent: this high absenteeism meant that refuse vehicles could not be manned.

The paradox here is that in both the areas mentioned above, the unemployment figure was around 10 per cent, and councillors were concerned to hear from the Department of Employment that the unemployed did not want to be either dustmen or busmen. With the current rate of social security payments to men with two or more children, or with graduated unemployment benefit, it was found that many men preferred to wait weeks until more suitable employment appeared.

While there is absenteeism in other industries, it is probably highest in the public sector, where sick-pay schemes are better, where there is a shortage of labour and little competition for the job, where there may be routine or unpleasant or thankless work, and where the work itself may attract those who prefer a steady level of pay with ample time off with pay.

The problem cannot be met by the General Practitioners. They have abdicated their responsibility by saying that it is up to the employer to deal with absentees, as their first duty is to their patient. The most effective method would be to develop more effective consultative committees which could also deal squarely with the problem of the persistent or regular absentee, and to link the considerable savings of money to improved bonus schemes which, in turn, could be enhanced by work study and productivity bargaining where possible.

5

The universities

The role of the universities in a modern society is shaped by politics
and public expectations. The development of mass education,
reinforced by government money and promises, has meant a large
expansion of higher education. From a pre-1939 figure of some
50,000 students, the numbers rose to over 80,000 in the post-war
bulge. This was accompanied by large capital expenditures on
sites, buildings and equipment. Public moneys were channelled
through the University Grants Committee (UGC), whose terms of
reference in 1946 were to: 'Enquire into the financial needs of
university education in the UK. To advise the Government as to
the application of any grants made by Parliament towards
meeting them; . . . to collect information, to advise, to assist
universities.'

The UGC are the body through which the government pays
university salaries.* There has been, since 1947, a system of
national scales for which the Association of University Teachers
(AUT) had long campaigned. But the feature which distinguishes
university salaries, and against which the AUT had been campaigning in vain, was that there were no negotiations in which the
employee representatives met the employer, or the paymaster,
face to face. The procedures, as far as they were formalised in 1955,
were that the AUT representatives went forward with a claim
approved by the AUT conference to the Committee of Vice-
Chancellors and Principals (VCC). The claim was discussed and
then the VCC went on to meet the UGC, who in turn met the
Treasury representatives. In one instance in the early 1950s, when
two senior MPs approached the UGC to express concern about low
university salaries, the UGC replied that they were responsible to
the Chancellor and not to parliament. The Chancellor told the two

* See the Robbins Report (Cmnd 2154), Part I of Appendix IV, on universities and their
relation to central government.

MPs that the country could not afford, in 1953, to 'provide the additional grants to increase university salaries'.*

Attempts by the AUT during the 1950s and 1960s to change these arrangements, known as 'the stately minuet' or 'the Whitehall bicycle', met with little success when confronted by the cheerful complacency of both Chancellor and the VCC, both expressing satisfaction with the procedures (ibid., p. 171). As Mr Butler pointed out, in reply to a parliamentary question: '. . . the relationship between the governing bodies and the academic staffs of the universities is, in important respects, different from that between employers and employees. This relationship is unique and I should be sorry to see any attempt to change it. Its effect is to make inappropriate the development of negotiating machinery of the normal type' (ibid., p. 172). He then went on to describe the convoluted negotiating procedures, or meetings, outlined above.

A curious feature of the salary award of 1957 was that Professor R. G. Allen acted as 'adviser and consultant to both sides' (ibid., p. 173), which indicates an unusual degree of agreement over the criteria to be used in salary determination. Later developments were to show a return to different sets of figures with different interpretations of them advanced by both sides. This hardening of official attitudes, which replaced the concordat of 1957, was due partly to growing government concern over the inflationary cost-push element in wages and salaries, and a determination to stand firm in the public sector. This attitude showed sharply in July 1961, when Mr Selwyn Lloyd, then Chancellor, announced a six months' 'pay pause' just as a UGC recommendation for a university salary increase emerged. The university teachers were caught, as they were to be on subsequent occasions, along with other public servants, in the jaws of the government machine, while hundreds of wage rises in the private sector then, as now, went by unnoticed.

As in other periods of 'credit squeeze' and 'pay pause', the government was cool to arguments based on cost of living and comparability. In this situation, the AUT moved into its next negotiations about salaries in a wider context, facing the newly created National Incomes Commission. NIC's instructions resembled those of the White Papers, and even of the anti-incomes policy Inquiry into the Electricity Workers' Pay Claim of January 1971. These terms of reference included 'the national interest', linking pay increases to the 'long term rate of increase of national

* H. Perkin, *Key Profession. The History of the Association of University Teachers*, Routledge & Kegan Paul, London, 1969, p. 139.

production', 'manpower needs' and the effects on other employments, and ended with the traditional phrase which is the stand-by of politicians and civil servants: 'The desirability of paying a fair reward for the work concerned.'*

Professor Fogarty, who was the chief salary negotiator for the AUT hearing before NIC, has written: 'The universities' case was the first in British incomes policy, and hitherto the only one, in which all the parties including the staff organisations appeared and a full hearing was possible.'† It should be said that this was the last occasion for years to come when the claim of the university teachers was virtually met in full. It was claimed that salaries fixed in April 1963 were short of 'fair comparison by some 15–25 per cent'. The award gave increases ranging from 5 per cent of the minimum of the Assistant Lecturer Scale, up to 22 per cent in the 'permissible average' of the Professorial Scale. The career grade of Lecturer had increases ranging from 12 to 17 per cent, which meant that most received over 15 per cent. The government accepted the award, but subsequent treatment of salary claims showed that no future government was prepared to allow a genuinely independent tribunal to award so large an increase in 'real' salaries to the universities. While the AUT thought that they had not reached true comparability, they used the 1964 award as a benchmark in future years.

The NIC award showed that if public pay is held down for a period, the resulting increase is disproportionately large and upsets a number of other groups who read about the award without finding out about the time period involved. The AUT were fortunate in that NIC also had to consider the future expansion of higher education under the influence of the Robbins Report.‡ The report wanted an objective of '197,000 full-time students . . . in 1967/8, and of 218,000 in 1973/4' (op. cit., p. 7). The great increase in student numbers meant a corresponding increase in numbers of university teachers required, given a staff/student ratio of 1:7·5, as it was in 1962/3. NICs calculations then moved to the number of recruits of high quality (as measured by degree results) required for university teaching, assuming that industry and the civil service would be competing for such graduates.

The Treasury opposed a large salary increase arguing, as they were to do subsequently before the PIB, that 'there had not been

* National Incomes Commission Report No. 3, 'Remuneration of Academic Staff in Universities and Colleges of Advanced Technology' (Cmnd 2317), March 1964.
† M. P. Fogarty, 'The National Incomes Commission', *British Journal of Industrial Relations*, November 1964, p. 361.
‡ Committee on Higher Education, October 1963 (Cmnd 2154).

any marked decline in the attractiveness of university teaching or any real difficulty in retaining teachers in that career' (op. cit., para. 43). NIC accepted the AUT argument on this point, that low salaries would have a long-term effect on the quality of university teaching, although the numbers recruited might be sufficient: 'It is commonplace in academic and public service careers that legitimate dissatisfaction with levels of salary takes a very long time to reflect itself at all accurately in rates of wastage.' There are many reasons for this, especially the difficulties facing those in middle years who hesitate over making a sudden transition from one career to another. NIC's conclusion was that: 'There has been a decline in the position occupied by university salaries in the overall pattern of relativities' (ibid., para. 48) and that this would affect future prospects for universities.

The phrase 'overall pattern of relativities' lies at the heart of any incomes policy, especially for those employees in the public sector. It underlines the principle of 'fair comparison' as refined by the Priestley Commission on the civil service, 1953–5, which argued that jobs or occupations being compared with each other should be capable of comparison in their 'duties, responsibilities and conditions of service' (ibid., para. 75). As NIC indicated, this would require an analysis of job content which had so far not been carried out. The AUT reply was that the Treasury should have carried out such research and placed the results before the commission. The Treasury sidestepped the point by saying that they might have done so had they been the employers of university staff, but as the independence of the universities was cherished by them, it was not their business to carry out job analysis.

NIC rejected the AUT argument that less than a quarter of university staff were working in the arts and humanities, whereas three-quarters were in the sciences: social sciences, applied sciences and medicine, where direct comparisons could be made with similar work outside the universities. NIC replied that 'similarity is not to be looked for in the functional content of their work but in the competition between the relevant occupations from the recruitment and retention of staff drawn from the same source of supply' (ibid., para. 78). For good measure NIC added that the job comparison argument would have been more valid if the AUT had been ready to accept differing salary scales for these groups of professions. On the contrary, the AUT had argued for the treatment of university teachers as a single profession, and the commission agreed with this view.

The main points dealt with so far include fair comparison and recruitment and retention of staff. This latter aspect of labour market pressures is extended by a discussion of migration, particularly the one-way movement to the United States. While the proportion was small (1–2 per cent), the quality was said to be high. The commission's answer was that the future expansion of British universities should improve promotion and research prospects. The quota of junior staff to senior staff was also considered, this being expressed as the ratio of senior staff (Professors, Readers, Senior Lecturers) to junior staff (Lecturers and Assistant Lecturers).

The 'quota' had been established in 1947 by the UGC as 'a convention to govern the ratio between Senior Lecturer and Reader posts and other non-professorial posts in order to assist in securing comparable conditions in all universities'. The ratio was set at 1:4, and was raised to 2:7 in 1958. One intention of the 'quota' appears to be to prevent the higher-status universities from attracting the better men from other universities by offering them senior posts. Some colleges and universities did promote more than the strict quota, while others left their quota unfilled. The UGC told the commission that they were considering changing the ratio to 1:3.

Another AUT complaint, which has been repeated from time to time, was the need to create more professorships. The percentage of professors to others had dropped from 19·5 in 1938/9 to 11·9 in 1961/2 (ibid., Table 6, p. 32).

It will be seen from these discussions that university staffs were concerned with more than pay matters. They were also interested in promotion possibilities. While the Treasury agreed that this was relevant and that a solution must meet 'the academic needs of the universities', they were also concerned with 'the protection of public funds'. The latter phrase is the vital one. Numbers of universities would like to promote staff but are restricted by the 'quota'.

The aftermath of NIC

The universities felt that NIC had given them some measure of justice, but the commission was to disappear after a short life. The large, though justified, increase to university teachers was partly due to the, by then, customary government policy of encouraging economic expansion and higher incomes in an election year, and to the government backing of the Robbins Report on higher education. The report had proposed an initial ten-year expansion period ending in 1973/4 and forecast 218,000 full-time university places, with a further large expansion to follow (Committee of Vice-Chancellors' Report on the Quinquennium 1962/7, January 1967).

The period 1961/2 to 1967 had also seen a considerable increase in student numbers, from 113,000 to 185,000. These had added to the numbers in existing universities, as well as entering a number of new universities which were created in the greatest university expansion of the twentieth century. The larger numbers were due to an increase in the students who stayed longer at school, as well as to the 'bulge' in the age group resulting from the 'immediate post-war increase in the birth rate' (ibid., p. 4).

Arguments arose in academic circles over the proposed plans between the expansionists and the Conservatives. The latter argued that greater numbers would lead to the dilution of the university product as the numbers of highly intelligent young people were limited. Articles were written on the 'more means worse' theme, although the most trenchant comment was made by a Scottish professor to the author: 'We'll have lassies who would make good domestic servants flooding in demanding to be lawyers, doctors and, ugh, sociologists.'

The effects of greater student numbers on university staff would, if staff numbers had remained the same, have been a worsening of their conditions of work, more students per teacher and therefore less staff-student contact, less time for personal research, a fall in the quality of teaching and, finally, a greater amount of administration. Both university staff and vice-chancellors were opposed to deterioration in standards and these were to be maintained by a staff/student ratio of around 1:8, although this figure was not fixed and had levelled off at 1:8 for the 1960s. In this respect, the British universities were more fortunate than those on the continent, especially France, where the staff/student ratio was much higher, personal supervision was almost unknown, universities were badly overcrowded and students erupted in riots.

The present and projected rise in staff meant a much larger salaries bill for the government. With the development of incomes policy, the government kept an official and anxious eye on salary increases as part of their vigil over the public sector where comparability in remuneration was a main factor in negotiations.

By April 1966, the AUT claimed that university salaries were 15–20 per cent behind the NIC level. But salaries rose by only 5 per cent, which was regarded on their side as an unsatisfactory interim increase, and there was much discussion in AUT and university government circles as to the form of inquiry or negotiating machinery which would decide salaries in the future. The Labour government, having set up the PIB, decided to give this task to them. In consultations with the government, the VCC asked that there be 'regular salary reviews' at 'fixed intervals. We also expressed the view that it would be undesirable that the method of determination of academic salaries should, except in the short term, be different in character from that of other staffs in related fields, such as the Civil Service and the medical profession, and we received assurance that this was not the intention' (ibid., p. 29). This was an example of the meaningless promises that are sometimes made by governments as subsequent events were to show that the government and the PIB viewed academic salaries in a different light to those in the civil service and the medical profession.

At this time a number of AUT branches were arguing that it was more important to have proper negotiating machinery than a salary award. They reasoned that once they could negotiate face to face with the UGC, or some independent body, they could soon reach a satisfactory settlement. The Labour government, like previous Conservative governments, had no intention of allowing this. The October Bulletin of the AUT reported:

Negotiating Machinery
The officers have had further discussions with the Secretary of State, who made it clear that there can be no prospect of an independent review body of the type the Association and the Committee of Vice-Chancellors wanted (p. 6).

The AUT were also considering what lines of argument might be deployed before the PIB. By the end of 1966 some members were advising the executive to follow recognised trade union practice and demand a higher percentage award than they could realistically hope for. This view was rejected as unworthy of academics, and it was decided to go forward with a claim based on the ascertainable facts. Judged by the criteria of the PIB, the university staffs were in a difficult negotiating position. They could not claim to be lower-paid workers, apart from some junior staff who were, in any important sense, far above the 'low-paid' category described, though rarely defined, by the Board.

The productivity argument, to which the Board would be more sympathetic, might prove a double-edged weapon for the AUT. Productivity in universities was difficult to define, as a university was not a factory with input, throughput and output. While the quantity or numbers of the students was measurable, their quality, or that due to the teaching input, was more elusive. One simple measure, that of increasing numbers of students while keeping staff numbers constant, was opposed by the AUT, although they were to argue in 1968/9 that the worsening staff/student ratio being forced on them by a standstill in staff expansion was equivalent to a rise in productivity. Another measure, that of increasing throughput or student numbers by more terms in the year, or a longer working day, was also criticised on the grounds that the savings would be small (especially in science and applied science facilities, where the workshops were in constant use throughout the year). Another difficulty was that discussions about productivity might deliver university staffs into the hands of the government, who might offer higher salaries for a worsening staff/student ratio or other efficiency measures, which would affect university standards in the long run. Nevertheless, the AUT at this time were conscious that higher productivity, or the willingness to co-operate with measures to improve efficiency, was the main way to get higher rewards under incomes policy. This emerges in the AUTs view of the PIB report on Scottish teachers' salaries, where they say: 'Another principle which emerged was that improvements in pay might be possible by making improvements in productivity, even for professional groups like teachers. This may mean that, in any future negotiations, productivity and conditions of service could arise' (ibid., p. 6).

The labour market argument, that unless salaries were raised the numbers and quality of university staffs would fall, would be countered by the Board arguing that, as university salaries rose, employers needing comparable labour would simply raise their salary offers in competition. More probably, the Board would give its customary reply to the undermanning argument: that firms and industries were not short of labour; they were simply not making the most effective use of the labour which they had. An international variant of this was the 'brain drain', but the Board would require statistical evidence of a substantial migration, which might be difficult to get.

The AUT decided to base their case on the proposition that university staffs were the 'key profession' who, in turn, trained most of the other professions and entrants to industry. They were entitled to a fair share of the rising national income which they were helping to create, otherwise men of quality and intelligence would not enter university teaching as a career, with consequential effects on the professions and industry.

One argument was that a job evaluation survey would show that university teachers were underpaid in relation to the duties and responsibilities of their work, a return to the case presented to, and rejected by, NIC. Some academics were doubtful about this, arguing that the universities had a common salary structure and that job evaluation would give a different weighting to the respective posts of Professor of Physics and Professor of Greek.

The more sophisticated level of analysis now needed for the presentation of a salary claim meant that the convenor of the salaries and grading committee of the AUT had to be an economist, as Professor Fogarty (who presented the claim to NIC) was. Second, the amount of time needed to gather, analyse and prepare data on comparative salary levels and movements meant that the convenor would need to be already doing research in such a field, or be paid to compensate him for the time lost from other work which he might do. In modern terms, especially under an incomes policy, it was unrealistic for a group of amateurs from various university disciplines to match up to the full-time economists of the Treasury. This position was underlined in the salaries and grading committee's report to the AUT central council in December 1966, which said that in the past, the general secretary had collected data, with 'outside paid assistance, as required' and drafted a case based on job comparability and career earnings. 'At the Executive, however, some members took the view that the incomes position had changed radically, that future claims would have to be based upon job evaluation (analysis of work content and levels of responsibility borne by different grades) and that it was impossible for anyone but a technocrat to prepare a claim so based.'*

The council debated the lack of progress towards negotiation machinery as the government had refused to give them an independent review body. 'All it would offer was a standing reference to the Prices and Incomes Board (PIB).' The AUT had some reservations about the reference as they thought the Board would confine itself to salary levels and not to the 'length of scales, the maintenance of promotion prospects and career earnings'. The association also wanted the proposed sub-committee to contain members with knowledge of, and acceptable to, universities, and that the AUT should have access to 'all written evidence submitted to the PIB and be present during all oral evidence'.

The AUT policy on subject differentials had one gap, that of lecturers on medical subjects who had a medical degree. The high salaries earned by medical consultants and by many GPs had set up

* Minutes of 100th Meeting of the General Council of the AUT, 21 December 1966.

pressures among university medical staffs and the AUT had, in recent years, conceded the need for some salary differential. However, at the May Council of 1966, the association had voted against subject differentials 'and two previous policy decisions which accepted substantial differentials for medical teachers with a medical degree had been rescinded'. This led to considerable anger and disquiet among clinical teachers and a series of mis-understandings led to many resignations by them from the AUT. In fact, the AUT position was that of seeking comparability between clinical salaries and comparable hospital staff: 'part of their total remuneration referable to their teaching duties should be the same as that for any other university teacher of a similar grade and that the rest should be paid for by the NHS in some way' (ibid.,). This was the two-tier solution.

The council agreed that the salary claim should proceed on traditional lines, as had been done with the case presented to NIC, i.e. comparability and competitive salaries. It was agreed that it would be best to wait until the end of the 'severe restraint' period, in June 1967, although there was strong criticism of the need to wait.

The AUT and the PIB

A long period of delay now took place over the government promise to refer the salary claim to the Board, which they made as early as November 1966, having previously imposed a total 'freeze' on all incomes in July 1966. After much discussion and recrimination, the reference was finally made on 30 October 1967.

Part of the government explanation for the delay was due to the difficulty of finding the two special members with a knowledge of universities who were to serve on the PIB committee. One of the two appointed, Mr Gerard Young, wrote to *The Times* following complaints after the publication of PIB Report No. 98 on university salaries, and stated that the Board had to wait seventeen months. 'The delay was not the Board's fault; it was due to arguments between the parties—teachers, universities, government—about alternative procedures for a settlement' (*The Times*, 17 February 1967). Neither the AUT nor the Vice-Chancellors accepted the explanations for the delay.

Concern about the dragging feet of the government or of the PIB was expressed throughout 1967 by the AUT. Various pressures were used by university staffs to interest either the newspapers or parliament, and eventually a parliamentary question succeeded in prising a date from the government. Due to the delay in the salary claim, the AUT had now a considerable leeway to make up in comparative salary rates. In November 1967 they were estimating that employees' earnings had risen by 20 per cent, which made the original claim of 10 per cent too low, and that a 15 per cent claim was necessary to restore a competitive salary. The association intended to claim that the award should be backdated to October 1967. Though the PIB reference had been announced, there was to be a further delay before the two 'special members' were appointed.

In an information circular to local secretaries, the AUT general secretary wrote that it was a bad time to submit a claim to the PIB, 'but that it would be wrong, when other sectors were getting normal salary awards, if university teachers alone decided to sacrifice themselves: they have, after all, had only 5 per cent increase in 4 years'. The circular contained a salary note from Professor Fogarty giving the basis for the claim of 10 per cent being increased to 15 per cent. This was based on the Cornmarket and Graduate Appointments Register figures, which gave the median employment salaries for M.Sc. and Ph.D. graduates. The movement of salaries for this group justified the 15 per cent claim, especially for younger university staff, who could be attracted away from the universities by industry and commerce.

By mid-1968 there were signs that, some two years after the government promise of a hearing for the university salary claim, the glacier was calving. A circular (11 July 1968) by the general secretary stated: 'After many letters to the Prime Minister, various other ministers, and the Chairman of the PIB, there are signs of (slow) movement at last. Moves are definitely being made to select the special members. . . .' The AUT negotiators had their first meeting with the PIB on 19 September 1968. The Board took some three months to hear and examine the salary claim. The resulting report will not be forgotten by university staffs, nor is it likely to be forgiven.

In the light of the earlier government pledge that university salaries would be dealt with in a similar manner to that of the civil service and the medical profession, we note that the report (No. 98, 'Standing Reference on the Pay of University Teachers in Great Britain', Cmnd 3866, December 1968), referred to both the Franks (now Plowden) Advisory Committee on the salaries of higher civil servants and the Kindersley Review Body on the salaries of doctors and dentists. In fact, the PIB was not independent and free to exercise its judgment in the way that those two other review bodies were.

The report pointed out that the AUT claim asked for an increase 'to restore that competitive equivalence between salaries and prospects in the universities and in other occupations drawing on the same pool of recruits. . . .' They noted that NIC had been influenced by this argument. The PIB were not convinced and made two main objections: the first was that recent income increases had been inflationary and an award based on comparison with them would 'add further to that inflation'. Their second objection was against the need to raise salaries to assist recruitment and retention of staff (the labour supply argument). The Board found no shortage of recruits, though their quality might have fallen slightly, and no outflow from the profession.

The nub of the report centred on its rejection of comparability and the infamous (to the AUT) para. 38: 'We recognise that any attempt to break the endless chain of increases because others in general have had increases may seem hard to those waiting at the point where the chain is broken.'

The claim was set against the five White Paper criteria already mentioned, and the Board rejected all arguments 'apart from the quality of newly recruited staff' and 'efficiency or the lowering of costs per student'. The report, in spite of having two members with 'special knowledge' of the universities, displayed an astonishing ignorance as to what university teachers did. While they were correct in saying that salary and career structure is mainly dependent on successful research and publication, and that teaching is rarely recognised or rewarded, they did not successfully attempt to define either 'research' or 'teaching'. The suggestion stated: 'To counter this bias towards research we recommend that each university should have freedom within, say, 4 per cent of the total annual salary bill for the relevant grades, to make discretionary payments to all grades of non-clinical staff below the grade of professor . . . designed to reward extra teaching load, quality of teaching, and, in exceptional cases, administrative load.'

This suggestion, accompanied by a derisory award of 5 per cent, split between different grades, with assistant lecturers receiving 10–17 per cent, lecturers 4 per cent at the top of the scale, and professors 2 per cent, united the profession in their protests. While the AUT has been handicapped, as no other professional group is, by a few members who write to the newspapers before or after any salary award saying that they are already well-paid, or over-paid, the suggestion that teaching standards might be assessed by student vote or questionnaire, was rudely received by all. The report showed no understanding of long- and short-term effects of lectures, of the nature of the subject, of the correlation between teaching and examination success. Professor Perkin, in his book on the AUT, called the PIB report 'These ill-conceived and half-digested arguments', while correspondence and articles in newspapers were critical. One vice-chancellor resigned in protest and the AUT stated that it had been discussing for years ways of improving productivity, efficiency and teaching in universities.

The government accepted the low award, but tactfully decided to do nothing about the recommendations on teaching. Feelings ran high at the AUT council meeting and a number of delegates debated the possibility of strikes or other sanctions. It was clear, however, that the PIB and the government had chosen their sacrificial victim, 'the weakest link in the chain of inflation' with care, and that university teachers had little strike effectiveness. A strike of staff would only remove lectures and supervision from students, who could substitute library and other work for a period. It was also felt that public opinion would be unsympathetic, as it would be to another possible sanction, that of refusing to set examination papers, or to mark them. While this discussion took place before the school teachers' strike, it was clear that a strike which affected pupils and, indirectly, parents would have most success where young children were involved and in areas where the mothers went out to work. One sanction suggested for university staffs was that they might refuse to do research for the government, or sit on government advisory committees. None of the methods suggested were accepted, as it was argued that an effective strike needed two main ingredients: (a) that the strikers have some effect on the product, or service, or on the public, or the government. As shown above, university staffs lack power in this area; and (b) that the union, or group, is prepared to take united action in support of its claims. There was no certainty that the AUT members were ready to strike, or would follow a lead given them.

The AUT now turned its energies against the differential payment for teaching, although some colleges treated the matter a little differently from others. They also lobbied MPs officially and unofficially to have the 4 per cent awarded for teaching excellence distributed as a salary increase. This was eventually agreed upon by most universities and partly by the government. Besides the 4 per cent residual payment, the pressure was to get a further salary revision in 1969, and, fundamentally, to get proper negotiating machinery for salaries, as the PIB was now discredited in the eyes of university staffs. The three items were known as the package deal and agreement was reached by the AUT, the VCC and the UGC on

N

these counts. The search for negotiating machinery began to achieve some results. An AUT circular of April 1969 said that:

> The three parties agree on the machinery they ask the Government to set up. This will cover academic and related staff. There will be two levels. At Level A the AUT and the VCC will sit on opposite sides of the table to hammer out views to be presented to the Government on salary and staff structure revisions, together with the costing of the proposals. . . .
>
> At Level B the negotiations would be direct with the Government, and the AUT and the VCC would sit on the same side of the table. . . .
>
> If at Level B the AUT or the UCC or both could not agree with the Government, the matter would be referred to independent arbitration machinery.

While this form of machinery is sometimes found in private industry, where the most common form of negotiation is that the union representatives face the employers, who are directly responsible for paying them, the universities had a different set of problems. The legal employers of university staffs are the university councils, who do not deploy sufficient power or funds to make major policy decisions. The government, with and through the UGC, provide the major part of the funds for development and salaries but claim not to be the employers of university staff. While a number of decisions relating to individual salaries and grading (subject to the quota of 35 per cent senior staff to junior staff) are made by VCs and principals and their college committees, they are not, properly speaking, the effective employers of their staff. The problem for the AUT had been to bell the cat, or define the paymaster with whom they wished to negotiate. As it was unlikely, under an incomes policy or not, that the government would allow the VCC to bargain as employers, and as the UGC were not anxious to assume this role, the negotiating machinery described above, with its two levels, and some representatives of the government on the B or higher level, seemed to be the most suitable. Even so, it was some long months later before the government could agree to the new machinery.

Universities and productivity

One result of incomes policy and the confrontation with the PIB was that the universities began to examine methods of increasing productivity or improving efficiency. A Joint Conference, the first of its kind, was held in March 1968 on productivity, and was attended by university staffs and by vice-chancellors and principals. Universities had to face the criticism of MPs who wanted to contain the large and mounting bill for higher education; their case rested on the assumption that student output from universities could be doubled with the same buildings and staff, by using buildings more intensively for more hours per day, and by re-arranging terms so as to have a flow of students throughout the year. Some MPs talked of university buildings and equipment standing idle for six months yearly, but became restive when told that this was a description of parliament, not of universities where science and applied science buildings were in constant use throughout the year.

Some vice-chancellors agreed that more terms per year need not mean more working days for the staff, but a re-arrangement of the working load; three terms yearly and the fourth term free for research. This arrangement would need more staff, and was criticised as leading to poorer teaching, less research and less student supervision. The four-term year was said to be bad for the university as a community, as it would fragment student political and social activities. The strongest criticism of productivity concepts came from those who argued that universities were not degree factories.

There was agreement on the difficulties of defining productivity, using the ratio of physical output to physical input. The product had to be defined: numbers of students passing examinations, grade of degree, research published. These were difficult to measure and such estimates are subjective. However, the universities still had to meet some cost criteria, as millions of pounds of public money was spent on them. The conference had the effect of making universities conscious of cost and productivity criteria, and led in some to an extension of the hours in which classes could be taken. There was also a work-diary sent out by the VCC, or rather three diaries, each to cover a week in the Michaelmas term 1969, the Easter vacation and the summer vacation 1970.

The work-diary had to be filled in at half-hourly intervals under the appropriate letter:

A—Time spent on work with, or for, undergraduates.
B—Graduate course work time.
C—Time spent with those doing graduate research.
D—Personal research time.
E—Unallocable internal time: 'Any administrative and

committee work not allocable to undergraduates, graduates, or personal research.'
F—External professional time.
Private and Free Time—Apart from the commonsense definition of this, it included 'other such activities which, while "work", neither derive from your university post nor contribute to your professional status in that post'.

This attempt to measure the efficiency, or work-spread, of staff aroused some opposition and a flow of letters to newspapers. One important objection was that staff had not been consulted in advance: although the AUT had co-operated in the first survey they had not been consulted over the dispatch of subsequent work-diaries. Other objections centred round the difficulties or inherent absurdities of measuring efficiency or productivity in a university, which most academics view as a community or a way of life, and not a broiler house for students.*

Work-diaries by themselves can only record the time spent by staff in different activities. Unless a common standard of performance in the time is assumed, it would be necessary to look at the performance of students as an output from the teaching input. This problem was examined by a Joint Conference of the VCC and the AUT: 'Assessment of Undergraduate Performance', March 1969. A quotation from one of the vice-chancellors shows the difficulty of measurement: 'Most candidates represent themselves in their papers as much less competent and well-informed than they really are.'† Some delegates questioned the use of examinations as a means of assessing work done throughout a course of study. Only two departments appeared to have done some research on predicting 'the usefulness of a student to future employers'.

The National Union of Students said that differences in standards of marketing 'cast serious doubts on the comparability of degrees in different subjects. It would be difficult to prove that teaching was better or worse in different subjects.' The Robbins Report was quoted to show that the proportion of firsts among students graduating in 1962 was 3 per cent for Social Studies, 7 per cent in Modern Language, 12 per cent in Classics, Physics and Chemistry, and 14 per cent in Mathematics. The conference agreed that traditional forms of imparting and testing knowledge were not satisfactory and numbers of people reported that they were experimenting with new forms and new methods.

---

* For a discussion of this see W. Campbell Balfour, 'The Academic Working Week' *Universities Quarterly*, November 1970.
† D. G. Christopherson, *The Engineer in the University*, E.U.P., London, 1967.

The 1969 council meetings of the AUT were critical of the PIB, and it was argued that they should refuse to appear again before the Board or to submit a claim to them. It became clear that there was no possibility of this happening as no negotiating machinery had been evolved. Until this new machinery was developed, and agreed upon by all the parties concerned, including the government, the university staffs were compelled to remain as a standing reference with the Board under the Prices and Incomes Act. The reference was referred to in full in the preamble to both reports on the pay of university teachers where, after agreeing 'that the present machinery for the review of the remuneration of these academic staffs is unsatisfactory', the government, under Section 3(2) of the above Act, 'instruct the National Board for Prices and Incomes to keep under continuous review the remuneration of the academic staff of universities in Great Britain'.

Until this order had been revoked by parliament, the AUT had to continue, however reluctantly, to negotiate with the Board. A number of unreported meetings took place between university negotiators and the Board, and the AUT executive gained the impression that the Board thought that Report No. 98 had been rather severe on university staffs and that a further submission late in 1969 would receive a more benevolent award. As the AUT secretary pointed out in a general letter,* several awards had taken place which had underlined the harsh treatment of university staffs, 'There appeared the Kindersley Report giving medical people increases based on the principle of fair comparison, and shortly after this the Government itself as an employer gave increases to its own staff, also based on the principle of fair comparison.' He argued that the PIB had rejected the 'fair comparison' argument of the AUT and 'to do so on a second occasion would be sheer victimisation of university teachers'.

This attitude was supported by the VCC in their submission to the PIB (21 November 1969). Over the five and a half years since NIC, university salaries had risen by 12–13 per cent, whereas other earnings had risen much more. The awards of the two major review bodies (civil service and doctors) were mentioned as having given large increases which the government had accepted. The expansion plans of the universities meant that more staff would have to be recruited and their quality would need to be sustained by 'a fair and reasonable salary structure'.

The second submission of the AUT to the PIB argued that university salaries had fallen far behind the general level of

* 'Salaries and Negotiating Machinery', 1 October 1969.

earnings over the period 1964–9 (the NIC award of 1964 was still being used as a benchmark of 'fair comparison' with other industries and occupations) and that the real income of staff had been cut when real national income had risen by some 9 per cent. A rise of 35 per cent in earnings in the manufacturing industry and of 33 per cent in the salaries of professional, executive and managerial staffs had taken place. Compared with this, the public sector salaries had lagged behind, with the range of awards between 13 and 32 per cent. The universities were at the bottom of the pay table based on their increase for lecturers of 13 per cent. The Secretary of State for Employment and Productivity, Mrs Barbara Castle, had admitted 'some anomalies in the treatment of different groups in the public sector'.* The Kindersley Report gave university teachers in clinical departments increases based 'on broad comparability grounds whilst other university teachers have not'.

The case of the AUT rested on pay comparison, pay structure and productivity. The comparisons mentioned above were developed in more detail, arguing that the results were similar whether the base year chosen was 1964 or 1966. Tables were given to illustrate this (e.g. Table 8).

Table 8 *Percentage rises in earnings in universities between 1964 and 1969*

Position	April 1964	April 1969
University Lecturer (top of scale)	100	113·8
Senior Lecturer, College of Further Education (top of scale)	100	130·1
Registrar (Hospital) (top of scale)	100	139·2
Economic adviser (civil service)	100	124·0

(Source: AUT Salary Submission, December 1969.)
Primary and secondary school salaries had moved from 100 to 132·2 over the same period.

The comparison of earnings was developed in much greater detail than the few examples given in Table 8, and the point made that a number of the services and occupations mentioned drew from the same pool of recruits as did the universities. Unless salaries were brought more into line with the general level, the quality of university teachers recruited was bound to deteriorate,

* *Hansard,* 13 February 1969, Vol. 777, No. 57, Col. 1608.

while 'It is clearly in the national interest that standards be maintained in a profession whose crucial task is to educate and train many of the future members of the professional and managerial class.'*

On pay structure the AUT asked that the award should vary between grades. The previous award had given most to young entrants, but had done little for the higher grades, whose chances of promotion had deteriorated sharply. The ratio of senior posts (Senior Lectureships, Readerships and Chairs) to junior posts was set at 35 per cent. This fixed ratio was preventing the promotion of people of merit, and in fact a number of universities had not filled their ratio, preferring to recruit junior staff to deal with rising numbers of students. The changing age structure of university staff was now making the promotion blockage more acute as an increasing percentage of lecturers were reaching the top of the scale and could go no higher due to the quota of 35 per cent. The percentage thus 'blocked' was approaching 50 per cent in some faculties in most universities.

This aspect of salary structure had been underplayed by Report No. 98, where it was assumed that the major increase was needed at the bottom of the lecturer scale to attract recruits. This assumed that once in the universities, the recruits would stay. Critics said that the Board failed to discuss what the effect of worsening promotion prospects and narrowing differentials higher up the scale would do, and that young lecturers would 'leave the profession for the more lucrative climes of industry, commerce and the Civil Service, before job opportunities start to decline on account of age'.† The writers claimed that numbers of academics would now begin to look overseas for greater job opportunities, and produced a table based on the proportion of university economists in different teaching grades to demonstrate this. The comparisons were made with Canada and Australia, but it is evident that opportunities for academic promotion were even better in the USA. Two criticisms that might be made of this analysis are, first, that it was based on economists and that other specialisms might not compare so well, and second, that they did not compare like with like, as teaching patterns and the mode of university life differs between the UK and the other countries mentioned.

The third point in the salary submission was based on produc-

---

* AUT Salary Submission, December 1969, p. 3.
† D. C. Corner and A. J. Culyer, 'University Teachers and the PIB', *Social and Economic Administration*, Exeter, April 1969.

tivity and 'more exacting work', measured as a rise in output, i.e. numbers of students, without a corresponding rise in staff. This was shown by the change in the staff/student ratio, which had shifted from 1:7·8 in 1965–6, to 1:8·4 in 1969–70. As fewer teachers had been employed in relation to the increase in the number of students, the unit cost of teaching students had fallen. This was equivalent to a 7·7 per cent increase in productivity. A point was also made that university teachers now had to read more to keep abreast with current developments in their field.

The submission ended with a request for increases of 10·5, 13 and 15 per cent on the lecturer scale, and 15 per cent on all points above. These figures 'would increase the university salary bill by 15 per cent'.

The Board examined these arguments and claims in Report No. 145.* They drew attention to developments since Report No. 98, in which their main theme had been the fund for discretionary payments designed to encourage teaching performance. The rejection by the government, the UGC and the universities of this proposal was referred to obliquely: 'these bodies decided that there should be further increases in the basic rates of pay, these increases resulting from amendments to our suggestions about the provision for discretionary payments. The 4 per cent of the salary bill suggested by us for discretionary payments to non-professional staff was reduced to 1⅓ per cent, the other 2⅔ per cent being used to increase the basic pay. . . .' There is no mention here of the storm within the university profession over the suggestion, of AUT reaction and their hostility to the scheme, or how 'the majority' who had 'gone ahead with their schemes' had implemented them. The Board insisted that the discretionary payments had been meant to help the national problem of a rapidly rising salary bill in universities ('some £83m a year, more than one-third of the annual recurrent expenditure on universities') by using teaching staff more effectively (Report No. 145, p. 3).

The reiteration of this policy by the PIB demonstrated two of its basic faults; the first was its failure, in a second report on any industry or group, to describe accurately what the effect of its proposals had been; the second was its apparent inability to learn from past mistakes, as when the discretionary payment scheme was rejected, and its general 'lack of feel for the situation' which might have been overcome if there had been more meetings between the Board and university staffs. The Board was not a substitute for an

* 'Standing Reference on the Pay of University Teachers in Great Britain', Cmnd 4334, April 1970.

effective bargaining machinery where suggestion and counter-argument can be examined round the negotiating table by people in the industry, occupation or profession. This was clearly demonstrated in the Board's reports on university pay.

The report said that the universities had no difficulty in recruiting staff, and they quoted the interim report of the Higher Education Research Unit (HERU), though they avoided a discussion of the points made by HERU showing the wide differences in the numbers of applicants, with some branches of engineering and statistics having difficulty in recruiting compared with large numbers competing to enter arts subjects, especially English. This could have been inferred from the HERU statement implying the various markets which university staff face outside their profession as 'possessors of a wide variety of special skills, the relative demand for which, in other economic sectors, varies considerably' (p. 19). The issue here is whether such special skills are readily transferable, and the report does not examine this, beyond saying that recruitment and retention present no problems.

On pay comparisons, the Board thought that these could be misleading as people have different satisfactions and greater freedom in universities than they would find in other occupations; they implied that staff accept a lower salary because of this. This theme was stated but not explained. On comparisons inside the public sector, they agreed that there were different criteria being used and that the government, like 'a large industrial concern' was having to make tactical settlements in the knowledge that one award influences others. They referred to Report No. 98: 'the application to different parts of the public sector of different criteria by different bodies will result in unfairness' (p. 5).

The report did not deal with the AUTs figures claiming a 15 per cent increase, but simply gave an award of 9 per cent. This appeared to be a tactical and political award, made in an Election year, with the figure of 9 per cent chosen as being less than 10 or 11 per cent, which would have given more impetus to other salary claims in an inflationary situation.

The productivity and 'more exacting work' claim was rejected on the grounds that there was no real evidence of increased effort and that the staff/student ratio varied widely between departments and faculties.

There was cold comfort on the salary structure claim. The Board conceded that promotion prospects had worsened in the short run, but pointed to greater prospects with future expansion. They made the important point, as a pious hope, that the UGC and the government might 'remove the fixed ratio of senior teachers to total teachers; we recognise however that this might entail some increase in the finance made available to universities' (p. 7). Professors were not to have a differential increase as their outside earnings were higher than those of lecturers. The Board failed here to look at different specialisms, as applied scientists and some social scientists have greater opportunities of outside earnings than most professors in the arts faculties have. Finally, an important exemption from the 35 per cent quota of senior staff was to be scarce medical lecturers. They were not to be given higher rates for their scarcity, but universities could place them higher up the salary scales. The 15 per cent award was 'across the board' and the AUTs attempt to improve differentials from the middle to the top of the profession was turned down. The award was sugared and the protesters disarmed by the phrase that 'a further interim increase for university teachers will be needed for the academic year 1970–1' (p. 6).

The salary increase was accepted with some grumbling by the AUT, though it confirmed them in their belief that they should cease to use the PIB and press to have their own negotiating machinery. Two resolutions on this theme appeared before the May 1970 Council, but the executive were able to report that negotiating machinery had been agreed upon with the different parties concerned.

The achievement in getting such machinery for university staffs had taken fifty-three years, as the AUT had been striving for this since 1917. Successive governments had been reluctant to depart from traditional methods, and their remarks have been quoted. Staff who spoke to MPs in opposition found that their zeal for reform dwindled as they disappeared in the labyrinths of Cabinet decisions when in power.* It appears that the government was cool about the two-tier negotiating system. They thought that in the first stage the VCC, acting as employers, might not be tough enough and award 10 per cent, whereas the government might only wish to finance a 5 per cent increase. This implied that the VCC needed an information link with the government as to the amount they were prepared to offer. One alternative appeared to be an Index of Comparative Salaries, drawn up by the Civil Service Research Unit; but as the PIB had already declared against cost-of-living and other automatic indices, this seemed unacceptable to the government.

---

* The writer spoke to a high-ranking Labour Cabinet Minister in 1968, who told him grimly: 'I think you'd better stick to the PIB. If you negotiate directly with the government or the Treasury, you'll find they drive a very hard bargain.'

Later in the discussions the framework of the new negotiating machinery emerged. There would be two committees: Committee A—university authorities and the AUT. This would deal with matters relating to salary, promotion prospects, salary structure, etc. There would be an independent chairman, who would have the power to arbitrate a single proposal if there were different views. There would be five representatives from both sides, with the UGC representative giving guidance and accepting advice; Committee B—the government, university authorities and the AUT.

The chairman of Committee B, appointed by the Secretary of State for Education and Science, was to sit with the chairman of Committee A, along with three representatives of the university authorities and three of the AUT. Government representatives would be present, along with the representatives of the UGC. Failure to agree on proposals from Committee A by Committee B, could lead to arbitration on agreement by both sides ('such agreement not to be unreasonably withheld'). Either the AUT or the university authorities could put the case at arbitration: 'An arbitral award will be binding, subject to the overriding authority of Parliament' (AUT Circular, p. 323, May 1970).

This was the negotiating machinery used for the first time by the AUT to test the recommendation of the PIB in April 1970 that there should be an interim award for salaries paid from October 1970. It was decided that the claim should be simple, 'across the board', and based on comparability and the cost of living. The size of the claim was to be in the range 10–15 per cent, though an increase in inflation by the date of the negotiations would lead to an increase in the figure claimed. Larger questions as to comparability within the public sector, career earnings and prospects, recruitment and retention would be examined in the major salary structure review which had been promised for 1971.

The negotiations took place in November 1970 and the AUT, with the pace of wage and salary increases accelerating, raised their claim to around 20 per cent. The discussions in Committees A and B were confidential, but an AUT circular ((LA/40/SC), December 1970) says that 'After three meetings, a compromise figure of 13 per cent was proposed to the DES on condition that a major salary review' was promised for the next year. 'The DES offered 8 per cent, but after negotiations coupled with the possibility of arbitration' an agreement on 10 per cent was reached. This was retrospective to 1 October 1970.

The figures reached by the two committees are interesting.

Government objections in recent years had been that the VCC on Committee A might simply agree with the AUT and present a united front to the government as paymaster. In fact, Committee A reduced the 20 per cent claim to 13 per cent, which indicates that they might have gone even lower than this, had they not thought that Committee B might reduce the figure yet further. It is also possible that they thought that Committee B would accept the 13 per cent figure reached by Committee A without argument.

The negotiating procedures are still different from those practised by trade unions and employers in the private sector, and even in most of the public sector. It is difficult to see why they should be confidential and why university staffs should not be able to read and evaluate the arguments, or at least the counter arguments, in Committees A and B. One of the reasons for this is given in the AUT circular of December 1970 describing negotiations: 'During the latter stages it was clear that a number of governmental pressures were being exerted on the negotiations.' This would be consistent with the Conservative government's policy of de-escalation of wage claims in the public sector, and the AUT negotiators thought that arbitration would take some time and that the climate of government opinion could only become less favourable. The 10 per cent salary increase was accepted by a large majority at the December 1970 Council as the only one possible in the circumstances.

From the beginning of incomes policy in April 1965 to the end of the PIB in late 1970, university staffs (career grade of lecturer, top of scale) received only 5 per cent in April 1966, 4 per cent in December 1968 (followed by months of pressure and argument, prising another 4 per cent by April 1969) and 9 per cent in April 1970. This was an increase of 24 per cent over a period from April 1964 to October 1970, and was less than the rise in the cost of living over the same period, and considerably below the rise in earnings of manual workers and professional, managerial and executive groups.

The frustration of university staffs was sharpened by the large increases given to higher civil servants by an independent committee and to top salaries by the PIB, and by the 30 per cent award of the Kindersley Committee to the medical profession in June 1970. Their feelings were expressed in the resolution passed by the December 1970 Council commenting on their first award through their new negotiating machinery, in which they stated that the 20 per cent demand 'was fully justified' on comparability, productivity and cost of living increases. They intended to 'press vigorously for further substantial increases as part of the major salary structure review proposed by the PIB and agreed in the new settlement'.

The experience of university teachers with the PIB had been to disillusion many who agreed in principle with an incomes policy. They found in practice that salaries in the public sector had been 'squeezed' while groups who could exercise power, fairly or unfairly, had gained during this period. The effects of their experience, to state the positive effects first, were to make them, and the universities, more conscious than before of relative cost-effectiveness and unit costs, of staff/student ratios, methods of teaching, assessment of student performance, and of productivity criteria in general.

Other effects were less easy to categorise. Some methods, longer terms, more terms in the year, greater use of buildings, had been examined and found to be of marginal use. There are signs that interest in productivity in universities reached its peak in 1969–70 and may now be declining again as it becomes evident that dramatic savings in cost or increases in productivity are not possible without changing the nature of British universities.

University staffs became more militant, at least in council meetings, over this period. Strike action and other forms of sanction were discussed, and a national ballot was taken on the issue. There are proposals to affiliate to the TUC. Thus the effect of incomes policy was to make the AUT more aware of bargaining strategy and tactics, as their vulnerability under a restrictive incomes policy became clear.

6

The airlines

The weakness of a policy which attempts to hold down incomes in the public sector is easily seen in an area where the employees have scarce skills, or a monopoly of such skills, or where their action in large or small groups has the effect of making the entire service unusable. This has been evident in the movement of wages and salaries in airlines and airports.

The two major airlines in Britain, which between them carry most of the passengers, are BEA (British European Airways) and BOAC (British Overseas Airways Corporation). The names explain the routes and areas, with the latter providing the longer-distance flights. Air transport of passengers and freight has been expanding rapidly, with one estimate running at an increase of 10 per cent per annum over the last ten years. The economies of scale which are possible with the Jumbo Jets and other large aircraft are that if all other characteristics are held constant, each doubling of aircraft size will produce a 15 per cent reduction in seat–mile operating costs.

Some of the economic problems faced by airlines are that the larger aircraft lower unit costs, and the more flying time they operate, the more the fixed costs of operation can be spread. These are the reasons why charter flights can be considerably cheaper than the regular flights. There is government regulation of routes, and fares are agreed by the International Air Transport Association (IATA). Government regulations are a framework to maintain safety standards which might be endangered by cut-price airlines. Recently changes have taken place in the quasi-monopoly of the two big airlines. This was due to the Edwards Report, which recommended that some of the routes be given to private competitors, provided they had the resources to handle the routes satisfactorily, and to make a reasonable profit. Critics of this change have pointed out that the big airlines are committed to set times and routes and face the problems of a fluctuating demand. Smaller airlines can charter planes to groups and clubs and 'cream off' some of the traffic and fly at new capacity.

Several western countries now have a situation of spare capacity, or empty seats, in their airlines. Profits have fluctuated considerably over the past fifteen years, and have fallen in the past four years from 1966 to 1970. While the number of passengers carried has grown, costs have risen and passenger traffic is making more use of charter flights and reduced-cost flights. IATA is now going through a reappraisal of its pricing policy, which would allow some reduction of fares. The airlines have also begun to try to cut costs and the aircraft manufacturing industry is facing a difficult time, as we have seen from the collapse of Rolls-Royce and its effect on parts of the US air industry.

The air travel industry has its employees in two distinct groups: those employed in airports and those working for airlines. Airports are publicly-owned and operated by the British Airports Authority (BAA), local authorities, or by the Board of Trade. The pay and duties of airport staff vary greatly according to the size of the airport and the traffic it handles. The PIB Report No. 128* surveyed thirty-five airports; the BAA own and operate four—Heathrow, Gatwick, Stansted and Prestwick, while the Board of Trade operate eleven: 'Belfast and all the public airports in Scotland, other than Prestwick and Glasgow'. The other twenty are run by local authorities. The BAA was set up in 1966 and took control then of the two major airports, Heathrow and Gatwick. Of the others, Manchester and Glasgow have a considerable amount of traffic, but most local authorities run their airports at a loss, maintaining them partly for local prestige and national communications, and hoping that air traffic will increase in the future.

There is a division of function at the airport as the airport authority looks after the physical capital, buildings, grounds, runways, and the handling of passengers, luggage and cargo; they also provide for safety measures such as fire and crash services, and marshalling aircraft. The airlines confine themselves mainly to cleaning and maintaining planes, although they may, in some airports, take over some of the services performed in others by the airport staff.

The numbers and allocation of airport staff are shown in Table 9.

The basic grade in an airport is described as a 'general or airport hand'. Their duties vary according to the size and activity of the airport but are summarised as 'labouring, loading, baggage handling, marshalling, left luggage, indicator boards, flare path,

* 'Pay of Ground Staff at Aerodromes', Cmnd 4182, October 1969.

Table 9   *Numbers and allocation of airport staff*

Position	BAA	Local Authorities	Board of Trade	Totals
Operatives	1,362	1,364	131	2,857
Craftsmen	400	142	18	560
Foremen	226	135	150	511

tow guides, etc.' In smaller airports the 'hand' might have a much wider range of duties, from driving to fire service and rescue work.

Negotiations for airport staff are conducted through the National Joint Council for Civil Air Transport (NJCCAT), though the BAA has its own negotiating machinery. Local authority negotiations are conducted through the NJCCAT and related committees. The NJCCAT has a system of national sectional panels which determine the pay of different working groups, from tradesmen to storekeepers, but since 1967 there has been a general purposes committee which settles with all the panels instead of dealing with them separately.

Ground staffs in the airlines and airports put steady pressure on the employers right from the beginning of incomes policy, although the PIB's strictures on productivity and the airlines' own awareness of overmanning and under-utilisation of labour led to agreement on more efficient working. These agreements involved changes or modifications in working rules. The sequence appeared to begin with the BOAC agreement on 1 December 1964, followed by BEA some two months later. These were three-year agreements, which consolidated previous pay rates into bigger annual basic salaries. Further increases were to take place in October 1965 and 1966. BOAC gave around $7\frac{1}{2}$ per cent to foremen and inspectors, while BEA gave their comparable staff a little less.

British United Airways (Gatwick) concluded a three-year agreement in March 1965, with increases of 5·7 per cent, with future increases to come in March 1966 and 1967. The following year, the second stage of the agreement was disrupted by a twenty-one-day strike at Gatwick which was followed by a 10 per cent increase in basic weekly pay. At the same time BUA reached agreements with the TGWU and the AEU for a 6 per cent increase for labourers, semi-skilled and skilled. This was the second stage of a three-year agreement begun in March 1965, similar to the others described above, which had given increases in basic weekly rates of some 17 per cent along with a reduction of hours. Porters and loaders in BEA also signed a three-year agreement for the same time-periods as the other groups, with productivity agreements over rationalised shift working, inter-job flexibility and method study (*IDS Panorama April 1965–July 1966*, p. 39).

The agreements and figures shown above demonstrated the co-ordination of negotiations, even when different companies and occupational groups were involved. It can be seen that the pay increases were at least double the 'norm' of $3\frac{1}{2}$ per cent, and higher for some groups.

Workers at Heathrow have the highest pay among airport staff, although basic rates are common in the BAA ground staff. In 1967 the BAA industrial staff had 5–7 per cent increases and six months later, January 1968, another 4 per cent. One year later there was a three-year productivity agreement, on 1 January 1969, which gave a $4\frac{1}{4}$ per cent increase, with $4\frac{1}{2}$ per cent due a year later. This agreement was in line with the Tier I productivity agreement of the NJCCAT. In October 1969, BAA negotiated another agreement of 7 per cent, or minimum 30s weekly extra. This was in line with the Tier II agreement of the NJCCAT, which contained some provisions for productivity bargaining in a local steering committee, after which the negotiations went to the national sectional panel for decisions on the amount of money.

Some inter-trade flexibility was introduced in the agreement of late 1964 and this was extended in 1969. The Tier II agreement awarded 30s weekly in October each year from 1969 to 1971 inclusive. This increase was 'across the board', so that differentials between grades remained unchanged.

Local authorities paid their airport workers $3\frac{1}{2}$ per cent in 1968, but as the workers' pay was lagging behind BAA there was industrial unrest, and Manchester and Glasgow staff (firemen and airport hands at the former, all at the latter except electricians) received 10s weekly in late 1968 as an interim payment towards future productivity negotiations.

The PIB Report No. 128 pointed out that comparability of rates between airports caused unrest among staff, although the differences were sometimes due to one airport having a productivity agreement and the others not having one. Different authorities and different processes of negotiation existed, and settlements were made at different times. The existence of the huge airport at Heathrow meant that staff there could exert pressures on authorities to make continual adjustments upwards in the pay structure, and the effects of such changes worked through the other airports. The end result had been that 'substantial differences' existed in the

o

'basic pay of comparable ground staff at airports both within owner groups . . . and between them' (pp. 9–10). There were also increments and allowances which were more favourable to BAA staff so that they earned more than did staff in local authority or Board of Trade airports. Firemen and draftsmen earned more than did operatives.

The situation is an unstable one as there is frequent comparison between employees of airlines and airport staff, whose duties are sometimes similar as are the duties of staff at all airports. This has led to the BAA and the NJCCAT staying close together in the terms of their settlements. However, there was industrial unrest at several airports in 1968, 1969 and 1970.

Increases based on productivity are mainly dependent on the more flexible use of labour and in reducing the size of the labour force. Changes in working hours are dependent on the traffic peak time at the airport. Planes are subject to delays and the pressure of work ebbs and flows. There is no doubt that inter-job flexibility could be greatly extended, and the labour force reduced still further, but there are limits to this as safety regulations require a minimum complement of staff in some operations.

Collective bargaining and the airlines

Airlines and airports do not operate in a free market, where prices can be adjusted to meet market forces. There is a long history of detailed government regulation which has laid down where airports are to be located (the controversy and subsequent inquiries over the proposed siting of airports, such as Stansted, and the Reckitt Commission on the third London airport illustrate this), where the planes are to fly and what routes they are to follow. The government has regulated competition in the industry so that some routes are allocated to particular airlines, thus avoiding the intense competition and possible dangers if two British-based airlines flew the same routes from the same airports. There are also regulations as to the price which can be charged to passengers, although in the case of the airlines this is laid down by an international conference (the International Air Transport Association).

In spite of government regulations, there is a certain amount of competition between airlines. This does not arise through direct price-cutting between different airlines, British or foreign, using British airports, but through the widespread use of charter flights or package trips, which offer transatlantic flights under specified conditions and agreed dates, at nearly one-third of the regular flight charges. Clubs and organisations have been formed, such as the North American Families Association, and many others, which use the wide range of flights now offered by chartered planes.

The airline industry has a high degree of unionisation, as employees have discovered their negotiating power as a tightly-organised group. For a number of reasons, some based on questions of national defence, others on national status, and others on the importance of air travel to high-ranking executives in industry, commerce and politics, there has been less resistance to wage and salary increases amongst airline and airport employees than there has been in more labour-intensive industries, for whose product consumers can often find effective substitutes. A strike affects an airline immediately, as its service for passengers is highly perishable. While some flights which are cancelled can find the same passengers a few days, or a week or two later, the majority of passengers can and do transfer to other airlines. The revenue lost to the strike-bound airline is largely unrecoverable.

Another union bargaining pressure is the highly-integrated nature of the airline service operations. Maintenance work has to be carried out, and planes cannot fly without fitters and engineers, as well as mechanics and others who refuel and service the aircraft. In addition to this, there are Board of Trade regulations which require that there be numbers of fully-trained employees to man and service the equipment for rescue and fire service. The weekly earnings of firemen are from 20 to 25 per cent higher than those of operatives, and come close to those of craftsmen, although the firemen work, or are on duty, an average of only two to three hours more than the other groups.

In smaller airports, as in the larger ones, there is division of duties. The airport staff (who tend to be lower paid than airline staff, as their skills and duties are of a lower category), provide porterage, loading and unloading, marshalling and other ground-area tasks. Airline staff do the internal checking, fuelling, cleaning and maintenance of the planes.

Airline staff outnumber airport staff by a large majority on nearly all airports. On one of the smaller airports the airline employees numbered eighty against the airport's fifty. On large airports the ratio of airline to airport staff would be higher still. A minimum complement for an airline would be: passenger reception and load control, cargo superintendents and clerks, catering staff, engineering (the largest group of employees).

The men usually work shifts, as planes fly round the clock, especially in the larger airports. There are seasonal fluctuations in the amount of traffic, with winter (except for the Christmas vacation traffic out of London) being less busy than the spring and summer months. There are peak and off-peak hours for arrivals and departures, and smaller airports have a good deal of idle time as compared with Heathrow where there is a steady flow of planes.

Some airlines use critical path analysis of the flight cycle from arrival to take-off. The plan of operations for an approaching aircraft is that units such as re-fuellers, traffic staff, loaders, engineers, catering and customs, are notified by operations control. Before an aircraft departs, the catering unit will have loaded meal packs, already made up, and a bar, uplifted and placed in customs an hour before departure, ready for loading. On the cargo side, before departure, the manifests have been finalised and the weight passed to load control for the load sheet. Trucks are loaded and ready for transit to the plane. Passengers are checked in, baggage and passengers weighed (or estimated), the weights being added to the load sheet. Load control takes over and the known weights for the different factors are filled in. Fuelling is carried out and weights and payload estimated. Maintenance or service checks are also carried out. The aircraft is also swept and cleaned.

This analysis of the different tasks needed to handle arrivals and departures of aircraft becomes more crucial when the plane has to be 'turned-round' as quickly as possible so that it can take off with another complement of passengers or cargo. In the peak season, or peak hours, airlines plan to have as many flying hours from their aircraft as is possible. The co-operation of the different groups of airline and airport staff is essential to the operation. Only pilots can fly a plane, but without most of the cycle of operations described above being carried out, the aircraft cannot take off.

The withdrawal of labour or 'work to rule' of various groups of ground staff has caused disruption of varying degree. Even in a small northern airport, the refusal of general hands to sweep or clear the snow from the runways can prevent a plane departing or arriving.

Unions have become more militant in their actions and closed Heathrow Airport (London) for the first time by an industrial dispute on 3 March 1970. Later the airport was only open for twelve hours. The BAA had to notify airlines that no incoming flights would be accepted and no passenger flights could depart. The firemen on strike were demanding on extra 12s weekly shift pay on top of their take-home average pay of £38 a week (*Guardian*, 3 March 1970). Gatwick and Stansted airports were also affected, as all three are operated by the BAA.

The firemen are a strategic group for airline companies, as
engine fires on the ground, either on take-off or on landing, can
spread quickly to the fuel tanks and cause great loss of life and
financial loss. Without stand-by fire services, pilots will not fly.
The loss to Heathrow through a firemen's strike can be great, as it
is the 'sixth busiest airport in the Western World, in terms of total
passengers handled annually (14·3 million in 1969)' (*Financial
Times*, 4 March 1970). It also has a large number of aircraft
movements with aircraft passing through, so that there can be,
even in February, 600 or 700 aircraft movements daily (ibid.). The
firemen have less effect on cargo flights, of which Heathrow has a
high number, being second only in value of goods handled to
London and Liverpool ports. The strike caused accusations of
'blacklegging' as fire officers, members of the Institute of Professional Civil Servants (the firemen being in the TGWU) manned the
fire equipment. Further difficulty for the airlines was the decision
of the motor transport section not to remove slush from the
runways, in support of the strikers. This action delayed many
flights and others were diverted to other airports.

As the dispute developed, the strike changed into a 'go-slow'
since the firemen stated that they would deal with accidents and
emergencies, but vetoed other duties such as general maintenance,
administration and training. The cumulative effect of the 'go-slow'
or 'work to rule' was that, for the airlines, it could have eventually
led to disruption of flight schedules, especially if the 'work to rule'
had spread to other groups, who could then have refused to do any
work not done by the firemen. The advantage of a 'work to rule'
from the firemen's viewpoint, is that they still receive pay near their
normal earnings, while frustrating the airline's wish to run a
normal service.

The dispute was made sharper by the BAA's legal action against
a shop steward. This action arose from his opposition, on behalf of
Heathrow workers, to the BAA decision to give a ground handling
contract to General Aviation Services (GAS) of North America.
This dispute had begun the previous summer (1969) when the
steward was said to have induced airport staff to prevent GAS staff
entering the airport. The steward was accused by the BAA of having
induced a breach of contract by an employee of his Contract of
Service. The BAA said that there was no trade dispute at the time.
The union denied this and claimed that the senior shop steward
was simply carrying out the decision of the membership taken at a
mass meeting.

The firemen's dispute arose from a rational exercise by the BAA to reduce the number of pay grades from 200 to some twenty. While most workers benefited, the firemen decided to stand aside from the agreement. *The Times*, in discussing the dispute, pointed to the web of differentials and the fact that the BAA 'has direct responsibility over only 2,500 employees in the 45,000 who make up the community of Heathrow' (23 March 1970).

The GAS dispute and the firemen's dispute could be seen as an example of the growing power of the shop stewards, which had been evident for years at the airport. The court of inquiry of 1958, which followed a strike of BOAC maintenance men, had criticised the shop stewards who took unconstitutional action without consulting the union: 'BOAC admitted that over a long series of unconstitutional incidents, the shop stewards had produced a run of successes as a result of which they had no doubt come to be regarded by the workers as astute leaders' (ibid., cf. *Financial Times*, 20 March 1970).

These successes led to constant pressure by the shop stewards on BAA and the airlines. The GAS dispute illustrates the way in which disputes over one issue are traceable to another. BAA chose GAS as an independent handler with international experience. While the major airlines had their own cargo and passenger services, and smaller airlines use these, BAA thought that there was need for an independent ground handling agency. The issue became political as the unions called the move 'denationalisation by the back door' and claimed there had been no consultation with them. Underlying the dispute was the workers' fear of redundancy, or loss of earnings and promotion prospects by BEA and BOAC workers. There was evidence suggesting that Heathrow Airport was overmanned and a new company might set different manning and work standards. The TGWU tried to get an agreement that if their members lost work which went to another company 'then employees shall be paid as though they were performing that work'. There was fear that GAS would cut employee earnings considerably as their quoted rates 'according to one senior airport official . . . have been as low as 40 per cent of BEA rates' (*Financial Times*, 20 March 1970).

In this situation, the Heathrow shop stewards supported the group who could put most pressure on management, in this case the firemen. The union's tactics have been to play off one employer against another, as wages and conditions vary between airlines, contractors and sub-contractors, while the employers have tried to form a more unified bargaining front.

Strikes and disputes, especially the latter, have been common in the last four years, in spite of the Memorandum of Agreement drawn up by the NJCCAT and the unions. The Agreement, covering one of the smaller airlines, had a preamble stressing the need for productivity and efficiency in a highly competitive sector serving the public by seven-day continuous working and co-operation in technical change: 'In the light of these understandings, the Employer and the Employee undertake that no strike or lockout shall take place.' The Agreement referred to flexibility of working and working outside one's normal occupation when necessary.

The vagaries of aircraft traffic with its unpredictable peaks in times of bad weather or emergencies were faced in the Agreement by clause 12(b): 'When operational conditions require it, workers . . . may be called upon to work overtime and to work when rostered on statutory holidays as part of the normal cycle or shift. Refusal to do so without a reasonable explanation acceptable to the employer shall constitute misconduct.'

The Agreement ran for three years from June 1968 and contains the standard clause that, in the event of disputes, 'employees will continue working in such a manner as will ensure the punctual completion of work programmes. . . .'

The Agreement with the various clauses on flexibility, job transfers when necessary, overtime when required, and normal working to complete tasks when there was a dispute, appeared to make a 'go-slow' or 'work-to-rule' a breach of contract. The airlines have claimed that recent (1970–1) actions on the part of the unions have frustrated the airlines' attempts to run their service efficiently and have caused inconvenience and annoyance to the air travelling public.*

Another agreement, dealing with work-study, states that 'The high capital cost of the aeroplane and its component parts demands the achievement of short elapsed times for all forms of work.' This factor, the high capital cost of aircraft, and the need to cover capital costs by the highest possible number of flying hours, shows the vulnerability of the airlines to the sort of union pressure which often stopped just short of a direct strike.

During 1970 there were further strike threats in July by the British United employees; in August a storemen's strike over pay in BOAC and BEA, as well as other types of industrial action by other groups, notably the pilots. The airlines became more resistant to wage pressures when the new Conservative government showed its

---

* These refusals to continue normal working sometimes occur at peak travel times, such as holidays, an example from the past being 'The sudden refusal of BEA loaders to work at Whitsun, wrecking the holidays of thousands of people, and acting in breach of agreement, in order to secure an improvement in already relatively good pay.' Professor B. C. Roberts, 'Outlawing the Unofficial Strike', *Daily Telegraph*, 21 July 1965.

support for employers' refusals to pay high percentage wage increases. BEA and BOAC refused to offer more than $4\frac{1}{2}$ per cent in early December, and the TGWU recommended industrial action. The BAA had made a similar offer, also rejected, to their staff.

The industrial action proposed by the unions concerned did not mean the traditional strike with withdrawal of labour. The new form, which may become more frequent, is to withdraw labour while still working and being paid by the employer. This includes a ban on overtime working and a 'work to rule', which means working as slowly as is possible and observing 'rules' which may not exist, which would slow down the servicing of engines. Other forms affect the airport vehicles: 'many workers have been disrupting the airlines' services by working to rule—for instance, by refusing to drive apron vehicles with faults like bent windscreen wipers, broken reflectors, or wrong tyre pressures' (*Financial Times*, 21 December 1970).

This form of protest was also used by bus crews, and inspectors in municipal transport alleged that such faults could be deliberately caused by the drivers, as well as others not mentioned above. The point is that 'work to rule' involves deliberate non co-operation in running or maintaining the service and many opportunities can be created to do this.

The December 1970 dispute lasted until mid-January 1971, although the unions did not have the whole-hearted support of their members, so that both BOAC and BEA managed to keep services going even though flights were sometimes delayed. The union and management representatives frequently appeared on television, where the inability of the interviewers to unravel the issues can only have confused the issues in the minds of the public. At one stage the issue was almost 'arbitrated' by the interviewer as percentages were offered by one party to another.

The unions, when interviewed, insisted that the offered increase was only $4\frac{1}{2}$ per cent and therefore much too low. Yet the 'Tier II' productivity deals led to 10 per cent on basic rates and 16 per cent on earnings. The offered $4\frac{1}{2}$ per cent, along with the later 'Tier II' increases later in the year, would bring 'the total percentage rise for many groups of workers to between 24 and 30 per cent or more during the 24 months between the end of 1969 and the end of 1971' (*Financial Times*, 21 December 1970). As the majority of airline employees are relatively highly paid and lost money through the use of work sanctions, the sanctions were withdrawn by a slight majority decision at a mass meeting of employees. This decision was against union advice, but may have shown a feeling that Christmas was not a good time to ground the aircraft.

Airline pilots

While airline employees are highly paid, pilots receive as much as cabinet ministers.* They defend their high salaries by pointing to the long and expensive training, the hazards of the occupation, the unique skill required, as well as their responsibility for expensive capital equipment and passengers' lives.

Pilots are training mainly at two commercial schools, Hamble and Oxford, and many are sponsored by an airline, with training being paid for 'with or without an arrangement whereby he returns a proportion of the cost of the course out of his salary after joining the airline'. 'British trainees who are sponsored by an airline—at present only BOAC and BEA are doing so—are being trained under a government-assisted scheme whereby the Board of Trade contributes 25 per cent of the total cost of training up to CPL/IR standards† and the airline recoups a proportion of the remainder of the cost from the pilot.'‡ The cost of such a course varies between £4,500 and £6,000, but projected changes in training may raise the cost by a further £2,000. BOAC and BEA have selection boards which screen applicants and choose 'between one in six and one in ten—approximately 100–160 from the 1,000 or so passing the preliminary selection' (ibid., p. 36). There is a lengthy seniority ladder to climb after the pilot is trained and joins the company, with a time scale of ten to fourteen years before the captain's seat is reached. Nearly one quarter of the 1,200 pilots in BOAC are in their forties and fifties.

The pilots are a tightly organised group. Evidence before the Scamp Court of Inquiry (Cmnd 3428, October 1967) into the dispute between the British Airline Pilots' Association (BALPA) and the NJCCAT showed that BALPA's membership was 93 per cent in BOAC and 86 per cent in BEA. By August 1969, BALPA had negotiated a union shop with BOAC, whereby all new pilots joining the corporation had to join the union. Part of the agreement was that BALPA dropped its objection to working with non-union pilots. Pilots already working and non-union members would receive a 'joint approach from BALPA and BOAC to persuade them to join the

* This was written before Parliament voted itself a large salary increase in December 1971.
  Commercial Pilots Licence and Instrument Rating.
  Flying Review International, March 1970, p. 35.

union. BOAC stewards and stewardesses had already agreed a closed shop agreement between the corporation and the TGWU.*

The strong bargaining position of the pilots was buttressed by the union shop agreement. The high capital cost and the skilled operation demanded of aircraft make the pilot virtually irreplaceable, so that the company threatened with a strike faces huge losses, both in the maintenance and depreciation costs of the aircraft, and from the losses of passengers to other airlines, as well as cargo-carrying losses.

Threats of strike action by the airline pilots had preceded the setting up of the Scamp Inquiry. BALPA belonged to negotiating machinery under the national sectional panel for pilot officers of the NJCCAT, and the dispute arose from the wish of BALPA to withdraw from the NJC on six months' notice. The other unions in the NJCCAT did not wish BALPA to withdraw as it would harm the negotiating machinery. The employers agreed with this decision and told BALPA that they would have to submit their notice at the next meeting of the full NJC. BALPA then refused to take part in the council's proceedings. The pilots then sought to negotiate separately with their employers, who refused to do so. BALPA argued before the court of inquiry that they wished to negotiate separately with the airlines as they had highly technical matters to discuss 'which were not the concern of the NJC'. The employers found this view 'surprising' and did not wish to see BALPA leave the well-established council.

BALPA stated that they wished to withdraw because of delays in their negotiations over the years. This was partly due to the fact that the employers' representatives had to negotiate with other groups as well and did not have the technical expertise to deal with pilots' problems. This had led BALPA to negotiate with individual employers satisfactorily: 'the agreements had been reported to the Pilots Sectional Panel but this had been no more than a formality. BALPA therefore wanted in future to conduct all their negotiations directly with employers, outside the machinery of the Council' (ibid., p. 15).

Much of the Scamp Inquiry dealt with an analysis of the complaint about inadequate bargaining machinery, but the bones of the complaint appeared to be that the pilots would be able to 'whipsaw' employers against each other and to push up salaries and improve conditions more quickly. The court of inquiry asked BALPA to reconsider their decision to withdraw from the NJC.

The court's decision had little effect on BALPA, who were bent

* IDS No. 74, August 1969.

on separate negotiations. After an exchange of letters with BOAC in which the corporation suggested that BALPA should accept the recommendations of the Scamp Report and said that they did not wish to negotiate separately with BALPA as this would bring the corporation into dispute with the other unions in their negotiating machinery, BALPA informed the Ministry of Labour, on 1 November 1967, that they were leaving the joint working party. The NJC continued in the meantime with the changes to their constitution.

On the same day on which BALPA had told the Ministry of Labour of their decision, they decided that the BOAC pilots should begin to work to rule, although, being a professional association, they named this restrictive action a 'restriction of co-operation'. This sanction was backed up a month later by a decision to strike on 8 December. The strike lasted for forty-eight hours. It was the first by BALPA and was designed to place the maximum pressure on BOAC as the airline was preparing to carry large numbers of passengers over the school and Christmas vacation period. The Minister of Labour reacted with astonishing speed* by setting up a court of inquiry (see Cmnd 3551, February 1968) under Lord Pearson on the first day of the strike. The Minister's decision was doubly surprising in that the Scamp Court of Inquiry had published its recommendations on the airline pilots only two months before. The Pearson Report outlined the history and development of BALPA's dispute with BOAC in the same way as the Scamp Report had done. BOAC gave a list of the nine most common causes of disputes, 'namely: job security, bad communication, poor industrial relations, hours of work, working conditions and discipline, problems about trade union status, frustration with negotiating machinery, pay and external causes such as sympathetic strikes' (ibid., p. 10), but argued that the only two causes which had figured recently in disputes with the pilots were pay and external causes. The employers went through some of BALPA's complaints and submitted that pay was the underlying reason for the dispute, hidden under arguments about separate negotiating machinery. BALPA had asked for a 100 per cent pay increase in August 1967. The pay claim was linked to the policy of the International Federation of Airline Pilots' Associations (IFALPA), to which BALPA belonged. The argument was that pilots' pay was determined in an international market and that there should be a prevailing level of salaries throughout the world. This comparison

---

* This speed of action can be contrasted with Mr Carr's decision as Secretary of State for Employment to allow the Post Office Strike of 1971 to drag on for many weeks, and shows the government's view of the relative importance of these two public services.

was usually made with reference to the pay of American airline pilots, who were the highest paid, and was linked with a demand that all aircraft should be operated by all-pilot crews. BOAC pointed out that they had been selected by BALPA for the first pay battle, as they were the largest and most profitable airline, and other rates and conditions followed their agreements.

The report shows a conciliator's desire to achieve a just and lasting settlement, but shows a naivety about labour economics and industrial relations tactics. Doubts were expressed by the court of inquiry about BALPA's 'militant conduct' and possible 'extremist ambitions' in which they 'might wish to achieve a position of unrestricted power, in which they would be able to act as judges in their own cause and enforce their own judgements in their own favour by threatening and, if necessary, bringing about "go-slows" and strikes which would cause heavy damage to the business of the employers and therefore to the industry and the national economy'. The court questioned the vice-chairman of BALPA and were satisfied that BALPA did not have 'extremist ambitions'. This statement avoided any analysis of the ability, as distinct from the BALPA disclaimer, to push pilots' salaries far above their level at the time.

The same willingness to believe the good intentions of BALPA was shown in the court's rejection of employers' claims that the pilots could use possible bargaining tactics, such as 'leapfrogging', 'whipsawing', 'picking off the employers one by one'. The report doubted that BALPA could force separate deals through with different employers, as the employers had been used to working together under the NJC system. This judgment shows an inability to understand the possible tactics and power exercised by BALPA.

A number of proposals were made which would improve the national sectional panel (airline pilots) of the NJC, and as the NJC had already been making certain changes it was concluded: 'A resumption by BALPA of membership of the NJC would now be innocuous for BALPA and would have considerable advantage for them, and is really the only solution to this unfortunate impasse' (p. 37).

One feature of the Pearson Report which distinguished it from the Scamp Report was its attempt to discover what the qualifications and activities of pilots were. Even here the court of inquiry displayed a lack of knowledge of comparative job evaluation, as there was little attempt to relate the degree of skill required and risks involved to those in some other occupations or, more appropriately, to speculate on the numbers who might be able to fly planes if trained. The central point of their job analysis was that the aircraft 'may be worth up to two million pounds and may have valuable cargo on board. It may be carrying up to 200 passengers as well as the pilot and the rest of the crew.' A slip or bad judgment could lead not to 'a mere accident, but a major disaster' (p. 19). Details of the other difficulties of an airline pilot's life were less convincing. Cramped working conditions, changes in temperature, time spent away from home, are much worse for other workers—miners, steeplejacks, seamen, whose pay is much less and whose individual industrial hazards may be greater than those of airline pilots. Their conclusion was that: 'Pilots do not need to have an exceptional quantity of theoretical technical knowledge, but there is something special and indeed unique in their practical experience and their essential task of flying aircraft, which is highly responsible and highly exacting' (p. 35).*

The Pearson Report was disappointing, as it showed little understanding of the BALPA control over the supply of pilots and their monopolistic bargaining position, or of the pilots' attempts to maintain the flying crews at a higher number than BOAC thought necessary. It might have been pointed out that the demand for pilots' services is inelastic, and that while substitution between airlines is possible for the passenger, the airline cannot replace pilots. The inquiry might also have looked at the relationship between pay increases to BOAC pilots and those to BEA and other smaller airlines.

The first hard look at the bargaining position of BOAC pilots came with Report No. 88 of the Prices and Incomes Board ('Pay of Pilots Employed by the British Overseas Airways Corporation', October 1968, Cmnd 3789). After the Pearson Report, BALPA rejoined the NJC and reached an agreement on a three-year settlement. This was after BOAC had refused to negotiate a 'completely new agreement for service', demanded by BALPA. The new agreement offered 'increases in pay of 10 per cent on 1 January 1968, $7\frac{1}{2}$ per cent on 1 January 1969 and $7\frac{1}{2}$ per cent on 1 January 1970, and certain measures are to be taken to increase the pilots' productivity' (PIB Report No. 88, p. 1). Differences in opinion over the cost savings involved led to the agreement being referred to the PIB.

Before this BALPA had followed its now customary action before an inquiry and had ordered a 'restriction of co-operation' campaign, which was later followed by a strike lasting two weeks. While the

* The skill of pilots and the risks involved were summed up in a negotiation heard by the writer in Chicago in the 1950s. When the employers objected to the high salary claim and said 'You pilots are claiming a bigger salary than doctors', the AALPA representative replied: 'Doctors can bury their mistakes. We get buried along with ours.'

Board were studying the reference, Professor Wood chaired meetings between BOAC and BALPA. The Board now found itself looking at a different situation than existed before their reference.

The Wood agreement changed the system of payment from an annual salary to an hourly rate of pay. There were also to be 'blocks' of work which would be bid for in order of seniority, and the less senior were to be protected by a minimum guarantee of pay. The PIB report estimated that the cost of the new system would add about 10 per cent to the salary bill for pilots. It was anticipated that the same flying operations could be carried out with a 'reduction of 15 to 20 per cent in flying staff', which would be phased out over several years. It has already been noted above that some 20–25 per cent of BOAC pilots were in their forties and fifties, so that normal retirement would have accounted for most of the redundancies, while recruitment could have been slowed down or reduced.

One major defect in the PIB report was that it only told us what the scales of pay were for pilots, i.e. from a second officer's starting salary of £1,540, then up the thirty-nine steps to £5,880 as a senior captain, first class. We were not told what average earnings were for each group of pilots on the scale, or what the expense allowances were, or the pension arrangements.

The 'bidline' system meant that senior pilots could choose the amount of flying they wished to do, and junior pilots could take up the 'blocks' of work left by them. An air transport journal, commenting on the report, noted the disadvantage of allowing 'voluntary overwork in the pursuit of money, thus bringing yet another financial factor into the problem of air safety'.* The report's view that larger, heavier, or faster aircraft should not automatically lead to a rise in pilots' salaries ('A change in pay should reflect changes in job content identified through techniques of job analysis') was met with the journal's comment that 'The PIB Report goes way out of its depth when it deals with the size of crews for particular aircraft.' Yet in our view this should have been tackled by the Pearson Report as well as by the PIB report.

The PIB report had as little effect on BALPA as the Pearson and Scamp Reports before it. For a union which had renounced extremist methods before Lord Pearson, BALPA still contrived to make the running well in front of the more avowedly militant unions. By April 1969, the newspapers were estimating that a strike could cost BOAC some half-million pounds daily, and that the airlines should not be mean over an extra few million pounds for

Flight International, 7 November 1968, p. 736.

the airline pilots, nor insist on fewer pilots per plane. Mr Clive Jenkins acted as mediator in the dispute between the two groups, a classic case of poacher turning gamekeeper. BOAC offered to raise the senior captain's pay from £5,880 for a minimum 660 hours up to £6,300, but the pilots demanded £7,500 for 600 hours. A settlement was reached at £6,750, a 15 per cent increase on basic pay, allegedly to be spread over the next three or four years. Extra hours worked could bring pay up to £8,837. The PIB returned to the airline industry in November 1969* and its survey criticised the pay agreement of April described above. The Board did not agree that the 747 (the jumbo jet) would be more difficult to fly than the 707s and similar planes, and doubted whether airlines should pay different rates for different aircraft. At this time BALPA were demanding a rise for 747 pilots from £7,000–£8,500 up to £13,000. BALPA were critical of the Board's report and banned pilot training for the 747. Some critics of the airline pilots could not agree that they should receive up to 50 per cent more pay for flying an aircraft which was said to be no more difficult to fly than the 707s, or that BALPA should use the pay of American pilots as a lever with which to raise their own pay.

The PIB Report No. 129 had also said that the expected productivity gains of the April 1969 settlement had not materialised. Instead of the number of pilots being reduced by some 13 per cent, their numbers had increased by some 2 per cent. Another suggestion, which had appeared in Report No. 88, was that rates of pay should be based on job analysis. As with the earlier suggestion, little attention was paid to this. The Board disagreed with the BALPA demand that flight crews should have a complement of four (American and foreign airlines aim at three-men air crews) and the demand that if airline pilots did reduce the crew from four to three they should receive a compensating salary increase.

BALPA also rejected the Board's suggestion that there should be a full-time mediator working continuously with the corporation and the pilots. The ban on 747 training was carried on into 1970 and the pilots also refused BOAC's proposal that they should go to arbitration. BOAC pilots received an immediate strike ballot on the question of hourly pay to third pilots.

The refusal to train for or to fly the jumbo jets continued through 1970, and the big jets remained on the ground. For a short time in April, when BOAC offered £11,500 a year, the training ban was lifted, but it was reimposed after a disagreement in which BOAC

* PIB Report No. 129, 'Pay of Pilots Employed by British Overseas Airways Corporation', Cmnd 4197, November 1969.

claimed that the pilots had accepted the principle of two-pilot crews. BALPA countered by saying they had understood management to accept the three-crew principle (*Guardian*, 26 August 1970). BALPA were claiming a salary of £13,500 for senior captains and the *Guardian* commented: 'Those of us who are not expecting a 50 per cent rise this year will simply have to accept that pilots possess a rare and still rather mysterious set of skills which puts them in a seller's market they are determined to exploit.' This seemed to be fair comment.

The militancy of the airline pilots set a mark for other airline staff to follow. While fitters and loaders did not compare themselves directly with aircrew, cabin crews did, and by February 1971 the British Airlines Stewards and Stewardesses Association were refusing to negotiate over pay and conditions for the 747 until they were recognised as aircrew, as they were by the Board of Trade, and given pensions closer to those of pilots, who received two-thirds of their salary as pension on retirement after thirty years' service. Yet it is difficult to see BOAC or other airlines being strike-bound by cabin crews to the extent they could be by aircrews.

The bargaining power of BALPA can be seen by looking at the pay increases which they achieved, from £5,880 for senior captains in 1969, to some £12,000 for 747 pilots only eighteen months later. No other group of employees in the country matched this leap forward, which was partly due to the long training, risk factors and skill of the pilots, but more particularly to the tight union shop of BALPA and their determined exploitation of their labour monopoly.

Recent setbacks in the aircraft industry, the collapse of Rolls-Royce in early 1971, the uncertain future of the RB211, the poor prospects for the Lockheed L-1011 jet with Rolls-Royce engines, all point to a contraction in aircraft production. This is partly reflected by the depression in which airline companies find themselves, especially in the United States, where many airlines lost millions of dollars in 1970. The economic depression in the USA reduced the volume of air traffic, while the contemporary disease of 'stagnation', a combination of sagging demand with high wages and cost inflation, has led to rapidly rising costs for airlines. The airlines also complain that too many flights are competing on the same routes and that charter planes are creaming off a large number of passengers. Airlines also find that they have placed too many orders for new and large aircraft of the jumbo jet type, for which the expected passenger demand has not yet materialised.

It seems likely that the early 1970s will see the airlines moving

Advertisement in *The Times*, 28 January 1971

Interruption of BEA *services*

The facts you should know

1 For the first time in twenty years BEA has been forced to suspend practically all its services as from January 26th, as a direct result of an industrial dispute involving maintenance staff.

2 Despite the cancellation of its operations BEA will continue to operate a reservation and information service booking passengers and cargo with other scheduled airlines as necessary.

3 Maintenance men only are involved—the majority of staff are not associated with this action.

4 The strike has been brought about by the termination of their employment by 25 members of the Heathrow engineering base staff who were in breach of contract by refusing to undertake normal work on the preparation and despatching of engines for overhaul.

5 This industrial action was taken because BEA and other airlines in the national joint council are in dispute with the unions over the level of pay increases proposed for 1971. The unions believe the further $4\frac{1}{2}$ per cent increase in wages offers to be insufficient. BEA maintain that following the 16 per cent increase in average earnings during 1970 the $4\frac{1}{2}$ per cent offer together with other awards already agreed will lead to a very substantial uplift in 1971.

6 The unions concerned have refused to accept arbitration.

7 BEA deplores the inconvenience and hardship this stoppage must cause our customers. Every effort will be made to reach a solution acceptable to both sides as soon as possible.
Please watch newspapers and TV for further reports on the situation.

BEA

through a more cost-conscious period than in the years 1967–70. In such conditions managements may negotiate more keenly over labour costs, including pilots' salaries, than they have done previously. A recent example of this was the lengthy strike of pilots in the USA against the Mohawk Airlines, while in France a three-day strike by pilots was met by a refusal on the part of the three French airlines to let them man the planes on their return. This move by the airline management had the apparent support of the French government.* This may indicate a policy of resistance to wage demands in the public sector by governments in western Europe, of which the present leading example is Britain in 1971.

* *The Times*, 25 February 1971.

7

The public sector

The public sector has been defined* as comprising the civil service, local government, education, the National Health Service, the administration of justice, the probation service, the police, prisons and borstals, the fire service, the Post Office, the BBC. Post-war additions to the public sector include the industries which were nationalised after 1945: coal, gas, electricity, rail transport, civil air transport and recently, steel. It should be noted that the pre-war public service provided services rather than a product (and we shall deal mostly with this area), whereas the post-war development brought in large groups of manual workers with a more militant tradition towards wages which was reflected, and seen to be reflected, in the price of the product.

This last factor contributed towards the decline in the public standing of the public sector, but the change was inevitable, given the influence of full employment, mass education, and the welfare state. In the 1920s and 1930s the public service was a highly desirable job for the brighter or better-educated working-class or middle-class boy or girl. In roughly ascending order, these jobs were: municipal transport, clerical work in local government, the Post Office, the police, the civil service; while entering the BBC was like entering a church—less an occupation than a consecration of one's duties. The attractiveness of public employment was that it offered security in a time of mass unemployment, relatively high pay, a well-ordered promotion ladder based on education and training, and a pension. Post-war changes in employment with the accompanying inflation and a rapid increase in manual workers' pay levels, the wide spread of education creating more recruits for white-collar jobs, the resulting fall in white-collar salaries, and the falling attraction of public service pensions through inflation and social security, combined to diminish the pre-war attractions of the public service.

* Hilda Kahn, *Salaries in the Public Services in England and Wales*, Allen & Unwin, London, 1963.

Inflation places the public service in a bargaining straitjacket, as it inevitably lags behind the private sector in wage/salary increases. It is easier for large numbers of private firms to give increases and pass these on to the customer than it is for the public sector, whose industries are much in the public eye and the newspaper, and whose deficits and salaries have to be met from taxation and rates. This situation is illustrated both by the attitude of government in monetary or industrial crises, where Ministers declaim the need to restrict public expenditure and public salaries using what influence they have on arbitrators and committees, and by the actions of councillors on local authorities, who, in the words of Galbraith, 'are extremely reluctant to set a bad example' (by conceding wage demands to the staffs under their control); 'but one should not be surprised if here we find one of the greatest modern sources of industrial and social tension' (*The Times*, 16 March 1970). The effects of incomes policy on the public sector have partly borne this out.

Another change in the attitudes towards pay in the public sector, which the government has tended to treat as a useful brake on inflation when necessary, is that public servants have changed greatly from their relatively passive and docile role to one of greater militancy and increased determination to join and be treated as trade unionists. This is seen in the growing membership of white-collar employees in the public sector. Britain will undoubtedly follow the developments in other countries of the western world. Professor Stieber writes that 'Government is the largest and fastest-growing industry in the United States. In 1965 ... the public payroll ... totalled ten million—three million more than in 1955. By 1975 government employment is expected to increase to about 15 million and comprise one out of every five employees in the country.'[*]

Stieber points out that one result of this is that trade union organisation among public employees has increased and that the three fastest growing unions in the decade (1955–65) 'were exclusively in the public employee field'.

Other western countries show this trend towards white-collar unionism: 'In France, where overall union membership figures are always difficult to ascertain, white-collar unionism seems to be at least as well developed as its blue-collar counterpart. In Sweden, the clearest case of successful white-collar unionism, some 70 per

[*] J. Stieber: 'Collective Bargaining in the Public Sector' in *Challenges to Collective Bargaining*, Lloyd Ullman (ed.), New York, 1967, p. 65.

cent of non-managerial white-collar workers are in unions as compared with 80 per cent for blue-collar workers.'*

As employees join unions in the expectation that their wages and working conditions will improve, this has led to more pressure on public service unions to keep abreast with increases in the private sector which have been given wide publicity. Public servants, conscious of their weaker bargaining position, have become more militant in their demands at their annual conference, with consequent results leading to more militancy in hitherto peaceful groups such as the teachers, local government workers, nurses, ambulance drivers, and surprisingly, doctors in 1970. Even the police moved a motion at their conference demanding the right to strike, which was defeated. This is a phenomenon which is more common in other countries of the western world, such as Italy, France, and Sweden in early 1971. (The latter country having been held up to Britain for years as an industrial relations model, found itself with its civil service, teachers and part of its army on strike.) One aspect of the new militancy in the public services is that, instead of the union officials leading the members in demands for higher wages, in the last two years of incomes policy, 1968–70, it was the rank and file who forced the union to raise their demands. This development was not unexpected. Union leaders are more aware of the arguments for wage restraint than their members are, and, in some unions, might listen to arguments about the national interest and the necessity of moderating wage demands. Unions like the NUGMW pursued moderate policies, as they had been in favour of an incomes policy; but the dustmen forced them to become more militant.

In spite of the public servants becoming more militant, most of them tended to lag behind the wage increases achieved by the more powerful bargaining groups in the private sector. This showed itself in two ways: one was the smaller percentage increase which most public service groups tended to get until the last year or so of incomes policy; the other, and more significant, fact was that the intervals between pay awards in the public services tended to be longer than in private industry. By 1970, the Labour government appeared to be following a policy of allowing large increases for public servants, as we shall see below. One labour correspondent summed the change up as follows: 'Certainly the public servants, having fared worst under the Government's incomes policy, are now having their positions improved. But the larger

* A. Kleingartner: 'The Organization of White-Collar Workers', *British Journal of Industrial Relations*, Vol. VI, No. 1, p. 81.

rises being allowed generally elsewhere mean that many of them will still be behind many industrial workers in the pay league' (*Financial Times*, 25 March 1970). There has always been a tendency for wage increases in the public services to follow behind those of outside industries, as this is the method by which the principles of 'fair comparison' are established. An incomes policy, however, tends to press harder on the public services and the nationalised industries as they are more in the public eye, and rising prices or taxes are more easily noticed and complained about than is the case in private industry. While it is not easy to trace the course of pay movements, we shall note some of the effects of incomes policy.

A survey of changes in wages and salaries for the period 1965–6 (*IDS Panorama*) pointed out the difficulties in trying to classify the great variety of settlements: some dealt with minimum rates, some with standard rates, while some were long-term agreements covering a number of firms, and others related to a particular company. The majority of the settlements (60 per cent) were for a period longer than a year.

In the middle sixties the trend for non-manual government employees was for pay to be reviewed every two years or more, which put the public services at a disadvantage in comparison with many employees in the private sector who were able to bargain on a plant basis and received an annual award, as did the public industries at times.

Of seventy-four industries analysed by Incomes Data in 1965–6, nineteen settlements were around the norm, and forty-eight were above, with '18 of them being over 6 per cent' (ibid., p. 57). Of those on 'the norm' there were eleven in the public sector, ranging from local authority manual workers and Health Service ancillary staffs to electricity supply. This meant that these groups had failed to keep up with changes in the cost of living and that their real incomes had fallen slightly; the only group in the public sector which achieved a 6–9 per cent increase was the London busmen.

This relative 'squeeze' on the public services continued throughout most of the period of incomes policy, and was admitted by Mrs Barbara Castle in December 1969. Introducing the White Paper on Prices and Incomes in the House of Commons she said: 'The facts are that many employees in the public services have seen others in private industry get big increases through productivity bargains or just sheer wages-drift, advantages which they have not been able to enjoy. That is why there has been unrest in the public sector.' The White Paper on Productivity, Prices and

Incomes Policy after 1969 (Cmnd 4237) laid down principles about pay in the public services, saying that employees should be treated as fairly as those workers in the private sector who did similar work. Special problems arose because it was often difficult to measure output as a link between pay and efficiency in the public services, market prices were not given to the product or service, the employees tended to stay for a long time, and changes in pay which lowered their relative standard of living might not affect the labour supply for some years. Lastly, the government was usually directly involved in public service pay settlements so that there were pressures for equality of treatment throughout the public services.

The White Paper had little effect on wage settlements during the first few months of 1970, as what wages dam there had been was well and truly breached. The pace was set by the unions in the car industry over the Ford pay talks. With no attempt at linking pay to productivity, the union asked for a £10 per week wage increase, finally accepting half this amount, equivalent to an 18 per cent increase. This widely-publicised settlement was bound to increase the frustrations in the public sector and each succeeding settlement became a step on a rising spiral staircase: the teachers, the armed forces, the nurses, and the police, with the nurses receiving 20 per cent and the police $8\frac{1}{2}$ per cent. All those four awards were designed to attract recruits, with the Forces award increasing the gross pay of the private soldier by nearly 100 per cent (with new deductions for food and board). The Forces award introduced 'Factor X', which was an ingenious device invented by the PIB in order to give a large increase to the army. 'X' stood for the extra payment given a soldier because he may be exposed to danger.

Increases for the public sector grew in size; the gas workers achieved 14 per cent and postal workers $12\frac{1}{2}$ per cent in early 1970. British Rail awarded 11 per cent over five months without any reciprocal promises about productivity. By the end of March there were waves of wage claims either awarded or pending, with busmen ranging from 9 to 12 per cent and local government white-collar staffs up to 15 per cent (although considerably less for some of the grades). By the middle of 1970 the dockers were demanding a rise which would have taken them some 75 per cent above their 1965 position, while the airline pilots were using similar militant tactics to virtually double the senior salaries over the five-year period of incomes policy.

The ending of incomes policy, for all relevant purposes, came not with a whimper but with a bang. The Kindersley Report on the pay of doctors and dentists was received by the government in early April. The government delayed publication as the award would have great repercussions for the rest of the Health Service. The BMA threatened reprisals, and groups of young hospital doctors talked of strike action. Under great pressure from the BMA, assisted by the Conservative opposition in parliament, the report was published on 4 June. The award to doctors and dentists was 30 per cent, which the government would not meet in full, saying that it would pay the full amount to the junior doctors to meet the recruitment–emigration problem, but only half this amount to the senior doctors. The BMA told doctors not to accept the increases, to withdraw co-operation and not to sign sick notes. As a further twist to the knife in the government's side in the middle of a general election, a referendum was to be taken to see if doctors would resign from the National Health Service. During this period, the BMA was to be seen almost nightly on television news, protesting against the government's decision and the virtual collapse of medical morale.

The doctors and dentists' award has been mentioned in some detail as it marked the end of incomes policy with the passing of the Labour government. It also illustrates in a classic manner the weaknesses of incomes policy, in that economic predictions about the movement of wages and earnings can collapse under the attack of a powerful, strategically-placed group in the public services, backed by the mass media, underlining the inter-relation of economic, political and psychological factors—in this case many people thought that their health was threatened by the denial of money to the medical profession.

Before the general election the Conservatives argued that the award should be paid in full, even though, by any definition, it was inflationary, with a 'hedge' of 7 per cent against future price rises. After the election, the new Conservative government decided 'in the national interest' to pay the senior doctors 20 per cent instead of the Kindersley 30 per cent. This abrupt shift from electioneering tactics to the realities of power was to mark the new attitude towards inflationary wage awards.

The last year of incomes policy had seen a sharp rise in wage and salary awards. This illustrated the cumulative effect of inflation on wage demands, which now sought to recoup past losses due to price increases and to add an element for the amount lost through taxation on the new rates, plus an extra for future price increases. These claims were put forward in an atmosphere of mounting anxiety and frustration as unions and their members watched each new award closely and studied the effects on their comparative position.

The net results of the expectations of future rising prices and of high marginal taxation were that wage claims became progressively greater. The TUC analysed this trend in a paper to the National Economic Development Council (in January 1971) in which they said that a 14 per cent increase in pay was needed to achieve a 3 per cent increase in real terms. The minimum objectives of the unions were: '(a) to restore real pay of their previous settlement (usually twelve months earlier) and (b) to ensure that the level is retained for at least six months thereafter. Under current inflationary conditions, these objectives would require pay increases of 8 or 9 per cent. To secure some *real wage* increase over and above this needs a further increase rather higher than the desired increase in disposable income, because of the high rates of marginal taxation.'

The last statement illustrates the inflationary effect of high marginal taxation on wage claims. A 10 per cent wage award vanishes with a 7 per cent annual increase in prices and some 3 per cent in income tax on the award (the marginal taxation rate on increases for many workers is around 30 per cent).

The Conservative government 1970

The government began now, though denying any incomes policy, to operate a negative incomes policy by saying 'no' to wage increases in the public sector which they thought too great. This attitude was elevated into policy by the politicians and newspapers, who described the declared intention of giving each new group of wage applicants in the public sector less than preceding groups as 'de-escalation' or 'N–1' (N being the percentage increase the previous group of workers had received). The government, as paymaster in the public sector, argued that they must set an example to private industry by refusing to pay high percentage increases unless they would be absorbed by productivity gains or the unit costs of labour affected by the claim showed no increase. It was hoped that a resolute stand by the government against public sector wage claims would be quickly followed in the private sector.*

* Mr Aubrey Jones, ex-Chairman of the PIB was sceptical of this policy as early as 1 November 1970: 'Let me rule out one option straight away. That is the option that the Government, by sitting hard on prices and incomes in the public sector, will be followed in its shining example by the private sector. This is what Mr Selwyn Lloyd attempted in 1961–2. The private sector did not follow' (*Observer*, 1 November 1970).

Mr Anthony Barber, Chancellor of the Exchequer, made his position clear to the Overseas Bankers Club banquet in January 1971. He said he was against a freeze on prices and pay, which could only be a temporary dam, which could burst again. He had considered a voluntary policy of co-operation between government, management and unions, but did not believe this to be practicable. His solution was that 'if we are to defeat inflation there must be a substantial and progressive de-escalation in the rate of pay settlements. . . . But the British people must be under no illusion as to what this policy means. If it involves standing up to unwarranted strikes then in the general interest both the Government and the nation must be prepared to face them . . . we have repeatedly made it clear that the policy of de-escalation applies to the public and private sectors alike and that in no circumstances will the Government encourage or connive at unreasonable pay settlements' (*The Times*, 2 January 1971).

The difficulties facing the government on their policy were similar to those facing the Labour government under the Prices and Incomes period but were more wounding to the late runners in wage claims as the PIB had disappeared and there appeared to be no element of fairness in the de-escalation policy. Secondly, while governments have been able to exercise some direct control over wages in the public sector from time to time, they have had little direct control over the wages in the private sector. Although the Government were supported in the de-escalation by the Confederation of British Industries, this did not prevent Chrysler from giving an 18 per cent increase to their workers, at a time when the government was anxious that awards should be only 10 per cent or less.

While the government, as paymaster, can refuse to pay postmen an increase which would bring them into line with other comparable jobs, and risk the loss of revenue and years of deficit, private employers often do not choose to risk going into bankruptcy or losing important markets or customers. As the last twenty-five years have shown, most employers have paid wage increases and have passed on the increased price to the consumer.

The failure of the private sector to match the resistance shown by the government to its employees can be seen from an analysis of the settlements in the last few months of 1970. Of forty wage settlements, some twenty-two had had an increase less than twelve months before. Thirty-four of these had been in the private sector and the increases varied from 10 to 39 per cent, and affected over a million workers. This was well above the unofficial level of

10 per cent or less which the government was trying to establish as its unofficial policy aim. Significantly, among the high wage settlements was one of 14 to 35 per cent for the workers in the retail meat trade, with nearly 100,000 workers affected. This illustrates the capacity of the retail trade, especially with decimalisation imminent, to pass on increases in costs through increased prices to the consumer. Other increases ranged from 16 to 20, and 17 to 24 per cent, for other industries, with the Engineering Employers' Federation reported as having given an increase of 17 to 31 per cent to draughtsmen, 'their second rise in six months' (*The Times*, 27 January 1971).

The government's attempt to force the public sector to accept lower wage increases than those in the private sector faced the difficulty that these latter rises were widely reported and were available to trade union research departments and negotiators. It was in this climate of spiralling wages that the government faced up to the claim by the miners, who claimed that during the five years from 1965 to 1970 they had fallen from first place in the pay league to thirteenth place. To rectify this they were submitting a claim of 33 per cent. The NCB wished to make an offer of 12 to 14 per cent.

The miners' claim showed up the problem of pay in the public sector clearly. The NCB was in deficit of over £35 million, and the miners' full claim would cost £75 million in a year. The Conservative government was committed to a policy of making the nationalised industries as viable as possible and the NCB was committed not to go over a £50 million deficit.

Unofficial strikes began in South Wales, and the area delegate conference voted to bring out the 40,000 miners. The meeting also rejected the NCB's offer. There were strikes in other coal-fields and the National Union of Mineworkers called for a national ballot to see if there should be a national strike. The miners' leader, Lawrence Daly, told a rally that they were not only confronting their employers, they were also confronting the Conservative government. This illustrated the growing realisation of unions in the public sector that they had to contend with a government determined to influence the public corporations not to offer over a certain percentage. In the case of the miners, the government hoped that it would be 10 per cent. Yet the government realised that a lengthy coal strike would have far more serious effects than did the lengthy dustmens' strike. The latter caused inconvenience and minor health hazards, but the former could cause a major industrial crisis. While it was true that the long-term demand for coal was downwards, important sections of industry were still dependent on coal, and electricity stations would also be affected, with important results. Strategically, it was a good time for the miners to strike, as coal stocks stood at some ten million tons, less than half of the previous year's supply. The miners were also motivated by resentment and uncertainty, as there had been an extensive programme of pit closures, with some fifty a year being closed down between 1965 and 1969. But the miners were prepared to see more pits being closed if the remaining miners could have higher wages.

A settlement was reached in November when the national ballot showed a majority accepting the NCB offer of 12 per cent upwards. This was more than the government had wished, but they were faced by Lord Robens who insisted on exercising his judgment. Finally, for a variety of reasons, Lord Robens left the NCB and the government continued with their policy of trying to influence the chairmen of public corporations.

The government suffered another defeat in its de-escalation policy when, later in November, the hospital workers (250,000) received increases of 15 per cent. The government decided not to make an issue of the award, possibly for the reasons that it came close after the Scamp Report, with comparable grades and wage levels, that hospital workers are in the lowly-paid category, and that public goodwill would have been lost if they had fought wage increases to hospital workers.

The next battle over wages in the public sector, in which the government at last found an adversary against which it could rally public opinion, came with the electricity workers' claim of some 25 per cent. This claim followed awards over three years of $3\frac{1}{2}$ per cent, 5 per cent and 10 per cent. The Electricity Council offered 10 per cent, and the workers refused. (It was at this time that Mr Heath, in parliament, denied that the government had said that no wage increases should be over 10 per cent (*The Times*, 9 December 1970).) The electricity workers decided to work to rule, as they were, under the law relating to essential public services, forbidden to strike. The 'work to rule' was as effective as a strike, as it cut power supplies at peak periods such as early morning and in the evenings between 5 p.m. and 7 p.m., cutting off traffic signals and street lighting, causing traffic congestion and chaos.

The Wilberforce Report* on the dispute denied that the

* 'Report of the Court of Inquiry into a dispute in the Electricity Supply Industry', Cmnd 4594, February 1971.

government had forced its views on the court, or suggested a solution. The Treasury memorandum had convinced the court that inflation was spiralling rapidly and becoming dangerous. The court thought that the pay of electricity workers could not be looked at in isolation, as previous settlements had influenced related technical and clerical workers and also related public utilities. They believed that many unions were watching to see what kind of settlement the court would award, and the court favoured a moderation in wage demands. The wage claim based on greater productivity, which the electricity workers were pressing, was said to be difficult to measure, as it was almost impossible to distinguish between manual effort and capital input in the productivity ratio, or the number of men per million kilowatt hours sold. But productivity had been improved by the acceptance of changes in the organisation and methods of work and by the fact that the industry was achieving a growing output with less workers. The cost-of-living claim was acknowledged, even though the Treasury had argued 'A formula for determining the level of pay by providing an element for rises in prices since the last settlement, an element for anticipated rises in the period ahead and an element above this for a further substantial increase in real earnings would give a dangerous upward twist to the inflationary spiral.'*

The court's award was based mainly on the productivity increases in the industry, and the government calculated that the recommendations would add some 10·9 per cent to the wages bill as compared with the offer of 9·7 per cent by the Electricity Council. This was a judgment of Solomon as it satisfied the government as being around 10 per cent, and it satisfied the electricity workers who said the award would amount to some 16 per cent for them. In parliament the opposition, led by Mrs Barbara Castle, made a number of estimates which ranged from 13·4 to 15·5 per cent, which the government denied. Whatever the final figure which emerged, and this was difficult to assess as the amount would depend on the output of electricity workers over the year, the government were seen by the public to have resisted what might have been a major dispute and an inflationary pay award, and some observers saw this as a possible halt to the inflationary spiral.

The de-escalation process, or N–1, was still being enforced. It was applied with full rigour to the postmen, who became a classic case of the doctrine being applied to the public sector. The electricity workers were in a capital-intensive industry with a high capital input and corresponding rise in productivity, while the

* This had been done in the Scamp Report, which incensed the government.

postmen were in a labour-intensive industry where higher productivity was difficult to achieve.

Not all unions in the public sector were locked in conflict with the government, as a number were slipping quietly through the N–1 net. Some of these, between December 1970 and February 1971, were making their assessment of the strength of government resistance to their claims. Those who could settle, even at the bottom end of their pay claim, did so without recourse to arbitration, which might have given them 1–2 per cent more or might have stuck to the original offer and exposed them to public gaze or government criticism. The university teachers accepted a minimum figure of 10 per cent in December, and the industrial civil servants accepted 8 per cent (the government estimate). This award was the 'first of two major increases they will collect in 1971, yielding average pay increases of at least 17 per cent' (*Financial Times*, 24 February 1971). On the same date the nurses, who had been claiming 15 per cent, received 10 per cent, and a few days later the police received from 11 to 22 per cent.

The shift in relative wages

When we look at the movement in wages in the last three years of incomes policy, we find that some of the private sector industries averaged twice, or more than twice, the 'norm' of 3½ per cent yearly. Building craftsmen had an increase of 26·3 per cent in three and a half years and civil engineering construction craftsmen the same amount. Bakery workers' wages (weekly rates and hours) rose by 37½ per cent in just over four years. The drug and fine chemicals industry men workers, Class I, raised their minimum rates by some 22 per cent in four years. One large car firm gave increases of 20 per cent in eighteen months and another 25 per cent in two and a half years (Calculated from *IDS Panorama July 1969–June 1970*).

These figures disguise the amount of increase over the period, as they refer to minimum rates, and in all the industries mentioned (and there are many more) there are various other payments ranging from bonus to overtime which make earnings rise above basic rates. This is especially true in building and construction, and engineering, as men may work less and earn more by absenteeism leading to overtime, which can be time and a half or double time Sundays.

Estimates of the increases in average earnings can be seen from Table 10. It can be seen from this Table that earnings in building

Table 10 Monthly indices of average earnings of employees (GB). Percentage increases between chosen dates (Jan. 1966 = 100)

	1966 July	1967 July	1968 July	1969 Jan.	1969 April	1969 July	1970 Jan.	1970 June¹	% increase between Dates July '68 / July '69	July '69 / Jan. '70	Jan. '70 / June '70	Jan. '70 / April '70	July '70 / June '70
Food, drink and tobacco	104·7	111·1	119·5	120·7	123·6	127·5	129·5	146·3	6·7	1·6	13·0	4·5	14·7
Chemicals	102·7	107·8	113·5	120·3	121·3	126·0	130·1	144·0	11·0	3·3	10·7	7·1	14·3
Metal manufacture	104·8	109·2	117·1	121·3	122·9	125·2	132·3	143·1	6·9	5·7	8·2	4·9	14·3
Mechanical engineering								138·7			7·0	3·9	12·9
Instrument engineering	103·2	106·3	113·8	118·9	121·6	122·8	129·7	135·2	7·9	5·6	4·3	5·0	10·1
Electrical								138·6			6·9	4·3	12·9
Shipbuilding	107·8	108·4	118·0	119·8	125·6	127·9	137·5	143·1	8·4	7·5	4·1	1·3	11·9
Vehicles	106·0	106·0	117·6	122·8	126·2	127·9	135·4	146·6	8·7	5·9	8·3	4·5	14·6
Textiles	104·2	109·7	118·7	121·4	123·3	126·8	129·1	139·4	6·8	1·8	8·0	3·0	9·9
Leather, leather goods	102·5	105·6	114·2	113·8	112·0	122·4	122·0	130·3	7·2	−0·3	6·8	4·3	6·5
Clothing and footwear	106·3	106·5	115·6	117·5	119·4	119·9	125·0	133·0	3·7	4·3	6·4	5·2	10·9
Brick, pottery, glass and cement	103·4	107·4	115·0	122·0	122·6	123·8	129·7	138·8			7·0	0·1	12·1
Paper, printing and publishing	102·0	104·5	113·9	118·5	121·7	123·5	130·8	138·0	7·7	4·8	6·5	3·1	11·7
All manufacturing	104·1	107·5	115·8	119·8	122·6	124·6	130·5	140·5	7·7	4·7	7·7	4·0	12·8
Building and construction	110·0	116·5	123·7	123·1	129·6	132·1	128·5	146·0	6·8	2·7	13·6	9·6	10·5
Gas, electricity and water	104·7	105·1	111·9	113·0	120·1	121·8	128·5	135·1	8·8	5·5	5·1	3·9	10·9
Transport	106·4	109·1	115·5	122·6	124·5	127·0	133·3	146·8	10·0	5·0	10·1	4·4	15·6
Miscellaneous services	102·6	107·9	115·2	121·3	125·7	126·6	131·6	140·9	9·9	3·9	7·1	5·7	11·3
All industries and services	105·2	108·8	116·3	119·9	123·2	125·3	129·9	141·1	7·9	3·7	8·6	4·8	12·6
All industries and services (Seasonally adjusted)	103·0	106·5	119·9	122·7	123·0	123·0	129·9	137·7	8·0	5·6	6·0	3·5	12·0

(Source: *Employment and Productivity Gazette*.)

¹Calculate from new series.

and construction went up by 6·8 per cent in 1968–9 and 10·5 per cent in 1969–70. In chemicals the increases were greater, with 11 per cent and 14·3 per cent. All manufacturing earnings increased by 7·7 per cent in 1968–9 and by 12·8 per cent in 1969–70.

When we look at some of the industries which achieved spectacular increases, as distinct from firms which introduced productivity bargains and gave their employees rises of over 20 per cent, we find that the exhibition industry raised minimum wages by some 60 per cent in just over three years. This shows the effect of a strike threat two or three weeks before an exhibition or trade fair when the manufacturers have made their arrangements, invited many customers from overseas, and have sunk a great deal of money into the arrangements. Under these conditions the unions or groups of workers are almost in the same position as dockers with a banana boat in mid-July. By contrast, electrical contracting minimum wages rose only 19 per cent. But in these industries, as in a number of others, the important point is that the minimum wage often bears little resemblance to the earnings pattern; in electrical engineering, earnings rose by 30 per cent in four years.

Pay, however, does not guarantee quality, and the fact that earnings or pay rise by 7 or 8 per cent year by year does not mean a corresponding rise in productivity, quality or consumer satisfaction. For example, minimum rates in motor vehicle retailing and repair rose by 30 per cent in three and a half years, which means that earnings rose rather more; yet a *Which* survey into the standard of repairs carried out by a sample of garages showed that some 97 per cent did unsatisfactory or inferior work.

Earnings in a related industry, vehicles, where a barrage of newspaper criticism, hostile TV comment and a consumer shift to buying foreign cars showed that there was dissatisfaction with the product, rose some 40 per cent in four years. By contrast, in textiles, earnings rose by 35 per cent in the same period, and in clothing and footwear by only 27 per cent.

We can see from the relative differences in earnings over the period mid-1966 to mid-1970 that the industries which could raise productivity or use strike-power effectively, or could put pressure on the government or industry, were able to raise their earnings faster than others. Strikes in the vehicle industry are frequent and the manufacturer has an inelastic and buoyant demand for cars (though this may change in the next few years as more consumers acquire a taste for, or appreciation of, foreign cars).

Pay movements in the public sector

Wages in the public sector started to move forward rapidly in order to catch up on the ground lost to the private sector. The resistance shown by the Labour government to wage demands by public servants melted away in the last few months before the general election of 1970, and large increases were given, e.g. government industrial workers got increases of over 15 per cent.

The movement of white-collar salaries followed the same pattern of increases as that of the manual workers, as can be seen by comparing manual workers in local government with the white-collar grades. After being constrained by the productivity requirements in incomes policy, public servants started once again to rely heavily on the argument of comparability.

The new shift in the last year of incomes policy was not so much the percentage increase as the reduction of the time interval between the increases, e.g. 5 per cent at six months intervals adds up to a yearly 10 per cent or so. The industries with the longest intervals between awards were those with the lowest-paid workers, often under the aegis of wages councils, or the public servants, whose claims, unless they had the advantage of strike-threat power, or public sympathy, could be postponed for a considerable period. This can be seen from the effects of incomes policy on the following groups.

Increases for the police were held up for two and a half years until March 1967. Thereafter they moved more quickly as they became more insistent and young policemen voted with their feet and left the force. The time interval between their awards fell as follows; thirty months, eighteen months, sixteen months, twelve months. The four pay awards, beginning in March 1967 and ending in February 1971, brought the police about 49 per cent forward, probably the largest pay increase of any of the public services and indicating the public alarm with the rising crime rates and the success of the 'law and order' campaigns. The police also benefited from the fact that crime has a faster growth rate than any industry.

Nurses had to wait two and a half years, from June 1965 to October 1967, for their 4 per cent. Then, as in the case of the police, the intervals between the awards narrowed: twenty-seven months, fifteen months, then ten months. Their case, like that of the police, rested on shortage of recruits, the need to make the service more attractive, and strong public sympathy for their claim, assisted by their own militant campaign in putting it

Q

forward. The combined awards received by the nurses since 1967 amounted to an increase of 48 per cent.

The teachers did less well than either the nurses or the police. They also had to wait almost as long (two and a quarter years, until July 1967) for their first award under incomes policy. They then received $9\frac{1}{2}$ per cent, then $7\frac{1}{2}$, then a further 12 per cent. This made an increase of 35 per cent over the period, and the teachers were claiming over 30 per cent in February 1971, when they were offered 8 per cent by the authorities. They then dropped their claim to 15 per cent and matters remained in deadlock for many weeks. The time intervals were longer apart at first than the others above (twenty-seven months, then twenty-one, then twelve months).

The civil service clerical and other related groups in the civil service kept their position in the wages and salaries race fairly well. They were assisted in this by the pay research unit of the civil service which worked on a basis of comparability with jobs in industry and commerce and in the public services.

When we look at the time-lag between awards for manual workers in local authorities and the small amounts which they received in the first three years of incomes policy (in March 1967, they received 5 per cent after eighteen months, and 4 per cent six months later), we can see the pressures building up which produced the two strikes of dustmen and resulted in increases of 10 per cent after the first strike and 14 per cent after the second.

Government attempts to hold back wage increases in the public sector to compensate for increases in the private sector above the norm led to the pattern seen above: relatively small increases up to 1968 or 1969 followed by increasing resentment and union pressures, followed by larger increases, sometimes preceded by strike action, or threats of such action, and sometimes as a result of the increases got by others using such actions. Militancy which led to pay rises added fuel to the frustration of other employees who were worried about rapidly rising prices. One of the effects of this mood was to bring the normally peaceful local government white-collar employees to threaten to strike on election day 1970, when many thousands of them were to man the polling booths up and down the country. The threat was sufficient to tip the balance and their claim was speedily met, with increases for APTC staff of 12·5 to 13·1 per cent. The settlement followed months of discord and argument in negotiation after a relatively poor award and a repudiation of the agreement by NALGO members. The government were in no mood to risk a confrontation of an embarrassing nature before and during the election and let the award go through. It is clear that the present government, with more than two years of government behind them, are prepared to resist large wage claims. A distinction should be drawn between the periodicity of awards in the public services, which have been shown to be slow for the first three years of incomes policy, and those in the public sector industries where there is more of an industrial background and also a tradition of militancy which made the Labour government more hesitant to put the brake on negotiations. The railwaymen are a case in point as they have been used to an annual pay award, supplemented in recent years by productivity negotiations.

Generally speaking, public industries have followed the private sector practice of the annual wage round, whereas the public services mentioned above, as well as others, lost money on two counts: they lagged behind for most of the period in percentage increases and, second, they lost money due to the long intervals between pay settlements, when their previous awards were whittled away by rising prices.

Principles of pay in the public services

'Within the vast body of persons employed in the Civil Service, the National Health Service and the Public Corporations, no consistent standards are applied, and no coherent wage and salary policy emerges' (Baroness Wootton, Preface to Hilda Kahn, *Salaries in the Public Services in England and Wales*, Allen & Unwin, London, 1963).

The lack of principles and the triumph of expediency is still as evident today in the determination of pay in the public services as it was during Hilda Kahn's study of the pay situation in the 1950s. This has happened despite the repeated statements of the various authorities who have attempted to lay down principles, notably the Royal Commission on the Civil Service 1953–5 which produced the Priestley Report (Cmnd 9613, 1955), which defined 'fairness' as 'fair comparison', and stated: 'The primary principle of civil service pay should be fair comparison with the current remuneration of outside staffs employed on broadly comparable work' (p. 194).

A number of committees have considered principles for pay in the public services in a number of reports: civil service, education (Burnham Scales) and the Post Office. A fairly complex system of pay has evolved based on the employee's type of education (the kind of qualifications obtained, whether they were got through educational or professional or technical training), the age of the employees, whether they have to supervise others or not, and the responsibility for particular jobs (measurement is difficult here). The numbers of population in an area is one of the factors in local government pay, as is experience under the Burnham Scales in education. Numbers of employees in public services receive a pay supplement for being stationed in London. Nearly all public services have a salary scale with increments which vary from 4–5 grades to 19–20 grades. Underlying these factors, as a broad foundation, lies the principle of 'fair comparison'.

Comparability raises the important question of defining the comparable jobs. University teachers argued for comparability before the National Incomes Commission and were told: 'Instances of true comparability which may safely be acted upon are rare indeed. . . . Attempts which have been made by artificial means to produce an equation of reward between groups of which the work can be described as similar only on more or less violent assumptions do a disservice to industrial peace and make their inevitable contribution to inflation' (NIC, 'Remuneration of Academic Staff in Universities and Colleges of Advanced Technology', Cmnd 2317, 1964, para. 82).

In this case, NIC rejected the argument that the jobs of university teachers were comparable with other groups. Professor Fogarty, submitting the claim of the AUT to NIC, thought that comparability could be achieved by job evaluation which 'makes it possible to assess the level of work which given individuals or occupational groups are actually being called on to do . . . when pay data are added, the three factors of work, pay and capacity can be compared, if not with absolute precision, at any rate to a useful degree of approximation' (M. P. Fogarty, 'The National Incomes Commission', *British Journal of Industrial Relations*, November 1964, p. 368).

Whatever the merits of job evaluation, it has not been widely used as a basis for 'fair comparisons' in the public services. The main recommendation for its use in the civil service was put forward in the Fulton Report (Cmnd 3638, 1968), where it was seen as a tool for restructuring pay and grading. Yet job evaluation cannot be used as the sole measure of jobs within a firm, industry or service. It must respond to market forces, or comparability, and it will be challenged in negotiations with the union.

Critics of Fulton on job evaluation have said that 'A unified job evaluation scheme for the whole civil service may very well be impossible to institute. And even if it were possible, it could easily create more pay problems than it solved' (M. J. Fores and J. B. Heath, 'The Fulton Report', *Public Administration*, Spring 1970, p. 22).

The essential points of job evaluation centre upon the factors to be included in the assessment, what relative weight they will have, how the jobs compare with each other, and how the factor or points system shall be converted to money. Fores and Heath, in the above study, fault job evaluation in the civil service on almost all these points. They say that job evaluation rates the jobs not the person, whereas 'the civil service pay structure is one based on people, not jobs' (p. 17).

The Prices and Incomes Board showed an interest in job evaluation and published a report which described an increase of interest in the method, and its use by a growing number of companies. Some writers and businessmen see job evaluation as a means of setting up a national 'job grid' so that an incomes policy could be based on a scientific study of jobs and pay.

The PIB, as already stated, saw its main aim as that of linking pay to productivity, and its secondary aim as achieving social justice for the low-paid. What was its effect on the principles of pay in the public services, as outlined above? In its first year, in the report on electricity supply, it allowed the white-collar workers to follow the increase given to manual workers from a productivity deal. The Board justified this, not on the grounds of productivity, but on 'a sense of grievance' amongst the white-collar workers.

The report on railway staff had to admit that, as above, comparisons still had to play an important part, though it was hoped that these would diminish in future negotiations. Although a few concessions were made, the threatened national strike made these of little importance, and comparability continued to be a constant factor.

The armed forces and the higher civil service were successful with the comparability argument. The Scottish teachers were not. Nor had the Board much success in preventing comparability for the busmen, though they did so for a few strife-torn months. The industrial civil servants received an award on their pay having 'fallen out of line'.

The seven references in the public sector breached incomes policy on the issue of comparability and showed how deep-rooted the issues of relative comparisons were.

In later years, the Board resisted comparability for the local authority manual workers, suggesting increased productivity and incentives. The local authorities were slow to take the advice, and the long-term effects of throttling back on comparability led directly to the dustmen's strikes of 1969 and 1970 and the consequent raising of their wages unrelated to productivity.

The Board had uneven success in ousting comparability in its third year. More groups in the public sector began to use productivity concepts in their negotiations, but the success of this depended on whether they were capital-intensive or otherwise. Electricity supply workers claimed productivity increases, but as a capital-intensive industry they were bound to benefit from this line of argument. Busmen, as a labour-intensive industry, clung to the comparability arguments and resolved to sell their surplus men dearly. Nurses had big increases due to labour shortage and comparability.

Pilots in the public sector continued to soar through the incomes policy barrier, though their principles of 'fair comparison' were based on the pay of pilots abroad, particularly those of the USA. On the other hand, groups with little bargaining power, such as university teachers, had comparability rejected on the grounds that such claims were inflationary. Doctors and dentists had little difficulty in sustaining their claims based on comparability, as no government, Labour or Conservative, wanted to risk a clash with them.

The Board's report on higher civil servants could be said to mark the end of the attempt to dispense with comparability, as it agreed to increases up to 63 per cent over three years, in order to bring these salaries into line with industry and commerce.

This account of the Board's sorties into the public sector shows that it did not succeed in doing away with the doctrine of 'fair comparison', nor did it succeed in defining it, though it did much to spread the ideas of job evaluation and efficiency bargaining which involved some measure of job measurement.

Comparability and the cost of living, the latter claim remaining more muted through the years, proved to be more powerful and enduring grounds for claims in the public sector, than did either productivity or social justice. Comparability and the cost of living emerged in full flower, not only unscathed but triumphant after five years of incomes policy, in the Kindersley Report of mid-1970. The impression which one receives on reading the Kindersley Report is that this review body set out to discover arguments for raising the salaries of doctors and dentists; so that their objectives were far more wide-ranging than almost any other group in the country. Compared with the austere arguments of the PIB reports, Kindersley reads like an account of an American trial lawyer at work defending his client; they sought to attract recruits, to stop losses from emigration, to pay more for the higher work load, to make general practice more attractive, to improve the efficiency of the NHS by adjusting 'the very difficult manpower situation' and 'to improve the morale of doctors generally' as well as looking at comparable earnings.

The terms of reference of the review body were admitted to be very wide, but the Pilkington Commission who had paved the way for them had suggested that three factors which would always be relevant were 'changes in the cost of living, the movement of earnings in other professions, and the quality and quantity of recruitment in all professions'.

At the same time, the review body had to pay heed to the criteria of incomes policy. They surmounted this difficulty by restating their terms of reference, and saying 'we have a primary responsibility towards the community for the medical and dental professions.' This statement shows both the independence of the Kindersley Committee from incomes policy and also the high standing of the medical profession, since no other body or tribunal had made the same statement about nurses, medical auxiliaries, or the whole field of education.

The central part of the case for higher salaries for doctors rested on two main points, known in lower-paid circles as the labour shortage argument: how to recruit doctors and how to prevent them from emigrating while the NHS is increasingly staffed by doctors from the Commonwealth. The key point seemed to be how to prevent young doctors from emigrating to countries like the USA, where doctors are paid much more for less work.

The points of interest for the public services lie in the Kindersley Report's treatment of comparability. An estimate was made of careers earnings, which consisted of 'taking the average earnings of each age group, multiplying them by the number of years in the group . . . and adding them all together' (op. cit., p. 23). Having done this, which was a useful exercise in salary negotiation, they then drew a comparison with a similar exercise in 1955–6, and found that the compound rate of salary increase was only 4 per cent compared with $5\frac{1}{2}$ per cent for professions with reliable statistics; a series of calculations produced a claim of 30 per cent, based on rises in comparable salaries. This figure included a figure as an 'inflationary hedge' against comparative salaries rising, 'projected forward to March 1971, the mid-point of the forthcoming review period'.

The effects on the salaries in the public sector if comparisons going back for twelve years were admitted, would be a disruptive factor in negotiations. Miners have claimed that they fell in a few years from first place in the wages table to twelfth or thirteenth, but this had little effect on the government. The conclusion we can draw from the Kindersley Report is that the principles of pay in the public services depend partly on the bargaining power of the parties, and on public concern for, and government interest in, the efficiency of the particular service. Both the Labour and Conservative governments felt unable to pay the 30 per cent claim in full, although the Labour government agreed to 30 per cent for the young doctors, then decided there were 'compelling reasons' not to pay the senior medicals more than 15 per cent. The review body resigned and the 1970 Conservative government also decided not to pay the 30 per cent, but added 5 per cent to Labour's 15 per cent. A new independent review body was set up with the same terms of reference as its predecessor, though the comparability factor had become far more muted. The findings of the new body were to be honoured unless there were 'compelling reasons' for not doing so. The new government made some move towards unifying the research work of several review bodies in the public sector by creating the Office of Manpower Economics (OME, which partly replaced, with different functions, the PIB).

The aim of the OME, while the government still abjures an incomes policy, is to carry out *ad hoc* enquiries into manpower and pay movements. This means that pay movements and 'fair comparison' in the public sector will be dealt with in a fragmentary manner. Professor Fogarty's comment on this is as valid today as it was in 1964: 'But the Treasury, though it has been made to accept fair comparison under that or some other name as applying to a whole series of public services, has never accepted this or any other principle as applying to them all. It has insisted on fighting the case of each service one by one; the Civil Services, the Forces, the doctors and dentists, the police and probation service, the nurses and other health service workers, the school and university teachers . . . the railwaymen, the postmen, the busmen, and the power workers' (Fogarty, op. cit., p. 370).

The sudden death of the PIB, in November 1970, ended a Board which might, left for a few more years and provided with a workable incomes policy, have produced some bases for 'fair comparison' based on a realistic and accurate comparison of related salaries and wages drawn from its extensive inquiries into British industry. This vast body of work and information is presumably to be sterilised, and the public services will be left with little more basis for 'fair comparison' than the present work of the Civil Service Pay Research Unit. It is little wonder that arbitrators and negotiators in the public sector are groping around in a mist with different types of compasses when the following exchange could take place in parliament during the 1971 Post Office strike: in reply to a question 'Are the Post Office workers receiving a just wage? If not, they should be given a just wage', the Secretary of State for Employment, Mr Carr, replied: 'What people have not yet discovered is how, in this or in any other country, to find an impartial authority that will lay down a scale of relativity which seems to be justified in all the circumstances. If that were so, life might be easier but that is not the case' (*The Times*, 2 February 1971).

This is an unsatisfactory answer to a deep-rooted problem. The three million or so workers in the public sector cannot always argue productivity or profits in the way that unions in the private sector can do. The government is under an obligation to set up standards of pay and conditions which satisfy the concept of 'fair comparison'. Enough work has been done in the past ten years, partly by the Civil Service Pay Research Unit, and more particularly by the PIB to provide better foundations for comparability than have been possible before. A beginning might be made by the government commissioning research of this nature on the files of the civil service and, more particularly, of the PIB.

8

Retrospect and prospect

The attempt at an incomes policy between 1965 and 1970 was the most comprehensive attempt at influencing wages and salaries since 1945. Looking back at the objectives in the 'Joint Statement of Intent on Productivity, Prices and Incomes', it is hard to see, at first glance, what were its achievements in the five years. The new Conservative government announced before, during and after the 1970 election that incomes policy had been tried and failed. They were returning to the more traditional forces and competitive atmosphere of an economy where market forces and reduced government spending with less taxation would provide incentive and stimulus to raise productivity and increase real living standards.

The 'Joint Statement' of December 1964 set out a series of noble perspectives: 'a rapid increase in output and real incomes combined with full employment. More equitable distribution of the new wealth to satisfy social need and justice'. All this, as well as a pledge from the TUC and the employers 'to keep increases in wages, salaries and other forms of incomes in line' with productivity increases, while keeping prices stable. Re-reading the 'Joint Statement' we can see that exhortation is not policy, and that the TUC and the employers could not deliver what they had promised.

The failures did not lie in the Statement, although the phrases now read like clichés. An incomes policy can best exist in an atmosphere of confidence in economic policy and the knowledge that the economy is expanding. Several factors conspired against confidence or expansion. The first was the atmosphere of crisis when the Labour government took office in October 1964: the run on the pound, the famous £800 million trade deficit and the decision not to devalue the pound. There were also a large number of pending wage claims in the pipeline when the Labour government took over, so that a condition of 'built-in' wage inflation existed.

The prime minister told the House of Commons of the difficulties facing an incomes policy in August 1965: 'the immediate problems of differentials, of leapfrogging and outstanding claims, many of them undeniably strong, many of them conceded ... in principle before we came in. Let us remember that the most successful machinery for an incomes policy in the world, that in Sweden, took twenty years to evolve. Certainly, we cannot afford a tenth of that time, but do not let us dismiss ours as a failure after only three months. Equally, let us be clear that one cannot preach the doctrine of freedom for other people to exploit a seller's market and then exclude labour from it.'* These few sentences contain the essence of the difficulties that were to beset incomes policy over the next five years: outstanding and sometimes long-postponed claims, leapfrogging, especially in engineering and cars, and the exploitation of a seller's market for labour by some unions or strategic groups.

The greater rate of economic growth promised did not material-ise and the National Plan of 1965, which forecast a rate of growth of some 4 per cent per year, collapsed in a short time. Wages and salaries were to increase faster than productivity, and the resultant balance of payments crisis brought a run on the pound and the threat of devaluation being faced by the government. This forced the government into a prices and incomes 'freeze' followed by six months 'severe restraint'.

The July 1966 'freeze' followed the March election in which the Labour government had received an increased majority (100) in parliament from the electors. This victory encouraged unions in their belief that they could press forward with wage claims nationally, assisted by their annual conferences, which were usually held in the April or May period. The unemployment figure in June was low, about 1·2 per cent. Earnings had risen at some 8 per cent the previous year while output was only rising at 2 per cent per annum. In addition to these factors making for more inflation, the average weekly hours worked in industry fell from forty-two and a half to forty and a half. Overtime did not rise correspondingly, which had been one of the usual features of a fall in hours worked. This, to some observers, confirmed the impression that British industry as a whole was badly overmanned, a view put in its extreme form by W. Allen,† who stated that British industry was overmanned by a factor of two.

The July 'freeze' went with a government decision to allow unemployment to rise. They were influenced in this by the fact

* House of Commons Debates, *Hansard*, 2 August 1965.
† 'Half-Time Britain', *Sunday Times*, 1 March 1964.

that some unions and groups of workers were prepared to fight for their wage increases to the last ditch. The seamen's strike of May 1966 lasted for six and a half weeks and the government used this as a test case in resisting extravagant wage claims. The strike had a bad effect on sterling and was one of the factors leading to a run on the pound.

The aftermath of the July 1966 crisis was a movement by the government, albeit silently, towards the 'Paish line' which stated simply that with under $2\frac{1}{2}$ per cent unemployed, an incomes policy was not possible. With over $2\frac{1}{2}$ per cent, an incomes policy was not necessary. Whatever the refinements of this line of argument, the message was that more unemployment would reduce total spending power and more importantly, slow down the wage demands of the unions or local shop stewards in a situation of labour scarcity.

The argument for more unemployment (or 're-deployment' or 'labour surplus') as a brake on wage rises overlooks the fact that in many sectors of the industry where 'key' bargains are made, labour on strike cannot be replaced by the employer due to union pressures and controls. Nor, as has been increasingly pointed out by those who look at labour problems abroad, has higher unemployment been a brake on rising wages in the USA. Last, though Professor Paish could not have foreseen this, increases in unemployment pay and redundancy pay enabled large numbers of workers to stay unemployed longer than they had done in the past, while their higher purchasing power contributed to general inflation (which was also worsened by their lost production).

In spite of rising unemployment, the period of 'standstill and severe restraint' which slowed down the rise in the wage index, proved to be only a temporary breathing space, and there was pressure on the pound from the foreign exchanges from the middle of 1967 onwards. The growing crisis was heightened by a series of bad trade figures which were reflected in the balance of trade figures (worsened by the effects of the dock strike).

The relevance of the above discussion of economic pressures and effects is that the devaluation of 1967 was depicted as a defeat for the Labour government and a bad blow for the country. The Labour government of 1964 could have devalued on taking office, but they were still sensitive of being dubbed the 'party of devaluation' as they had been called in 1949. So they struggled to maintain the pound for three years, 1964–7, at its high parity figure of $2.80. The constant movements of 'hot' money, the bad balance of trade figures, and the frequent loans which were necessary from international bankers, showed the basic imbalance in the exchange rate. More importantly, there was the effect on the economy and on the morale of unions and management. Frequent warnings about restrictions on spending, on higher taxation, and the eventual rise in unemployment, all contributed to a general sense of frustration, of economic stringency, of powerlessness in the face of rising prices, almost of national humiliation. This showed clearly in the opinion polls, in the by-elections for parliament, and in the landslide against Labour in the municipal elections in 1967 and 1968, when the Labour Party lost virtually all the major towns and cities in Britain, including some which it had held for forty years.

The trade union support for an incomes policy was now breaking down; leading figures like Frank Cousins were attacking the policy, and more union leaders were critical of the PIB and its judgments. The support of the left-wing intellectuals was also turning sour, (one exception being the *New Statesman* which was at times in favour of a statutory incomes policy*), and one characteristic comment in 1968 was: 'the incomes policy has been damagingly punctuated by big rises for doctors, judges, cabinet ministers and other wealthy persons, not notably needy, or rapidly increasing their productivity, or in short (as opposed to artificially restricted) supply.'† The 1969 TUC congress passed a resolution opposing 'anti-trade union legislation' and 'interference in trade union affairs'. They demanded the repeal of the 1966 Prices and Incomes Act.

In the three years 1964–7, the Labour government had squandered the goodwill and potential support for an incomes policy expressed in their two election victories, by struggling to keep the pound at its high parity figure. This inhibited plans for economic expansion and led to an excessive respect for the balance of trade figures, whose downward plunge into deficit led to an atmosphere of growing gloom and falling confidence. Ideally, an incomes policy needs an atmosphere of economic expansion, hope and confidence. This could have been achieved if Labour had begun by devaluing either in 1964, or in 1966 when there was widespread evidence that the public supported the standstill on incomes rises. As this stimulus was not given to the economy before late 1967,

---

* The *New Statesman* argued for greater regulation of incomes and profits and wrote of the injustices 'of a wage structure determined by purely market forces, in which powerfully organised bodies of men can extract wages greatly in excess of their deserts and at the expense of their fellow men ... free-for-all trades unionism is the enemy both of socialist planning and natural justice' (p. 574, 21 October 1966).
† M. Lipton in *Matters of Principle* (by Tyrell Burgess *et al.*), Penguin, Harmondsworth, 1968, p. 24.

much of the work of the PIB was inhibited or damaged by the shifts in national and international economic policy. The high taxes imposed by the Labour government as part of the credit 'squeeze' increasingly affected workers' earnings, and wage claims rose to compensate for higher marginal taxation and other fiscal measures dealing with credit borrowing, purchase tax, and SET which raised prices.

Devaluation did give an impetus to exports and had further beneficial results in the long run. But recovery was slower than hoped, as periodic outflows of 'hot' money showed the nervousness of the international investors and the feeling that there might be another devaluation. Interest rates remained at a high point, which helped the inflow of funds but inhibited domestic expansion, so that the balance of payments position was still gloomy.

Average earnings continued to rise far in advance of productivity: they rose by 8 per cent in 1969, while retail prices rose by some 5 per cent. The increase in 'real income' in 1969 was about $\frac{1}{2}$ per cent, as compared with nearly 2 per cent in the previous year (London and Cambridge Economic Bulletin, published in *The Times*, 4 February 1971). The small increase in 'real income' led to more wage pressure by workers and unions in an attempt to raise their living standards.

In this atmosphere Mrs Barbara Castle brought in the Industrial Relations Bill (preceded by the White Paper 'In Place of Strife') which was an attempt by the Labour government to deal with the problem of unofficial strikes. Proposals that unofficial strikers could eventually be fined by industrial courts or by later criminal law enforcement, were dropped from the Bill in the face of trade union and Parliamentary Labour Party pressure. The government, faced with a collapsing incomes policy, wanted a legal check on unofficial strikes which they hoped would remove the mainspring from a number of wage pressures. As one writer pointed out about the Bill: 'It was also meant as a psychological substitute for the incomes legislation.'* The government's dropping of the so-called 'penal clauses' (sanctions against unofficial strikers) from the Bill was apparently taken as a weakening of incomes policy. Wage demands were pressed and granted in the last quarter of 1969 and continued throughout the period up to the general election of 1970. Average earnings rose from 8 per cent in 1969 to 12 per cent in 1970 with retail prices rising by over 6 per cent.

There is no doubt, in spite of evidence to the contrary, that most citizens thought that they had lived through a period of economic

* S. Brittan, *Steering the Economy*, Penguin, Harmondsworth, 1971, p. 407.

stringency and crisis from 1964 to 70, and that the policy on incomes and prices had failed. This last belief was a major factor in the defeat of the Labour government and the return of the Conservatives in June 1970. When the Labour government came to office in 1964, they inherited an over-expanding economy with rising wage demands and an £800 million deficit on the balance of payments. When they left office they passed on a situation with rapidly rising wage demands, a slowly-expanding economy and rapidly rising prices, with a compensatory strong balance of payments position. It could be said that they sacrificed economic growth, which would have raised real incomes faster, to 'keeping the pound strong' and the balance of payments safe. Yet the incomes policy had some effect on prices, as a Board member commented: 'Contrary to a widely held impression the Prices and Incomes Board did some of its most effective work on prices.' But this was defeated by rises due to devaluation and by taxation which raised prices.*

Incomes policy and its effect on collective bargaining

Thus far we have dealt with the macro-economic effects of incomes policy. In retrospect we can say that this aspect was always over-emphasised by economists and politicians in discussing and setting up the policy. One monetary economist, in debating with the writer, said that once the country agreed on the need for an incomes policy, the rest would be simple. The econometricians would calculate the growth rate of the economy and estimate the share of the different factors of production. The amount available for wages in the coming year would be announced and the unions or some joint committee or board would agree on the share-out. We argued that the macro-economic calculations were the simplest part of the exercise and that the most difficult part would be persuading the different unions or groups of workers to accept a 'norm', as the idea of a 'norm' was that some groups would get less than the 3 per cent and some would get more. This is, in fact, what happened. It was naive of the government, or the PIB, to argue that the idea of a 3 per cent or 4 per cent 'norm' was an average. The very existence of the figure X per cent became a target to beat, not a figure to accept as long as other unions were triumphantly achieving rises of 6 or 9 or even 12 per cent. The incomes policy also overlooked the difficulties facing trade union leaders who

---

* J. Mortimer, 'The rise and fall of the PIB', *Personnel Management*, London, February 1971, p. 21.

accepted the idea of the 'norm'. If they settled for an increase less than the 3 per cent, then their members, few of whom thought that their claim justified accepting less than the 'norm', would put pressure on them, or militants would arise at local level or in the national union who would then gain support. The shift of power in the trade unions from national level to local level, underlined by the Donovan Report, is reinforced by an incomes policy which gives local groups the opportunities to circumvent the agreements reached at national level, or at least to frustrate the national intentions of such agreements.

Economists, once they are convinced of the need for an incomes policy (and numbers are not), tend to overlook the difficulties involved in its micro-economic aspects as the different unions battle with employers for their relative shares of the available wages. One noted liberal economist puts the case with trustful simplicity: 'Given a reasonably affluent price level . . . workers may be more content to accept a moderate increase with stable prices than a larger one with the prospect of partial loss from rising living costs. Since the corporation is not experiencing rising costs, it can accept stable prices as its part of the bargain. All that remains is for the state to give a clear initiative in this regulation.'*

The reality is more complex than the dream. The Labour government did achieve a pact on paper between the unions and management at a national level. But though the industrial and labour generals signed, they were unable to impose military discipline on their troops. The TUC can lead, but there is no compulsion, or indeed tradition, which says that unions must follow; or even if the unions follow, as numbers did for a time, they themselves cannot or will not police all the local agreements which their factory branches make. The employers' associations for their parts, could only urge their troops not to set a bad example to others. Thousands of small employers did not consider themselves bound by such agreements and numbers of large employers found their way round and through the various labour-supply and pay difficulties which incomes policy had created for them.

One of the chief difficulties which the employers faced was the unofficial strike. As a militant shop steward once put it: 'I don't know of any difficulty with management that a short sharp strike won't cure.' While this statement is not true for all firms, it was true of a sufficient number to have made the number of unofficial strikes rise to 95 per cent of all strikes by 1968. The union attitude to the unofficial strike was equivocal: some union leaders conceded

* J. K. Galbraith, *The New Industrial State*, Penguin, Harmondsworth, 1967, p. 260.

that such strikes undermined the authority of the union and the credibility of any agreements that had been negotiated. Yet as agreements were not usually enforceable at law, most unions took the attitude that there must be some local reasons which justified the strike and were slow to condemn such actions until the strike (usually of short duration) was over. There were also some officials who used the strike as a bargaining lever with the employer, saying that while they disapproved of it and had told the men this, the men were so incensed about the delay in dealing with their claims that there was no chance of restraining them.

In spite of the failure to achieve widespread observance of a 3 or $3\frac{1}{2}$ per cent 'norm', the incomes policy had some beneficial effect on collective bargaining. The PIB had always insisted on linking pay to productivity as far as possible and spelt this out in many papers and reports over its lifetime. As a third, and officially neutral, party it had been able to enter firms and talk to both management and unions and then to make recommendations of a kind that neither of the two parties might have been able to make to each other. Even when these suggestions were not implemented, at least the fashion of arguing in terms of productivity or efficiency began to spread. The emphasis was not so much on increasing workers' efforts at the point of production, although the Board did look at payment by results schemes, but on changing working conditions and making more effective use of labour. In some instances, the Board made suggestions about increasing management efficiency, and as management consultancy is not highly developed in Britain, they were able to fill this role in an unofficial and informal manner. Those who did part-time work for the PIB were frequently struck by the slowness with which some industries appeared to follow, or wished to follow, the best practices in their field. There was a good deal of ignorance of methods which other firms were using successfully. The fault was not only that of management: unions and groups of workers had successfully resisted attempts to make more effective use of labour. The PIB reports were able to point this out and although their suggestions had little effect in an industry like printing or newspapers, there were other industries where such suggestions pointed the way towards productivity bargaining.

Productivity bargaining became a cult for a time. As McKersie put it, the Fawley Agreement became a quasi-religious book for British industry.* It could be added that a large number of subse-

---

* R. B. McKersie, 'Productivity Bargaining, deliverance or delusion', *Personnel Management*, September 1966.

R

quent agreements were far less successful than the Fawley Agreement had been, or that oil refining (Fawley) and other flow or process industries with high capital/low labour costs were the best areas for spectacular wage increases traded off against greater job flexibility and less manpower. Such industries also have a high growth rate and can afford yearly wage increases for workers without much difficulty. Discussion about productivity led to numbers of 'phoney' bargains where the employer got the bargaining without the productivity, and wage increases unrelated to productivity were approved by the Department of Employment and Productivity, not out of duplicity, but because the detailed figures for such calculations were not available. Some PIB investigators who went to firms were struck by the fact that frequently few figures were available to measure the relationship between pay and productivity, so that some rule-of-thumb assessment had to be made.

In spite of the 'phoney' bargains, there were many genuine advances made in a number of industries, and unions and negotiators began to recognise that they must make a number of suggestions about job flexibility and interchangeability, about retraining and training semi-skilled men to take on certain jobs, about overtime and absenteeism, and about unnecessary tea breaks (a sacred rite in British industry and one of the stumbling-blocks in many productivity agreements where the management complained that they were losing nearly an hour's work per day over this ceremony). The Board's study of hours of work, overtime and shiftworking (Report No. 161, Cmnd 4554) did much to convince industry that excessive overtime was a sign of managerial inefficiency, leading to slack work throughout the day in order to make overtime available, and making 'wage drift' inevitable.

The main advantage of productivity bargaining in this context was that it enlarged the area of collective bargaining and enabled management and unions to look at the totality of the work situation instead of arguing narrowly about wages and bonus rates. This was a new development in British industrial relations and was bringing the unions closer to the American form of collective bargaining.

Another promising development was that the unions began to display as much, if not more, interest in productivity bargaining than the employers did. The TUC's assistance was sought by the BBC to make a series of short films about productivity bargaining, where the principles were discussed and some cases examined. Thousands of booklets were printed and sold and hundreds of trade unionists were able to study the subject in day release courses sponsored jointly by the CBI and the TUC. Many of these were organised through universities and technical colleges. The effects of this mass education programme are difficult to estimate, as the television programme was shown at an off-peak time and was too simple for the active shop steward. Yet it did make many workers aware of the possibilities of productivity bargaining and they may have been less nervous about discussing this with management in negotiations.

One result of the wider interest in productivity was that the wide-reaching and often lengthy discussions between workers and management led to a greater exchange of ideas and information in some industries than had hitherto taken place, and the management had to agree to provide information about production and costs of a complexity they had not been asked for before. This helped to break down the traditional barriers of hostility and suspicion which had poisoned relations in some industries.

Over the period of incomes policy more and more unions declared their willingness to negotiate in terms of productivity, and a survey of union attitudes by Incomes Data Services Ltd, published in 1970, showed a contrast with the situation in 1966: 'Now the situation is very different almost all unions are ready to co-operate to negotiate productivity agreements at plant level or to negotiate guidelines nationally.'* At the same time, the survey said that few of them had the resources or staff to initiate such bargains themselves.

The TUC issued a booklet on the subject,† which dealt with the aims and characteristics of agreements, and dealt with a number of points such as gains to workers: 'The wages of all workers covered by productivity agreements have gone up. . . .' Wage structures in the plant could now be changed by job analysis and evaluation. They pointed out that most productivity agreements 'have been concluded in capital intensive industries where labour costs are small in relation to total production costs and the demand for the products of the industry is increasing' (ibid., p. 7). Bargaining in labour-intensive industries was more difficult and the purpose of the agreement was to reduce manpower. An interesting conclusion was that the line between joint consultation and negotiation could be crossed and the two processes merged, thus increasing 'union participation in the firm's decision making'. The support of the TUC for productivity bargaining helped the method to gain acceptance.

* IDS, 'Study on Unions and Productivity Bargaining', January 1970, p. 3.
† 'Productivity Bargaining', 1966.

R*

In practice there were a number of difficulties; while employers' groups and unions could agree nationally on pay and productivity guidelines, at local or plant level firms were reluctant to feed figures about pricing policy, production, profits and costs into negotiations with national or district union officials. While more information was sometimes given to the local shop stewards, management still felt that a high degree of secrecy was necessary on some figures, which some of their competitors or large customers would be glad to have.

The spread of productivity bargaining did not mean that this followed the guidelines of incomes policy. The PIB had meant this to be one of the cornerstones of economic growth: they returned to the theme several times with an interim report* and a full report† followed by another.‡ The advice of the Board and the DEP was that the benefits of the increased productivity should be a three-way split between employees, employers and customers with one-third going to each so that the customer shared in lower or stable prices. In practice this did not happen, as the unions were unwilling and the employer preferred to put the customer's share into profits. The IDS Survey said that 'Very little note is taken of any Government statements of policy on this question. . . . The productivity bargain is universally regarded as a means of negotiating higher pay on the best terms' (op. cit., p. 4).

Another defect was the failure on the part of management to achieve the productivity for which they had paid in advance. PIB Report No. 36 says that there is a good deal of ignorance about costs on the management side. Describing one well known agreement, the report says that 'the costing was rudimentary'. Some managements underestimated the difficulties of measurement which can be caused by changes in materials, product-mix and changing raw material costs.

Yet the fact that so many unions began to use the language of productivity, and acknowledge that such practices as excessive overtime, craft monopolies and restrictions on output, as well as a need for inter-job flexibility and a reduction of overmanning, existed, was a major step forward. The mutual recognition of problems is the first necessary step towards their solution, although a number of unions were attracted to productivity bargaining as a means of extending trade union control and power in industry rather than as a means of fighting inflation. Numbers of plant

---

* No. 23, December 1966.
† 'Productivity Bargaining', Report No. 36, Cmnd 3311, July 1967.
‡ 'Productivity Agreements', Report No. 123, Cmnd 4136, August 1969.

committees used these agreements to become virtually auto-nomous of national union control, and to strengthen their bargain-ing power. Productivity agreements demanded that long-term commitments had to be undertaken by the unions as to the points agreed on, and on the amounts to be paid.

By mid-1970, productivity bargaining had exhausted the impetus of its drive in the mid-1960s and many productivity negotiations were beginning to turn sour. There were several reasons for this. One of the first was that numbers of such productivity bargains resulted in a run-down in manpower. Even with a phased run-down, a halting of recruitment, earlier retirement and natural wastage, largely accepted in the mid-1960s with an unemployment level of some 1·2 to 1·5 per cent, men became more anxious as unemployment mounted to double this figure by 1969–70. Another reason was that the spectacular wage increases of 20–30 per cent were in many cases once-for-all productivity bargains; later bargains yielded more slender gains and unions came to prize jobs for their members more than small increases which could be bettered by straightforward strikes or strike threats. Third, there was the increasing militancy of important unions such as the Amalgamated Union of Engineering Workers (AUEW) and the TGWU with nearly three million members, who began to demand pay increases without 'productivity strings'. This attitude spread to other unions and 1970 marked the weakening of productivity bargaining as well as the collapse of incomes policy.

While a number of agreements were relatively successful, others broke down or were frustrated by local or factory groups who felt that unofficial strikes were necessary to resist certain changes or to improve their rates or earnings.

Incomes policy and strikes

The belief which goes with some substantial evidence, that many of our recent inflationary troubles are due to the cost-push effect of higher wages, has caused large numbers of people to point the finger at powerful trade unions or groups of shop stewards. This criticism is not confined to Conservatives, many of whom believe that inflation could be cured if wages could be restrained by supply and demand or by market forces and competition, along with the banning of the 'closed shop'. On the left, Labour govern-ment members and their advisers have also thought of ways of curbing trade union power to raise wage rates. The right's belief in market forces and the left's belief in an incomes policy both founder in the ability of groups to launch short, sharp, unofficial strikes in strategic places or at strategic times.

The Conservative Party were more strident in their 1970 electoral criticism: 'in terms of the actual number of strikes our postwar record is among the worst in the world.' The Labour government White Paper 'In Place of Strife' said that 95 per cent of all strikes were unofficial, that this was an increasing trend, and that they were short (2–3 days) in duration. The Donovan Commission was critical of unofficial strikes, although its report disappointed the public in not recommending legal restraints or sanctions on such strikes. In addition to those three reports, British newspapers, radio, and television appear to give strikes first priority,* so that the average citizens is bombarded with headlines and opinions about strikes, most of which are critical of the strikers and their claims, which by definition are inflationary and cause prices to rise.

There is an element of 'scapegoating' here, as this outcry has become a hardy annual: miners were striking during World War II, when strikes were virtually forbidden; dockers were striking in the late 1940s when the country was trying to find a peace-time footing; articles appeared on strikes in the 1950s, e.g. 'What is wrong with Britain's industrial relations? . . . A series of strikes . . . caused this question to be raised with growing impatience by the suffering British public.'† This statement could have been made at intervals for the past twenty or so years; the TUC and the CBI agreed on a joint investigation of strikes in 1964. However, the number of days lost through strikes has risen nearly five-fold since then, being 2,277,000 in 1964 and 10,970,000 in 1970.

The atmosphere of anxiety about strikes now, and the urgent nature of the remedies put forward, are due to a number of factors, of which one is the different nature and finance of the modern strike. The traditional view of the strike was that workers, usually on modest wages, went on short rations and endured hardships while the employer could afford to wait, or might hire other labour.

The situation today in industries where most strikes occur is very different from the older picture. If we exclude mining as a

---

* The British, more than most nations, appear to take a masochistic interest in criticising themselves. See in this context the perceptive remark of George Orwell: 'English literature, like other literatures, is full of battle-poems, but it is worth noticing that the ones that have won for themselves a kind of popularity are always a tale of disasters and retreats. . . . The most stirring battle-poem in English is about a brigade of cavalry which charged in the wrong direction' (George Orwell, *The Lion and the Unicorn*, Secker & Warburg, London, 1941, p. 19).
† 'Our Industrial Discontents', *Observer*, 14 August 1955.

special case (and the short, frequent strike in mining dropped sharply over the last ten or so years) then the strike-prone industries tend to be highly capitalised so that strikes are costly to the company, and other factors operate which make the employer wish to avoid strikes or disruption. Such industries as engineering, construction, metal manufacture, shipbuilding and marine engineering, air transport and docks (especially docks), usually have urgent customers or contracts, so that the unions or shop stewards are in a strong bargaining position.

Some large firms, and even medium ones in these industries, have heavy overheads on rent, interest, depreciation and salaries, as these have to be paid even if manual workers, who may be a minority group, do strike. Firms face a loss of customers who may buy expensive durables such as cars from other firms or foreign dealers. Such customers and overseas markets, which have taken money and years to build up, may be lost, and years pass before they can, if ever, be recovered.

In many firms and in some industries it has been easier for the employers to buy off a strike or strike threat by a wage increase which, in a capital-intensive industry, may only represent a small part of the total cost of production.

On the trade union/worker side, the threat of a strike may be sufficient to get the wage increase. If not, then a short unofficial strike can disrupt production, either by large groups (as in the case of the strike in the glass industry at Pilkington) or by small strategically-placed groups, such as the workers in a firm supplying brakes or other vital accessories for the car industry. Small-group strikes can often be the most disruptive, as eighty or so men in one process can put thousands in the factory out of work; likewise 300 drivers in a car-producing complex with 50,000 workers. One of the most ridiculous examples of this was the strike of the eight women lavatory attendants who managed to close a factory with several thousand employees, became known as the 'the loo ladies' and were the delight of the strike-sensation reporters.

To say that a strike is unofficial simply means that the union does not give it official support, but the union may give the strikers, or their leaders, much private support. Publicly the union will say that the strike is 'unfortunate' or 'the men are over-enthusiastic' or 'we are trying to get them back'. To the employer they will say that the unofficial strike shows how strongly the men feel about the issue. Newspaper criticism that unofficial strikes undermine the authority of the union miss the point, as this only happens where the union feels strongly that the men should go back. Few unions, if any, discipline members for unofficial strike action, so it is difficult to discover what any union really thinks about such strikes unless one is present at its executive meetings. Looking at the figures of strike benefits paid out yearly by unions who frequently have members on unofficial strike—e.g. the TGWU (docks, cars, buses, airlines and airports) and the AUEW (cars and engineering)— we can see that these large unions pay out little in strike or dispute money compared to state benefits. For example the TGWU, with one and a third million members, paid out £501,720 in 1969.* Even where a strike is made official, the weekly money paid is relatively small, ranging from the miners' 10s to the TGWU £4–5 and the engineers' £6. The classic example was that of the postmen, who were on official strike for six weeks and had no strike pay at all, as the union had no strike funds. Professor Turner points out that numbers of small short strikes are over before the union headquarters hear of them and that 'in about half the cases where strikes had begun without the union sanction and the union executive later became aware of them, it was decided that dispute benefit should be paid in retrospect'.† He then makes the point that the number of unofficial strikes is therefore much less than the official figure given and in his conclusions says 'The evidence that the pattern of industrial conflict in Britain is in some way different to that in other countries, as taking the form of frequent small strikes rather than a few big ones, is quite unconvincing.'‡

W. E. J. McCarthy, who worked as research director for the Donovan Commission, refutes a number of Turner's points and insists that Britain's strike problem is: '(1) A steady upward creep of small-scale unconstitutionalism which sometimes results in the creation of a strike-prone group in particular firms or plants. (2) The fact that sometimes unconstitutionalism results in the odd strike which causes a disproportionate amount of damage to the national economy and results in large numbers of workers who are not involved in it being laid off.'§

There is no doubt that McCarthy is right in his analysis. But there is still a mystery about how these many strikes, whether or

---

* *The Financial Times*, discussing the £133m held by all 328 registered unions, said: 'few unions would be able to last out long if they called all their members out on strike and paid them normal dispute benefit with no outside help' (7 December 1970). They might have added that few workers' families could last long on strike pay of £5 weekly. The Ford strike of early 1971 was more costly to the TGWU and the AUEW than almost any strike of the past five years, as it was lengthy and the two unions were paying out higher strike benefits than before.
† H. A. Turner, *Is Britain Really Strike-prone?*, Cambridge University Press, 1969, p. 22.
‡ Ibid., p. 44. Turner's detailed analysis merits reading in full.
§ W. E. J. McCarthy, 'The Nature of Britain's Strike Problem', *British Journal of Industrial Relations*, Vol. VIII, No. 2, July 1970, p. 235.

not they are legitimated later by the union, are financed. Unions pay out only a small proportion of their funds in dispute pay.

Strikes and state benefits

Recently it has been said that strikers, both official and unofficial, have their actions subsidised by the state and are able to stay out without the financial loss which they suffered in the past. One newspaper argued: 'for just as few other countries have so many unofficial strikes as Britain, so does practically no other make it so easy to stop work' (*Daily Telegraph*, 17 April 1969). The article went on to recommend that 'supplementary benefits should be confined to the families of official strikers'. This point of view, unacceptable to the Labour government and the TUC (although the Ministry of Social Security did consider the idea briefly), was put forward also by the president of NALGO in 1969, who said: 'Personally, I cannot help wondering if much of the real hardship has not been taken out of strikes. Social security benefits and income tax rebates provide a useful cushion' (*Guardian*, 11 June 1969). He agreed with the suggestion of the newspaper quoted above.

The Donovan Commission considered this aspect of state benefits to strikers and said: 'It is sometimes suggested that the sources of income open to strikers and those laid off as a result of strikes in the form of refunds of income tax, supplementary benefits for their dependents and so on, is such that it makes little difference to them if they are unable to draw unemployment benefit. We believe this suggestion to be ill-founded' (p. 256). Yet the only evidence the Commission offered was that, in the period 1962–6, only 8·4 per cent of the workers involved in stoppages of over two weeks received payments. While this Donovan view was correct at the time, it appears that the number has increased greatly since 1966, as the number of families receiv-

Table 11 *Supplementary benefits*

	1969 £ s d	1971 £ s d
Wife	3 14 0	4 3 0
Two children under 11 years	3 4 0	3 12 0
Rent allowance	3 10 0	4 0 0
Income tax rebate	3 10 0	3 10 0
Total	13 18 0	15 5 0

ing benefits, excluding families of workers laid off through strikes, has risen five or more times since 1964. As the authorities supply few figures, we can only make estimates.

A striker is not entitled to benefit for himself, but he can apply for his dependents. Income, strike pay and family allowance are deductible from supplementary benefits, but Table 11, on page 251, shows what a married man with two children under the age of eleven could be receiving.* The supplementary benefit paid to strikers' families had risen each year as follows:†

	£
1965	66,000
1966	128,000
1967	377,000
1968	334,000
1969	749,000
1970	2,500,000‡

Working days lost through strikes in the six years from 1965 to 1970 were:§

1965	2,925,000
1966	2,398,000
1967	2,787,000
1968	4,690,000
1969	6,846,000
1970	10,970,000

Strikes and Inflation

The strike has changed greatly over the past twenty years and particularly over the last decade. In the 1950s the Conservative government were anxious not to clash directly with the unions, and Lord Monckton became the Minister of Labour who could smooth out any dispute. The Cohen Committee, writing in 1958, and analysing the causes of the rise in prices and incomes, talked of 'the power of the Trade Unions in such a society as ours, particularly at times when Governments and public opinion generally are very anxious that industrial peace should be preserved.'||

* Information from the Department of Social Security.
† *Financial Times,* 17 June 1970.
‡ Secretary of State for Social Services, *Hansard,* 29 March 1971. He estimated that if new regulations about benefits and payments during strikes had been operative in June 1970, £1¼ million would have been saved. Recent legislation has reduced payments available to strikers and dependants.
§ *Financial Times,* 17 June 1970.
|| *Council on Prices, Productivity and Incomes,* HMSO, London, 1958.

During the 1960s trade union pressure mounted as seen both by the rising number of working days lost—eight million in 1969 and eleven million in 1970 (with the first three months of 1971 accounting for half the previous year's working days lost)—and by the number of strikes, most of which were unofficial, numbering over 3,000 in 1970. The notable factor here is that the number of strikes in mining dropped from around 2,000 to 200 in ten years, 1958 to 1968, while 'the frequency of stoppages in other industries, and particularly in the metal-working sector which is largely identified or associated with the engineering industry, has trebled'.*

In an inflationary situation the employer pays the wage increase and passes the added costs on to the consumer in higher prices. Numbers of firms and industries may raise prices within a few days of each other: oil companies, car firms, newspapers, engineering firms, banks, bakeries, steel firms, tend to do this. Customers grumble but pay, reserving their public outcries and protests for price rises in the public sector which, rightly or wrongly, serves as an inflationary scapegoat about which 'something should be done'.

From time to time strikers are told that the firm may go out of business, or that exports, or the customers, will suffer. As few firms had, by the end of 1970, closed down because of strikes, the threats appeared empty. Attitudes began to change after the Rolls-Royce redundancies in early 1971. In some situations, groups of workers might be prepared to see the firm go out of business if it could not meet wage demands. This would depend on: (a) the type of labour—whether skills were easily transferable or not; (b) whether alternative work was readily available in the area; (c) the length of service and age of the workers concerned. In category (c) workers might know that, even if the firm did close down, they would qualify for redundancy pay which, for the longer-serving workers, might range from a few hundred pounds to a maximum of around £1,000–£1,200. As this lump sum could amount to more than some would have at any time in their career, the fact that a long strike could lead to redundancy pay would be one of the unintended consequences of the Redundancy Act. Those who received little, or nothing, from redundancy pay would qualify for earnings-related unemployment benefit, as well as an income tax refund. We are not suggesting that most workers want to be redundant or unemployed; but in a strike situation there is now some 'cash buffer' even if the firm does close down, and this may influence a small number.

* Turner, op. cit., p. 24.

Most surveys or reports of strikes deal with the effect on the employer. We have shown here that, on the workers' side, the effects of strikes or closures is quite different from that described in the classical model with the interaction of labour supply and demand curves producing a viable wage at stable prices, traditionally with a reserve of unemployed. In the 1960s, instead of the strikers lasting out only a few days or weeks, and in extreme financial difficulty and actual want, there were circumstances where a combination of their dependants' social security and their income tax refund could enable them to stay on strike for two or three months (we are discounting the money which might be got by some, especially in industrial areas, from a wide range of part-time jobs, paid for in cash, which the Ministry of Social Security would find impossible to trace).

A modern theory of strikes would need an input of games theory. The employer looks at his costs—the labour/capital cost ratios, the product, whether it is durable, consumable, whether it could be stored, if demand could be postponed and recovered by future output, whether the markets (domestic or foreign) could be recovered or would be lost after having spent millions to establish them; he then makes his calculations and decides whether to pay, postpone or fight the wage demand.

On the union side, looking at the prospective strike from their negotiators' viewpoint, industries could be divided into roughly three groups; those in which strikes are likely to be successful, those where the outcome would be doubtful and those where the union or workers are likely to lose. On this basis engineering (especially cars), construction, metal manufacture, shipbuilding and marine engineering, transport and especially docks, emerge as the areas in which strikes are likely to be effective (as the strike record and pay increases of the late 1960s showed, in spite of incomes policy). The fact that employers in these industries knew that strikes were likely to be effective, and decided in many cases to buy off the strike, underlines the ineffectiveness of incomes policy against a combination of inflation and market forces.

There are areas where strikes are not likely to be effective, e.g. a wide range of clerical workers in local government, whose only effective threat can only be used when they staff polling booths on election day every four or five years; buses, where cities have allowed strikes to go on for weeks; teachers of secondary school children, where the strike would not be very effective.

As a result of the successful and well-publicised strikes in the industries previously mentioned, the area where strikes may or may not succeed has widened and workers urge their shop stewards or union officials to take militant measures before they fall too far behind in the wage race.

This has led to a 'psychology of inflation' being put forward, where people are worried and frustrated by rising prices and constantly watch the daily or weekly reports of wages rising around them. Economists, who were the high priests helping at the birth of the incomes policy in 1965, now tend to argue that they know the medicine for inflation, but the public will not swallow it. They, too, talk of handing the problem over to the psychologists or sociologists.

Traditional economic attempts to curb wage inflation are still being propounded, and are being used in practice. The Labour government allowed unemployment to rise from 1967 onwards (1·3 per cent in April 1966), and the Conservative government has raised the figure to its highest point in thirty years, over 3 per cent. Despite this, prices and incomes have continued to increase at a record level, and the failure of higher unemployment to prevent inflation has been ascribed to the cushioning effect of redundancy pay and earnings-related unemployment benefits, along with the argument that unemployment is more structural (declining, or changing industries) than cyclical.

The traditional argument now is that unemployment must rise still further. Professor Paish, writing in mid-1969 when unemployment was some $2\frac{1}{2}$ per cent, argued for 'a larger average margin of unused productive potential, and a higher average level of unemployment than those to which the post-war generation has become accustomed'.* Since then, there have been reports that unemployment might have to rise to 6 per cent (one and a half million), to break the 'inflation psychology' and then settle down at around 4 per cent, (one million unemployed), in order to slow down the rise in wages and prices.

Some writers have argued that there is a 'natural rate' of inflation (rather like the 'natural level of profits') above which wages tend to rise and cause inflation. This is linked with the 'psychology of inflation' which makes it necessary to raise the unemployment level some distance above its 'natural' level. Estimates are worked out on the Phillips curve to show that this could be between 3 and 4 per cent unemployed.

There is increasing doubt that there is a given level of unemployment at which wage increases would begin to level off, as the American economists have discovered. One American writes: 'It is

---

* F. W. Paish, 'Rise and Fall of Incomes Policy', Hobart Paper 47, London, 1969, p. 62.

possible to combine a politically unacceptable level of unemployment with a socially damaging rate of inflation.'* This is the real
crux of the problem for the government and their economists.
There is some level of unemployment at which the 'slack' in the
labour market and its side effects would cause a levelling off in
wage increases, but the concomitant rise in the collapse of firms
and their closures or bankruptcies would bring a strong criticism
of the Conservative government from its own supporters. Even a
later reflation of the economy in time for the next election would
hardly erase the memory of the first million unemployed since the
1930s.

While public revulsion at rising unemployment is not as strong
as it was in the past (the Labour government allowed the level
to rise from 300,000 to over 600,000), the question would be how
long it would be necessary to keep the level at around one million.
The new pattern of state benefits means that some men would
have a sum for redundancy, then earnings-related unemployment
benefit plus the flat-rate, along with family allowance and income
tax refund. At the higher level of manual worker pay (around £30),
the worker with wife and two children would collect some £18–19
weekly. This amount would protect the worker for up to six
months, after which his income would fall down to the social
security level of around £12–14. This amount is an improvement
on past standards but lengthy unemployment would involve
families in difficulties with hire purchase payments and running a
car, which would be necessary for increasing numbers of workers
searching for jobs.

Legal regulation over strikes

The economic and political difficulties of combating inflation by
raising unemployment and tightening credit are well known. With
the failure of a voluntary incomes policy, even with statutory
underpinnings, government thinking turned to curbing unofficial
strikes and regulating industrial relations by law. The Conservative
government made industrial relations reform one of their strongest
election pledges. They brought the Industrial Relations Act 1971,
on to the statute book, arguing from the experience of the Taft-
Hartley Act in the USA, and claiming that entry into the Common
Market would demand a legal backing for industrial relations, like
those of the Six.

Whatever the political consequences of trying to damp down

* J. K. Galbraith, *The American Left*, Fabian Society, London, 1971.

inflationary wage demands by legal regulation of industrial relations, the effects are not likely to be evident for some years as a
number of cases will certainly be fought through the courts with
workers and unions waiting to see what the judgments or consequences are. The most satisfactory position to emerge would be
one where the law was not invoked, where agreements began with
the clause 'Nothing in this contract will be enforceable at law' and
where both sides agreed to go to local arbitration, as they do in the
United States, for a speedy solution to their grievances. Those who
insist on the strict letter of the law in industrial relations will get
that and nothing more.

Return to incomes policy?

The incomes policy begun with such high hopes in 1965 had
virtually been abandoned by the time the Conservative government
came to power in mid-1970. The new government's emphasis on
market forces was expressed in their election manifesto: 'We
utterly reject the philosophy of compulsory wage control. We want
instead to get production up and encourage everyone to give of
their best.' Unfortunately, the emphasis on deflation as a first
priority, the pursuit of N–1 in the public sector with the determination to hold down wage awards even at the cost of lengthy
strikes, was bound to worsen the government's relations with the
unions.

An experienced financial commentator wrote of this policy:
'Ministers seemed almost to relish the thought of one or two strikes
in the autumn in key sectors which they hoped would bring
symbolic victories.'* The effects of the credit squeeze, the
increasing number of redundancies and the rising level of unemployment has, however, alarmed numbers who would normally
support the Conservative view that market forces would prevail.

The Times has stated its view that an incomes policy is necessary,
and is critical of the government's policy of restraining wages in
the public sector while exhorting employers in the private sector
to follow this example: 'There is no evidence so far that this is
reducing wage settlements in the private sector of industry. Of 40
settlements reported in the last four months the lowest was at 10
per cent and the highest 39 per cent' (28 January 1971). The
solution, said *The Times*, was a 'far reaching incomes policy' on a
voluntary basis with the co-operation of the unions achieved by
embarking on a more expansionist economic policy. A statutory

* Brittan, op. cit., p. 411.

wages and prices freeze might be necessary as the first stage. In March this theme was still being pressed and the editor explained why there must be both a voluntary element (to command general support) and a statutory element 'to deal with the flagrant cases of greed, the cases which exploit the consent of the majority for the benefit of small groups'. The paper reported a public opinion poll which showed that over half the population, and over half of trade unionists, would accept a wage freeze.*

The leaders of the Labour Party wish to return to some form of incomes policy, though they are handicapped in discussing what form this should take by the strong opposition to incomes policy expressed by powerful trade union leaders.

There is little possibility of an incomes policy of a voluntary nature being agreed in 1972, while the tensions of the Industrial Relations Act and high unemployment continue to make a consensus difficult. But continuing inflation and economic stagnation will make future attempts at such a policy inevitable. The major difficulty is that incomes policy is seen as wage restraint by the majority of trade unionists. This feeling is exacerbated in times of crisis when the policy is most necessary and explains why the many small unofficial strikes occur against the wishes of leaders.

An incomes policy will need a contractual basis for collective bargaining, otherwise small powerful groups may flout agreed decisions at any time. As Mr Callaghan has said: 'It is indefensible that a handful of men, by withdrawing their labour, can put 2,000 of their fellows in the same factory out of work' (*The Times*, 11 January 1971).

The ideal conditions for an incomes policy to function are when economic growth is evident in a rising standard of living and there is general confidence that this will continue. Unfortunately, these are also the conditions when neither politicians nor trade unions wish such a policy to be imposed. This leaves two other possible climates in which incomes policy would be discussed; the first is when the country has been through a bout of heavy unemployment and inflation combined, so that large numbers recognise that something must be done to remedy the situation; the other is when there is some urgent and visible economic or political crisis, such as a run on the pound, or serious balance of payments crises, or devaluation, or any two or all three of these events. In both these cases it would be difficult to introduce an incomes policy based on

---

* 5 March 1971. The 'wage freeze' was used by President Nixon in August 1971 for a three-month period, along with a 10 per cent surcharge on imports, to help the US economy.

general restraint. Numbers of groups or unions would feel that they had been left behind and that only when their claim was satisfied would they agree to the policy. This would start the wage claim spiral again. The only way to begin would be to have a statutory wages and prices standstill. This would demonstrate both the seriousness of the measures and the fairness of their application, allowing for the inevitable resentment felt by some groups who would have been stopped when they were about to have an increase.

There is a case for reviving the Prices and Incomes Board which would have in the meantime looked at the record of its five years of existence and decided what lessons to draw from this. They might discover that they had been too rigorous in their approach to wage claims and that comparability was important, or general ideas of what a 'fair wage' is when compared with other earnings. The new Board would have to make judgments and pronouncements about wage and salary awards to a greater degree than they did in the past, and justify their views by reference to commonly accepted standards.* This would be one of the ways in which to deal with the groups who led the breakthrough against the past incomes policy, by appealing over their heads to the general public and putting such groups morally on the defensive. This might have to be backed by an element of statutory law or fiscal sanction, e.g. by imposing a fine or payroll tax on amounts paid by firms above the agreed 'norm' which the Board had estimated.

Linked to this would be a policy of expansion set by the government to provide the general framework in which the policy would be possible. As part of this, productivity deals would be encouraged provided they were more accurately measured and evaluated than they have been in the past. The original rule of one third each for workers, employers and the public should be re-introduced, else there would be wide disparity between the men in capital-intensive expanding industries and labour-intensive industries such as the Post Office or education. Payment by result systems in industry would have to be tightened up to prevent groups of workers or employers indulging in 'wage drift' designed to circumvent incomes policy. Some statutory backing would be needed to prevent wide-spread evasion of the kind which took place in many firms during 1965–70. Wage inspectors might be used to make spot checks as they do in France. The very fact that such a group existed would make firms and unions more circumspect, especially

---

* An extension of job evaluation giving a 'national grid' for reference would serve as a point for comparisons.

in the building industry (although this would be one of the most difficult to inspect).

To gain the co-operation of the unions and establish the principle that living standards would not fall, some cost of living factor would be guaranteed against rises in prices. The idea was put forward by the Organisation for Economic Co-operation and Development in 1970, when they suggested that many large wage demands were fed by fear of rapid price rises, and they in turn led to further large wage demands. Fears of a fall in real wages would be lessened if there were automatic compensation for a cost of living rise. If we assume that the increase is limited to the cost of living and does not also contain a percentage increase related to an expectation of a rise in real wages then the proposal would have a downward pressure on the wage spiral. Increases in real wages would have to be related to the overall growth of the economy and the normal process of collective bargaining assisted by the Prices and Incomes Board, which would also be pronouncing on pricing policy and price rises.

These suggestions arise out of a survey of the experiences of the period 1965–70. But there is no magic panacea for inflation and wage-push inflation beyond trying to stimulate growth and providing the confidence and high employment policy which is necessary for an incomes policy to function. No democratic country has succeeded in achieving stable prices, full employment, and free collective bargaining along with growth, though some have come closer to this aim than others. It is a worthwhile objective for a civilised country.

9

Postscript: the XYZ of an incomes policy

The demand for an incomes policy has been with us for many of the post war years. Policies were put forward long before the Labour government of 1964, and after their relative failure with pay and prices the same demands for order and stability face the Conservative government. A variety of suggestions have been put forward, as well as a broadside from some economists who argue that an incomes policy is not only unworkable, it also encourages inflationary forces. The suggestions, like an electric wiring system, range from the positive to the negative, but they produce more heat than light.

The 1970 government were elected partly for their opposition to controls on wages and a promise to deal with prices. But their absence of policy was a policy in itself, and produced the equation N–1 in the public sector, where each pay settlement was meant to be less than its predecessor. This was the negative policy in the public sector mentioned above; it had failed under Selwyn Lloyd, caused trouble under the Labour government, and exploded, like a pressure cooker, with the bitter and successful strike of the miners in early 1972.

The strike was inevitable, given the fact that the Treasury were informing the public sector that the upper limit of pay and salary awards was 7·5 per cent per annum. As this was some 2 per cent below the rise in the retail price index (9·4 per cent between October 1970 and October 1971), and as a number of powerful or strategic groups in the private sector were able to get increases from two to three times the unofficial 7·5 per cent, public sector workers resented the cut in their standard of living. The postal workers strike was the major warning signal, but they lacked the industrial muscle and the money, as they had many women members who received little or no social security. The miners had muscle, and with a male membership, saw their families draw one million pounds weekly from the state. When it was clear that the mines might be closed for months, the government gave the Court of Enquiry a blank cheque, and the miners returned to work.

The country has now seen the collapse of two policies, the positive but unsuccessful one of 1964–70, and the negative one of 1970–72, even though this was buttressed by an unemployment figure of over one million.

As there are no longer experts producing, on a monthly basis, the ABC of an incomes policy, it might be useful to produce the XYZ. This does not mean the last word, but the winding-up of an era where it has been discussed and tried for a decade, and to point to some possible conclusions which might assist future attempts.

This takes the form of theories, X, Y, and Z. Theories X and Y (with apologies to McGregor, who used them for psychology) could be stated as follows:

Theory X represents the world as it is, not what we would like it to be. It is the world of the 'tough-minded'.

1 Many, though not all, groups of workers (or company directors or MPs) want to maximise their income.
2 Because many want to maximise earnings, efforts to keep their incomes below what they otherwise might be, will lead to subterfuge or evasion of incomes policy by the company, or absenteeism, 'go-slow', bonus 'fiddling' or other reactions by the men. Unemployment would have to rise to politically suicidal levels to change this situation.
3 Attempts to check breaches of incomes policy by statute will not work effectively, for the reasons in 2 above. The numbers of inspectors required would be counter-productive and the law would be ignored. For proof note the widespread disregard of the speed limit in Britain, in spite of 100,000 yearly being killed and injured on the roads. Or that Rhodesian trade flourishes in spite of sanctions.

Theory Y represents the world of the rational and the 'tender-minded'.

1 Many, though not all, workers accept that high wage demands are inflationary, raise prices, and are counter-productive.
2 There are enough of these to ensure a majority for a voluntary incomes policy, and measures could be devised to limit the ability of employers to raise profits and prices at the expense of wage restraint.

3   (a) 1 and 2 show that the majority of workers want fairness and equity above all in their daily lives. A National Board or Committee could decide arguments about relative wages and act as a public forum.
(b) The TUC agree down to 3(a), where they would insert an automatic cost-of-living increase, along with the demand that the Government abandon the Industrial Relations Bill.

Theory Z would make the following assumptions, based on hope and experience:

1   Views about the size of incomes are always views of the other man's income. Most people want at least 10 to 15 per cent more income than they have. This counters the statement that most people will accept an 'incomes freeze' for more than a short time.

2   Collective bargaining is the best method of rewarding groups of workers, providing that the link between output and reward is more closely measured than it is now, and that management becomes more efficient and raises overall output or efficiency.

3   1 and 2 will lead to an increasing gap in wages between labour-intensive and capital-intensive industries. The latter should be referred to the Monopolies Commission or a new PIB, and made to justify large wage increases or price rises, or both. Labour-intensive industries should be told to use less labour and mechanise where possible. The public sector should not be penalised at the expense of the private sector. Unions should be encouraged to enter yearly contracts, with restrictions on strikes, and disputes should be dealt with by local and speedy arbitration, instead of the traditional trial of strength.

The short term programme for an incomes policy:

1   There is a case for a revised Prices and Incomes Board with greater power over strategic prices.* Cost of living arguments could be defused by 'threshold' or cost of living agreements. These are widely negotiated in the Common Market countries. Arguments over differentials might be tackled on a basis of rationality by wider use of job evaluation. Stronger action should be taken against unofficial strikes, by legal or political methods although official trade union action is best.

* The CBI price initiative of 1971–2 was helpful. The new Board would be tripartite.

S

Local conciliation or arbitration should be urged on unions and industry as a rational substitute for strikes.

2 The above programme will not be effective unless it commands majority support, which needs moral, legal or political sanctions against the minority who exploit the restraint of others. A rising level of employment and economic growth is needed, as well as the feeling that the new wealth is being equitably shared. The alternative to finding rational methods of increasing wealth, sharing it fairly, reducing strikes and decreasing unemployment, is a long and bitter argument over the distribution of poverty.

Select bibliography

National Board for Prices and Incomes publications

No.	Reference	Published	Cmnd no.
	General Reports		
19	General Report April 1965 to July 1966	23.8.66	3087
40	Second General Report July 1966 to August 1967	31.8.67	3394
77	Third General Report August 1967 to July 1968	25.7.68	3715
122	Fourth General Report July 1968 to July 1969	29.7.69	4130
170	Fifth and Final General Report July 1969 to March 1971 (See also Supplement)	29.4.71	4649(-1)
	Specialist Reports		
36	Productivity Agreements	13.6.67	3311
65	Payment by Results Systems (See also Supplement 10.12.68)	14.5.68	3627(-1)
83	Job Evaluation (See also Supplement 10.12.68)	26.9.68	3772(-1)
123	Productivity Agreements	5.8.69	4136
161	Hours of Work, Overtime and Shiftworking (See also Supplement)	30.12.70	4554(-1)
169	General Problems of Low Pay	28.4.71	4648
	References on Pay		
2	Wages, Costs and Prices in the Printing Industry	17.8.65	2750

5   Remuneration of Administrative and
    Clerical Staff in the Electricity Supply
    Industry   25.10.65   2801
6   Salaries of Midland Bank Staff   24.11.65   2839
8   Pay and Conditions of Service of British
    Railways Staff (Conciliation, Salaried
    and Workshop Grades)   14.1.66   2873
9   Wages in the Bakery Industry (First
    Report)   19.1.66   2878
10 Armed Forces Pay   28.1.66   2881
11 Pay of the Higher Civil Service   28.1.66   2882
15 Scottish Teachers' Salaries   24.5.66   3005
16 Pay and Conditions of Busmen   26.5.66   3012
17 Wages in the Bakery Industry (Final
    Report)   9.6.66   3019
23 Productivity and Pay during the Period
    of Severe Restraint   15.12.66   3167
24 Wages and Conditions in the Electrical
    Contracting Industry   22.12.66   3172
25 Pay of Workers in Agriculture in
    England and Wales   2.2.67   3199
27 Pay of Workers in the Retail Drapery,
    Outfitting and Footwear Trades (See
    also Statistical Supplement 18.4.67)   9.3.67   3224(-1)
29 The Pay and Conditions of Manual
    Workers in Local Authorities, the
    National Health Service, Gas and
    Water Supply (See also Supplement
    4.5.67)   16.3.67   3230(-1)
30 Pay and Conditions of Limbfitters
    employed by J. E. Hanger & Co.   6.4.67   3245
32 Fire Service Pay   16.5.67   3287
35 Pay and Conditions of Merchant Navy
    Officers   2.6.67   3302
41 Salaries of Staff employed by the General
    Accident Fire and Life Assurance Co. Ltd   7.9.67   3398
42 Pay of Electricity Supply Workers   19.9.67   3405
45 Pay of Chief and Senior Officers (1) in
    Local Government Service and (2) in the
    Greater London Council   23.11.67   3473
48 Charges, Costs and Wages in the Road
    Haulage Industry (See also Statistical
    Supplement 8.3.68)   6.12.67   3482(-1)

49 Pay and Conditions of Service of Workers
    in the Engineering Industry (First
    Report on the Engineering Industry)
    (See also Statistical Supplement 6.3.68)   19.12.67   3495(-1)
50 Productivity Agreements in the Bus
    Industry   21.12.67   3498
51 Pay and Productivity of Industrial
    Employees of the United Kingdom
    Atomic Energy Authority   2.1.68   3499
54 Remuneration of Solicitors   8.2.68   3529
60 Pay of Nurses and Midwives in the
    National Health Service   28.3.68   3585
63 Pay of Municipal Busmen   26.4.68   3605
68 Agreement made between certain
    Engineering Firms and the Draughtsmen's
    and Allied Technicians' Association   16.5.68   3632
69 Pay and Conditions of Busmen employed
    by the Corporations of Belfast, Glasgow
    and Liverpool   23.5.68   3646
70 Standing Reference on the Pay of the
    Armed Forces   30.5.68   3651
74 Agreement relating to Terms and
    Conditions of Employment of Staff
    employed by the Prudential and Pearl
    Assurance Companies   21.6.68   3674
78 Award Relating to Terms and Conditions
    of Employment in the Road Passenger
    Transport Dept. of Rochdale County
    Borough Council   26.7.68   3723
79 Electricity Supply Industry National
    Guidelines covering Productivity
    Payments   30.7.68   3726
81 Pay Awards made by the City and
    County of Bristol to staff employed in its
    dock undertaking   23.8.68   3752
82 Report on an Agreement relating to the
    Pay of Sawyers and Woodcutting
    Machinists in the Sawmilling Industry   20.9.68   3768
84 Report on a Settlement relating to the
    Pay of certain workers employed in the
    Thermal Insulation Contracting Industry   8.10.68   3784
85 Pay and Conditions of Busmen employed
    by the Corporation of Dundee   15.10.68   3791

86	Pay of Staff Workers in the Gas Industry	24.10.68	3795
88	Pay of Pilots employed by the British Overseas Airways Corporation	29.10.68	3789
90	Pay of Vehicle Maintenance Workers in British Road Services	4.12.68	3848
91	Pay and Conditions in the Civil Engineering Industry	28.11.68	3836
92	Pay and Conditions in the Building Industry	28.11.68	3837
93	Pay and Conditions in the Construction Industry other than Building and Civil Engineering (See also Statistical Supplement 1.4.69)	28.11.68	3838 3982
94	Productivity Agreements in the Road Haulage Industry	5.12.68	3847
95	Pay and Conditions of Busmen employed by the Corporation of Wigan	6.12.68	3845
96	Pay of Busmen employed by the Corporation of Great Yarmouth	6.12.68	3844
98	Standing Reference on the Pay of University Teachers in Great Britain (First Report)	18.12.68	3866
99	Pay of Maintenance Workers employed by Bus Companies	2.1.69	3868
101	Pay of Workers in Agriculture in England and Wales	31.1.69	3911
103	Pay and Productivity in the Car Delivery Industry	18.2.69	3929
104	Pay and Conditions of Service of Engineering Workers (Second Report on the Engineering Industry)	20.2.69	3931
105	Pay of General Workers and Craftsmen in Imperial Chemical Industries Ltd	25.2.69	3941
106	Pay in the London Clearing Banks	28.2.69	3943
107	Top Salaries in the Private Sector and Nationalised Industries	25.3.69	3970
108	Pay and Conditions in the Electrical Contracting Industry in Scotland	20.3.69	3966
109	Pay of Salaried Staff in Imperial Chemical Industries Ltd	28.3.69	3981
110	Pay and Conditions in the Clothing Manufacturing Industries (See also Supplement)	17.4.69	4002(–1)

114	Pay and Duties of Light-Keepers	4.6.69	4067
115	Journalists' Pay	10.6.69	4077
116	Standing Reference on the Pay of the Armed Forces (Second Report)	16.6.69	4079
117	Pay and Conditions of Workers in the Exhibition Contracting Industry	18.6.69	4088
120	Pay and Conditions in the Electrical Contracting Industry	27.6.69	4097
125	Salaries of certain staff employed by BICC Ltd	24.9.69	4168
126	Remuneration of workers in Smithfield Market	9.10.69	4171
128	Pay of Ground Staff at Aerodromes	28.10.69	4182
129	Pay of Pilots employed by the British Overseas Airways Corporation	4.11.69	4197
131	Pay of certain employees in the Film Processing Industry	6.11.69	4185
132	Salary Structures	18.11.69	4187
134	Standing Reference on the Remuneration of Solicitors (First Report)	19.11.69	4217
140	Pay and Conditions of Workers in the Milk Industry	22.1.70	4267
142	Standing Reference on the Pay of the Armed Forces	25.2.70	4291
143	Hours and Overtime in the London Clearing Banks	27.2.70	4301
144	Bread Prices and Pay in the Baking Industry (First Report)	7.4.70	4329
145	Standing Reference on the Pay of University Teachers in Great Britain (Second Report)	9.4.70	4334
146	Pay and Conditions of Industrial Civil Servants	29.4.70	4351
149	Pay and Other Terms and Conditions of Employment of Workers in the Pottery Industry	21.7.70	4411
150	Pay and Other Terms and Conditions of Employment in the Fletton Brick Industry and the prices charged by the London Brick Company	23.7.70	4422
151	Bread Prices and Pay in the Baking Industry	28.7.70	4428
152	Pay and Productivity in the Water Supply Industry	4.8.70	4434

157	Standing Reference on the Pay of the Armed Forces (Fourth Report)—The Pay of Senior Officers	8.12.70	4513
162	Costs, Charges and Productivity of the National Freight Corporation	13.1.71	4569
164	Standing Reference on the Remuneration of Solicitors (Second Report)	1.4.71	4624
166	Pay and Conditions of Service of Ancillary Workers in National Health Service Hospitals	28.4.71	4644
167	Pay and Conditions of Service of Workers in the Laundry and Dry Cleaning Industry	28.4.71	4647
168	Pay and Conditions in the Contract Cleaning Trade	28.4.71	4637

General publications

Chapter 1

BEVERIDGE, W., *Full Employment in a Free Society*, Allen & Unwin, London, 1944.

FABIAN SOCIETY, *A Plan for Incomes*, London, 1965. The Fabian Society has published several pamphlets on this theme in the post war period.

FLANDERS, A., *The Fawley Productivity Agreements*, Faber & Faber, London, 1964.

HMSO, *The Economic Implications of Full Employment* (Cmnd 9725), March 1956.

HMSO, *Employment Policy* (Cmnd 6527), 1944.

HMSO, *In Place of Strife* (Cmnd 3888), 1969. The Labour government's views on the reform of collective bargaining.

HMSO, Royal Commission on Trade Unions and Employers Associations, 1966–1968, (Cmnd 3623), 1968 (the Donovan Report).

MCCORMICK, B. and SMITH, E. O. (eds), *The Labour Market*, Penguin, Harmondsworth, 1968. Contains much material on aspects of wages, inflation, unemployment, etc.

News Summary: Local Government Pay and Conditions, Local Authorities' Conditions of Service Advisory Board, 41 Belgrave Square, London S.W.1, (monthly bulletin).

OEEC, *Report on Rising Prices*, Paris, 1961.

PAISH, F. W., 'The Rise and Fall of Incomes Policy', *Hobart Paper 47*, London, 1969.

PHELPS BROWN, E. H., 'Wage Drift', *Economica*, vol. 29, 1962.
ROBERTS, B. C., *National Wages Policy in War and Peace*, Allen & Unwin, London, 1958.
TUC, *Productivity, Prices and Incomes*, London, April 1965.
TURNER, H. A. and ZOETEWEIJ, H., *Prices, Wages and Incomes Policies in Industrialised Market Economies*, ILO, Geneva, 1966.

Chapter 3

HMSO, NBPI Reports on the bus industry: Nos 16, 50, 63, 69, 78, 85 95, 96.

Chapter 4

BAIN, G. S., 'The Growth of White Collar Trade Unionism in Great Britain', *British Journal of Industrial Relations*, November 1966.
HMSO, Committee on the Management of Local Government (the Maud Report), 1967.
JACKSON, W. ERIC, *Local Government in England and Wales*, Penguin, Harmondsworth, 1969.
SPOOR, A., *White Collar Union, 60 Years of N.A.L.G.O.*, Heinemann, London, 1967.
WARREN, J. H., *The Local Government Service*, Allen & Unwin, London, 1952.

Chapter 5

FOGARTY, M. P., 'The National Incomes Commission', *British Journal of Industrial Relations*, November 1964.
HMSO, 'Report on Higher Education' (Cmnd 2154), 1963 (the Robbins Report).
HMSO, National Incomes Commission, Report No. 3, Remuneration of Academic Staff in Universities and Colleges of Advanced Technology (Cmnd 2317), 1964.
HMSO, NBPI Reports: Nos 98, 145.
PERKIN, H., *Key Profession. The History of the Association of University Teachers*, Routledge & Kegan Paul, London, 1969.
NATIONAL INCOMES COMMISSION, Report No. 3, *Remuneration of Academic Staff in Universities and Colleges of Advanced Technology* (Cmnd 2154), March 1965.

Chapter 6

HMSO, *Court of Inquiry* (Cmnd 3428), October 1967.

HMSO, *Inquiry into the Dispute between B.O.A.C. and B.A.L.P.A.* (Cmnd 3551), 1968 (the Pearson Report).

HMSO, NBPI Report No. 88, 'Pay of Pilots Employed by British Overseas Airways Corporation' (Cmnd 3789), October 1968.

HMSO, NBPI Report No. 129, 'Pay of Pilots Employed by British Overseas Airways Corporation' (Cmnd 4997), November 1969.

Chapter 7

FOGARTY, M. P., 'The National Incomes Commission', *British Journal of Industrial Relations*, November 1964.

FORES, M. J. and HEATH, J. B., 'The Fulton Report', *Public Administration*, Spring 1970.

HMSO, *Productivity, Prices and Incomes Policy* (Cmnd 4237), 1969.

HMSO, *Review Body on Doctors' and Dentists' Remuneration: Twelfth Report* (Cmnd 4352), 1970.

HMSO, 'Report of a Court of Inquiry into a dispute between the parties represented on the National Joint Industrial Council for the Electricity Supply Industry' (Cmnd 4594) (the Wilberforce Report), 1971.

HMSO, Royal Commission on the Civil Service 1953–55 (Cmnd 9613), 1955.

HMSO, NBPI Reports: No. 83, Job Evaluation; No. 8, British Railways Staff; No. 10, No. 116, Armed Forces Pay; No. 11, Pay of the Higher Civil Service.

KAHN, HILDA, *Salaries in the Public Services in England and Wales*, Allen & Unwin, London, 1963.

Chapter 8

BRITTAN, S., *Steering the Economy*, Penguin, Harmondsworth, 1971.

HMSO, Royal Commission on Trade Unions and Employers Associations 1965–1968 (Cmnd 3623), 1968 (the Donovan Report).

HMSO, NBPI Report No. 123, 'Productivity Agreements'.

HMSO, NBPI Report No. 161, 'Hours of Work, Overtime and Shift-working'.

MORTIMER, J., 'The Rise and Fall of the P.I.B.', *Personnel Management*, London, February 1971.

Index

Soc
HC
260
W24
B3

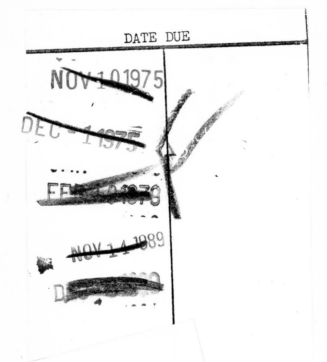

DATE DUE

NOV 10 1975

DEC 1 1975

FEB 10 1979

NOV 14 1989